THE HOLY PASCHA
GREAT FRIDAY & BRIGHT SATURDAY

TREASURES OF THE FATHERS OF THE CHURCH SERIES

Our paramount objective in this series is to introduce the believers to the trialogue of faith—the harmony among the Holy Bible, the Church Fathers, and the rites of the Coptic Orthodox Church. Through this symphony of discourse, the believer not only reads the Holy Scriptures, but understands it through the homilies, exegeses, and commentaries of the Church Fathers. This is a brief and simple companion to the Coptic Orthodox lectionary. We hope and pray that through this series, the Holy Bible, the Church Fathers, and the Church rites are not only introduced to each believer, but are experienced by the believer as a deep source of blessing, wisdom, and faith.

His Eminence Metropolitan Serapion
Editor-in-Chief

Father John Paul Abdelsayed
Father Ishak Azmy Yacoub
Father Moses Samaan
Series Editors

VOLUME I
Sunday Gospels of Tute-Amshir

VOLUME II
Sunday Gospels of the Great Lent

VOLUME III
The Holy Pascha

VOLUME IV
Sunday Gospels of the Holy Fifty Days

VOLUME V
Sunday Gospels of Baramhat-Nasie

VOLUME VI
Daily Readings for the Church Year

VOLUME VII
The Holy Theotokos

Cⲧⲛ Ⲑⲉⲱ Ⲓⲥⲭⲧⲣⲟⲥ

Treasures of the Fathers of the Church
Volume IIId

The Holy Pascha
Great Friday & Bright Saturday

A Guide to the Rites, Hymns and Readings of Holy Pascha Week

St. Paul Brotherhood Press
Coptic Orthodox Diocese of Los Angeles, Southern California, and Hawaii

THE HOLY PASCHA
GREAT FRIDAY & BRIGHT SATURDAY

SAINT PAUL BROTHERHOOD PRESS

—ɯ—

Coptic Orthodox Diocese of Los Angeles, Southern California, and Hawaii
Saint Paul Brotherhood

38740 Avenida La Cresta

Murrieta, California 92562

www.SaintPaulBrotherhood.org

First Edition, March 2004

Second Edition March 2016

Third Edition October 2017

ISBN 978-1-940661-34-6
LCCN 2015935334

If you are a Simon of Cyrene, take up the Cross and follow. If you are crucified with Him as a robber, acknowledge God as a penitent robber. If even He was numbered among the transgressors for you and your sin, do you become law-abiding for His sake.

Worship Him Who was hanged for you, even if you yourself are hanging; make some gain even from your wickedness; purchase salvation by your death; enter with Jesus into Paradise, so that you may learn from what you have fallen. Contemplate the glories that are there; let the murderer die outside with his blasphemies.

And if you are a Joseph of Arimathaea, beg the Body from him who crucified Him, make your own that which cleanses the world. If you are a Nicodemus, the worshipper of God by night, bury Him with spices. If you are a Mary, or another Mary, or a Salome, or a Joanna, weep in the early morning. Be the first to see the stone taken away, and perhaps you will see the Angels and Jesus, Himself...

If He descends into Hades, descend with Him. Learn to know the Mysteries of Christ there also, what is the providential purpose of the twofold descent, to save all men absolutely by His manifestation, or there also only to those who believe. And if He ascends up into Heaven, ascend with Him. Be one of those angels who escort Him, or one of those who receive Him. Bid the gates be lifted up, or be made higher, that they may receive Him, exalted after His Passion!

– St. Gregory Nazianzen

His Holiness Pope Tawadros II

118th Pope of Alexandria and
Patriarch of the Great See of Saint Mark

His Eminence Metropolitan Serapion

Metropolitan of Los Angeles
Southern California, and Hawaii

CONTENTS

NINTH HOUR: "THE ARREST"

ELEVENTH HOUR: "THE TRIALS BEGIN"

II
GREAT FRIDAY
"THIS IS HE WHO OFFERED HIMSELF UP AS AN ACCEPTABLE SACRIFICE..."

FIRST HOUR: "THE TRIAL"

THIRD HOUR: "VIA DOLOROSA: THE WAY OF SUFFERING"

SIXTH HOUR: "THE CRUCIFIXION"

NINTH HOUR: "THE CRUCIFIXION"

ELEVENTH HOUR: "THE FOUNTAIN OF LIVING WATER AND THE PASSOVER LAMB"

TWELFTH HOUR: "BURIAL"

III
BRIGHT SATURDAY
"HE LIFTS US UP"

IV
CONCLUSION
"COME, LORD JESUS!"

ABBREVIATIONS

AACS   *Ancient Christian Commentary on Scripture*, New Testament Series.

AACS-OT   *Ancient Christian Commentary on Scripture*, Old Testament series.

ANF   *Ante Nicene Fathers*, 10 vols.

BOG   Bede the Venerable. *Commentaries on the Gospel*, translated by L.T. Martin and D. Hurst, 2 vols., Kalamazoo, MI: Cistercian Publications, 1990.

CLC   St. Cyril of Alexandria. Commentary on Luke.

CS   Cistercian Studies. Kalamazoo, Michigan, Cistercian Publications.

CTD   St. Ephrem the Syrian. *Commentary on Tatian's Diatesseron*. AACS 2.

FC   *Fathers of the Church* Series. Washington, DC: Catholic University of America Press.

HOP   St. Ephrem the Syrian. *Hymn on Paradise*, translated by Sebastian Brock. Crestwood, N.Y., St. Vladimir's Seminary Press, 1990.

HPB   Holy Pascha Book, Holy Virgin Mary Church, 5th edition, March 2002, Los Angeles.

JCI   *Commentaire sur Isaie, sources Chretiennes*, v. 403, 1983, translated By Johanna Manley, assisted by Dr. C. P. Roth.

JTG   Fr. Pishoy Kamel. *From Jerusalem to Golgotha.* Santa Ana, CA: Archangel Michael Church, 2001.

NPNF   Nicene and Post Nicene Fathers Series.

ONT   *Orthodox New Testament.* Buena Vista, CO: Holy Apostles Convent, 2000.

PG   J.P. Migne, ed., *Patrologia Cursus Completus, Series Graeca.* 166 vols. Paris: Migne, 1857-1886.

PL	*Patrologia Latina*
PLS	*Patrologia Latina, Supplementum*
PPB	Fr. Pishoy Kamel. *The Passover by the Blood: The Holy Pascha*, Ontario.
SC	*Sources Chrtiennes*
SSGF	*Sunday Sermons of the Great Fathers*
TGM	The Blessed Theophylact, The Explanation by Blessed Theophylact of the Holy Gospel According to St. Matthew.

I

EVE OF GREAT FRIDAY
"Gethsemane"

Overview

"What? Could you not watch with Me one hour? Watch and pray, lest you enter into temptation. The spirit indeed is willing, but the flesh is weak." (Matthew 26:41)

As we approach the Crucifixion, the number and intensity of the events steadily increase. This evening's events include the Last Supper, the Eucharist, our Lord's final message to His apostles, His prayer at Gethsemane, Judas' Betrayal, and the round of trials. In the first hour, we read four gospels from St. John. For the remainder of the Evening of Friday and Great Friday, every hour contains four gospel readings, one from each evangelist.

The readings are as follows:

Hour	First	Third	Sixth	Ninth	Eleventh
Theme	Christ speaks with us and prays for Us	Gethsemane	Continuous Prayer	The Arrest	The Beginning of Trials
Prophesies	Jer. 8:17-9:6	Ez. 36:16-26	Ez. 22:23-28	Jer. 9:7-11 Ez. 21:28-32	Isa. 27:11-28:15
Psalm	Psa. 101:1,7	Psa. 108:1,2	Psa. 58:1,68:18	Psa. 27:3,4; 34:4	Psa. 2:1,2,4,5
Gospel	Jn. 13:33-14:25 Jn. 14:26-15:25 Jn. 15:26-16:33 Jn. 17:1-26	Mt. 26:30-35 Mk. 14:26-31 Lk. 22:31-39 Jn. 18:1,2	Mt. 26:36-46 Mk. 14:32-41 Lk. 22:40-46 Jn. 18:3-9	Mt. 26:47-58 Mk. 14:43-54 Lk. 22:47-55 Jn. 18:10-14	Mt. 26:59-75 Mk. 14:55-72 Lk. 22:56-65 Jn. 18:15-27

First Hour: "Christ Speaks With Us and Prays for Us"

Jer. 8:17-9:6; Psa. 101:1, 7; Jn. 13:33-17:26

Overview

On Thursday evening, after eating of the Last Supper and the Body and Blood, Christ gives His last discourse to us in the gospel readings (Jn. 14-17). This passage is so powerful that many Christians in the early Church and in the Church today memorized these three chapters. This message is a very special one, for it is only spoken to the disciples and it is only mentioned in the Gospel of John. In plain language, He speaks to them and announces His departure, recalls His ministry full of deeds, words, and miracles. He urges them to keep the commandments and to preserve unity among themselves. And at last, He prays for them.

In the First Hour prophesy of **Jeremiah**, the Lord explains how the sins of His people have saddened and perplexed Him. He is to the point of tears. This revelation of His saddened love for us continues throughout the readings of the gospels.

The **Psalm** of this hour also whispers in our ears the distress of the Lord, where we hear the Lord cry through David the Prophet, "My enemies have approached me all day long, those who deride me swear an oath against me."

Through this wonderful first hour of the evening of Great Friday, the Church reads from **Gospel** according to St. John (13:33- 17:26). This is the only time in the entire year that four gospel readings are read consecutively from the same evangelist! It is perhaps the longest continuous message of Christ mentioned in all of the gospels—even longer than the Sermon on the Mount. For this was not just a sermon, but a private lesson to His disciples. Even more, these passages contain the longest and most personal prayer from Blessed Son to the Heavenly Father. Here, He prays for us personally that we may not fall into sin and that we stay strong in the coming time of trouble and danger. We also see the Lord referring to Himself as Messiah, or the "Christ" directly (Jn. 17:3). The final three words of this gospel reading, "I in them," speaks of His desire for our every believer. As if it is His final request that each soul unites with Him in glory, righteousness, and salvation through the offering of His Body and Blood on our behalf.

The **Exposition**, as well, is wholly dedicated on this passage, and even begins by repeating part of Christ's prayer for us. Truly, this passage is one of the very special moments of the entire week. May we listen carefully and swim in the sea of His love during these readings.

To prepare us for this message of love, the Church adds the words "The Lord is my strength, my praise and has become my salvation" to the Paschal hymn "Thine is the power." This is another reminder that the Lord is preparing Himself and us for the Crucifixion. This is first mentioned in the Song of Moses after crossing the Red Sea (Exod. 15:2). It is also quoted in Isaiah 12:2 and by David in Psalm 119:14. Thus, the same God who delivered Moses and the Israelites will deliver the prophet from time of trouble. In the psalms, this verse appears a few verses before the declaration of the Resurrection, which we use in the Resurrection play, "Open to me the gates of righteousness, I will go through them..." (Psa. 119:19). Thus the Church uses one to commemorate the crossing of the Red Sea, a type of the Crucifixion; and the salvation of the Lord through His Resurrection.

Readings and Patristic Meditations

JEREMIAH 8:17-9:6

"For behold, I will send serpents among you, Vipers which cannot be charmed, and they shall bite you," says the Lord.

I would comfort myself in sorrow; My heart is faint in me. Listen! The voice, The cry of the daughter of my people From a far country: "Is not the Lord in Zion? Is not her King in her?"

"Why have they provoked Me to anger With their carved images—With foreign idols?" "The harvest is past, the summer is ended, and we are not saved!"

For the hurt of the daughter of my people I am hurt. I am mourning; astonishment has taken hold of me. **Is there no balm in Gilead, Is there no physician there?** Why then is there no recovery for the health of the daughter of my people?

Oh, that my head were waters, and my eyes a fountain of tears, that I might weep day and night for the slain of the daughter of my people! Oh, that I had in the wilderness a lodging place for travelers; that I might leave my people, and go from them! For they are all adulterers, an assembly of treacherous men.

"And like their bow they have bent their tongues for lies. They are not valiant for the truth on the earth. For they proceed from evil to evil, and they do not know Me," says the Lord. "Everyone take heed to his neighbor, and do not trust any brother; For every brother will utterly supplant, and every neighbor will walk with slanderers. Everyone will deceive his neighbor, and will not speak the truth; they have taught their tongue to speak lies; they weary themselves to *commit iniquity. Your dwelling place is in the midst of deceit; **through deceit they refuse to know Me**," says the Lord.*

I weep day and night for the people, who were led to perdition through wicked teachings. The ears of the simple have gone astray, and have got used to hear the heretic evils.

St. Basil the Great

Now is the right time for me to utter these words; yes, and even more so, than in the days of the prophet. If I do not lament for many cities, or for all nations; yet I grieve for a soul that parallels several nations, and is even more valuable. I am not grieving for the devastation of a city, nor for its captivation by the wicked; but for the devastation of your Holy Spirit...; and the destruction and the demolition of the temple that carries the Lord Christ...This temple is holier than [the temple of the Old Testament]; it does not glitter with gold or silver, but by the grace of the Holy Spirit; and instead of having in it the ark of the covenant and the two images of the cherubim, in the heart there are the Lord Christ, His Father, and the Paraclete.

St. John Chrysostom, *Exhortation to Theodore After His Fall*, 1.1 (NPNF 1:9, p. 91).

In this sense, the prophet talks to the ministers of the Church, calling them its walls and towers; saying to each of them, "O wall, let tears run down like a river" (Lam. 2: 18)... Do not cry for the dead, and do not lament on him; but cry, cry, on him who departs, as he is not coming back to see the land of his birth.

St. Jerome

Who can provide me with a fountain of tears, to mourn my deeds and my days? I am in need of a river of tears to cry for the harsh strikes that I deserve, for the sake of a life that I spent in sin! Break up, O Jesus, the stone that is my heart, to soften my inner man, and to create in him a fountain of deity!

St. Paulinus, Bishop of Nola

In extreme gentleness, the prophet Jeremiah carried the iniquities of his people in his heart, in his thoughts, and all his feelings to create in him an incessant fountain of tears, and bitter inner moans. In this he was a symbol of the Lord Christ, the suffering Servant, who carried our sorrows; yet with great difference between the two: Jeremiah, with a true love, bore them to a certain limit; then in almost despair, he sought to flee to the wilderness, away from everyone, to weep and moan! Our Lord Christ, on the other hand, carried our sorrows and sufferings, and did not seek to flee, but He went down to the wilderness of our life, to stay in our midst, and to bear on His shoulders every soul that could repent and return to Him; saying: "I am with you always, even to the end of the age" (Matt. 28:20). He descended to our world, and dwelt among us as one of us; and when He ascended to heaven, He did not forsake us, but carried us to let us share His glories.

Let us carry the Spirit of the Lord Christ. Let us desire to be among the people — however their iniquities are - to bear their sufferings, and to weep for their weaknesses; seeking through the assurance of faith, and the strength of hope, the work of the Holy Spirit in them. I wish we never flee from the road of the Cross, and never fear suffering.

Fr. Tadros Malaty, *Patristic Commentary on Jeremiah*

He rebukes them for their evil and lies, as well as their wicked deeds; running from evil to evil. Yet the reason he accused them is that they are unrighteous, that they do not know the Lord, and they are unfaithful.

St. Athanasius the Apostolic

PSALM 101:1,8

A prayer of the afflicted when he is overwhelmed and pours out his complaint before the Lord. My enemies reproach me all day long, those who deride me swear an oath against me.

"Hear my prayer, O Lord," is the same as, "Let my crying come to You." The feeling of the suppliant is shown by the repetition. "Turn not Your face away from me." When did God turn away His Face from His Son? When did the Father turn away His Face from Christ? But for the sake of the poverty of my members...

With their mouth they praised, in their heart they were laying snares for me. Hear their praise: "Master, we know that You are true, and teach the way of God in truth, neither do You care for any man. Is it lawful to give tribute unto Caesar or not?" And from where this evil repute, except because I came to make sinners my members, that by repentance they may be in my body? From there is all the abuse, from there the persecution. "Why does your Master eat with publicans and sinners? They who are whole do not need a physician, but they who are sick." Would that you were aware of your sickness, that you might seek a physician; you would not slay Him, and through your infatuated pride perish in a false health.

St. Augustine, *Commentary on Psalm 102* (NPNF 1:8)

JOHN 13:33-14:25

Little children, I shall be with you a little while longer. You will seek Me; and as I said to the Jews, 'Where I am going, you cannot come,' so now I say to you. **A new commandment I give to you, that you love one another; as I have loved you, that you also love one another.** *By this all will know that you are My disciples, if you have love for one another."*

Simon Peter said to Him, "Lord, where are You going?" Jesus answered him, "Where I am going you cannot follow Me now, but you shall follow Me afterward." Peter said to Him, "Lord, why can I not follow You now? I will lay down my life for Your sake." Jesus answered him, **"Will you lay down your life for My sake? Most assuredly, I say to you, the rooster shall not crow till you have denied Me three times.**

"Let not your heart be troubled; you believe in God, believe also in Me. In My Father's house are many mansions; if it were not so, I would have told you. I go to prepare a place for you. And if I go and prepare a place for you, I will come again and receive you to Myself; that where I am, there you may be also. And where I go you know, and the way you know." Thomas said to Him, "Lord, we do not know where You are going, and how can we know the way?" Jesus said to him, **"I am the way, the truth, and the life. No one comes to the Father except through Me.**

"If you had known Me, you would have known My Father also; and from now on you know Him and have seen Him." Philip said to Him, "Lord, show us the Father, and it is sufficient for us." Jesus said to him, "Have I been with you so long, and yet you have not known Me, Philip? He who has seen Me has seen the Father; so how can you say, 'Show us the Father'? Do you not believe that I am in the Father, and the Father in Me? The words that I speak to you I do not speak on My own authority; but the Father who dwells in Me does the works. Believe Me that I am in the Father and the Father in Me, or else believe Me for the sake of the works themselves.

"Most assuredly, I say to you, he who believes in Me, the works that I do he will do also; and greater works than these he will do, because I go to My Father. And whatever you ask in My name, that I will do, that the Father may be glorified in the Son. If you ask anything in My name, I will do it.

"If you love Me, keep My commandments. And I will pray the Father, and He will give you another Helper, that He may abide with you forever— the Spirit of truth, whom the world cannot receive, because it neither sees Him nor knows

Him; but you know Him, for He dwells with you and will be in you. I will not leave you orphans; I will come to you.

"A little while longer and the world will see Me no more, but you will see Me. Because I live, you will live also. At that day you will know that I am in My Father, and you in Me, and I in you. He who has My commandments and keeps them, it is he who loves Me. And he who loves Me will be loved by My Father, and I will love him and manifest Myself to him." Judas (not Iscariot) said to Him, "Lord, how is it that You will manifest Yourself to us, and not to the world?" Jesus answered and said to him, "If anyone loves Me, he will keep My word; and My Father will love him, and We will come to him and make Our home with him. He who does not love Me does not keep My words; and the word which you hear is not My but the Father's who sent Me. "These things I have spoken to you while being present with you.

John, from whose Gospel I have taken the passage introduced above, is not the only evangelist who details this incident of the prophetic announcement of his own denial to Peter. The other three also record the same thing. They do not, however, take one and the same particular point in the discourses [of Christ] as their occasion for proceeding to this narration. For Matthew and Mark both introduce it in a completely parallel order, and at the same stage of their narrative, namely, after the Lord left the house in which they had eaten the Passover; while Luke and John, on the other hand, bring it in before He left that scene. Still we might easily suppose, either that it has been inserted in the way of a recapitulation by the one couple of evangelists, or that it has been inserted in the way of an anticipation by the other; only such a supposition may be made more doubtful by the circumstance that there is so remarkable a diversity, not only in the Lord's words, but even in those sentiments of His by which the incident in question is introduced, and by which Peter was moved to venture his presumptuous asseveration that he would die with the Lord or for the Lord...

St. Augustine, *Harmony of the Gospels*, 2.3 (NPNF 1:6)

JOHN 14:26-15:25

*But the Helper, the Holy Spirit, whom the Father will send in My name, He will teach you all things, and bring to your remembrance all things that I said to you. Peace I leave with you, My peace I give to you; not as the world gives do I give to you. Let not your heart be troubled, neither let it be afraid. **You have heard Me say to you, 'I am going away and coming back to you.'** If you loved Me, you would rejoice because I said, 'I am going to the Father,' for My Father is greater than I. And now I have told you before it comes, that when it does come to pass, you may believe. I will no longer talk much with you, for the ruler* *of this world is coming, and he has nothing in Me. But that the world may know that I love the Father, and as the Father gave Me commandment, so I do. Arise, let us go from here.*

"I am the true vine, and My Father is the vinedresser. Every branch in Me that does not bear fruit He takes away; and every branch that bears fruit He prunes, that it may bear more fruit. You are already clean because of the word which I have spoken to you. Abide in Me, and I in you. As the branch cannot bear fruit of itself, unless it abides in the vine, neither can you, unless you abide in Me. I am the vine, you are the branches. He who abides in Me, and I in him, bears much fruit; for without Me you can do nothing. If anyone does not abide in Me, he is cast out as a branch and is withered; and they gather them and throw them into the fire, and they are burned. If you abide in Me, and My words abide in you, you will ask what you desire, and it shall be done for you. By this My Father is glorified, that you bear much fruit; so you will be My disciples.

"As the Father loved Me, I also have loved you; abide in My love. If you keep My commandments, you will abide in My love, just as I have kept My Father's commandments and abide in His love. These things I have spoken to you, that My joy may remain in you, and that your joy may be full. This is My commandment, that you love one another as I have loved you. Greater love has no one than this, than to lay down one's life for his friends. You are My friends if you do whatever I command you. No longer do I call you servants, for a servant does not know what his master is doing; but I have called you friends, for all things that I heard from My Father I have made known to you. You did not choose Me, but I chose you and appointed you that you should go and bear fruit, and that your fruit should remain, that whatever you ask the Father in My name He may give you. These things I command you, that you love one another.

"If the world hates you, you know that it hated Me before it hated you. If you were of the world, the world would love its own. Yet because you are not of the world, but I chose you out of the world, therefore the world hates you. Remember the word that I said to you, 'A servant is not greater than his master.' If they persecuted Me, they will also persecute you. If they kept My word, they will keep yours also. But all these things they will do to you for My name's sake, because they do not know Him who sent Me. If I had not come and spoken to them, they would have no sin, but now they have no excuse for their sin. He who hates Me hates My Father also. If I had not done among them the works which no one else did, they would have no sin; but now they have seen and also hated both Me and My Father. But this happened that the word might be fulfilled which is written in their law, 'They hated Me without a cause.'"

The disciples did not yet know what this resurrection was which He had foretold, when He said, "I go away, and come again unto you...". Now what they were to think of this? The Father, they knew, was mighty. So in other words He says to them, "Although you fear for me, that I cannot defend Myself, and you are not certain that I shall see you again after My Crucifixion, yet, at hearing that I go to the Father you should rejoice since I am going to One Who is greater than Me, and able to scatter all such tribulations." All this He said because of the timidity of the disciples...Because they were troubled at hearing of the hatred and strife they would meet when He was gone, He again comforts them by saying, "My peace I leave with you..."

St. John Chrysostom, *Commentary on John* (FC 28)

JOHN 15:26-16:33

"But when the Helper comes, whom I shall send to you from the Father, the Spirit of truth who proceeds from the Father, He will testify of Me. And you also will bear witness, because you have been with Me from the beginning.

"These things I have spoken to you, that you should not be made to stumble. They will put you out of the synagogues; yes, the time is coming that whoever kills you will think that he offers God service. And these things they will do to you because they have not known the Father nor Me. But these things I have told you, that when the time comes, you may remember that I told you of them. And these things I did not say to you at the beginning, because I was with you.

*"But now I go away to Him who sent Me, and none of you asks Me, 'Where are You going?' But because I have said these things to you, sorrow has filled your heart. Nevertheless I tell you the truth. It is to your advantage that I go away; for if I do not go away, the Helper will not come to you; but if I depart, I will send Him to you. **And when He has come, He will convict the world of sin, and of righteousness, and of judgment:** of sin, because they do not believe in Me; of righteousness, because I go to My Father and you see Me no more; of judgment, because the ruler of this world is judged. I still have many things to say to you, but you cannot bear them now. However, when He, the Spirit of truth, has come, He will guide you into all truth; for He will not speak on His own authority, but whatever He hears He will speak; and He will tell you things to come. **He will glorify Me, for He will take of what is My and declare it to you. All things that the Father has are My. Therefore I said that He will take of My and declare it to you.***

"A little while, and you will not see Me; and again a little while, and you will see Me, because I go to the Father." Then some of His disciples said among themselves, "What is this that He says to us, 'A little while, and you will not see Me; and again a little while, and you will see Me'; and, 'because I go to the Father'?" They said therefore, "What is this that He says, 'A little while'? We do not know what He is saying." Now Jesus knew that they desired to ask Him,

*and He said to them, "Are you inquiring among yourselves about what I said,
'A little while, and you will not see Me; and again a little while, and you will
see Me'? Most assuredly, I say to you that you will weep and lament, but the
world will rejoice; and you will be sorrowful, but your sorrow will be turned
into joy. A woman, when she is in labor, has sorrow because her hour has come;
but as soon as she has given birth to the child, she no longer remembers the
anguish, for joy that a human being has been born into the world. Therefore,
you now have sorrow; but I will see you again and your heart will rejoice, and
your joy no one will take from you. And in that day you will ask Me nothing.
Most assuredly, I say to you, whatever you ask the Father in My name He will
give you. Until now you have asked nothing in My name. Ask, and you will
receive, that your joy may be full.*

*"These things I have spoken to you in figurative language; but the time is
coming when I will no longer speak to you in figurative language, but I will tell
you plainly about the Father. In that day you will ask in My name, and I do
not say to you that I shall pray the Father for you; for the Father Himself loves
you, because you have loved Me, and have believed that I came forth from God.
I came forth from the Father and have come into the world. Again, I leave the
world and go to the Father." His disciples said to Him, "See, now You are
speaking plainly, and using no figure of speech! Now we are sure that You know
all things, and have no need that anyone should question You. By this we
believe that You came forth from God." Jesus answered them, "Do you now
believe? Indeed the hour is coming, yes, has now come, that you will be scattered,
each to his own, and will leave Me alone. And yet I am not alone, because the
Father is with Me. These things I have spoken to you, that in Me you may have
peace. In the world you will have tribulation; but be of good cheer, I have
overcome the world."*

[v. 8] The righteousness of Christ's disciples consisted in this, that they
believed that the Lord, Whom they discerned was a true human being, was
also the true Son of God, and that they worshipped always with a definite
love the one Whom they knew had been taken away bodily from them. The
righteousness of other believers—that is, of those who have not seen the
Lord in His human body—consists in this, that with their hearts they believe
and love Him Whom they have never seen with their bodily vision as true
God and Man. Unbelievers are convicted of this righteousness, which arises
from faith ...for when they hear the word of life in like manner with
unbelievers, they are unwilling to believe in a way which leads to
righteousness...

[v. 14] The Spirit honored Christ because through Him such great love
was enkindled in the hearts of the disciples that they cast aside fleshy fear
and resolutely preached the effect of the Resurrection of Him Whom they

fearfully fled at the time of His Passion. The Spirit honored Christ when holy teachers, filled with spiritual grace, worked so many and great miracles in Christ's name. The spirit honors Christ when by His inspiration He enkindles in us a love of the vision of Him, and when He impressed upon the hearts of the faithful that He is to be believed equal to the Father in His divinity...

[v. 21] He refers to the holy Church as a woman [in labor] on account of her fruitfulness in good works, and because she never ceases to beget spiritual children for God...As long as the holy Church devotes herself to the progress of spiritual virtues in the world, she never ceases being harassed by the world's temptations. But when she arrives at her reward, after triumphing in the struggle of her labors, she no longer remembers the distress that preceded it on account of the joy from the recompense that she has received. Just as a woman is glad when a human being has been born into the world, so the Church is filled with fitting exaltation when a multitude of the faithful are born into the life to come.

Bede the Venerable, Homily 2.1: *After Pascha, Homilies on the Gospels* (BOG 2, pp. 101, 104, 120, 121)

JOHN 17:1-26

Jesus spoke these words, lifted up His eyes to heaven, and said: "Father, the hour has come. Glorify Your Son, that Your Son also may glorify You, as You have given Him authority over all flesh, that He should give eternal life to as many as You have given Him. And this is eternal life, that they may know You, the only true God, and Jesus Christ whom You have sent. I have glorified You on the earth. I have finished the work which You have given Me to do. And now, O Father, glorify Me together with Yourself, with the glory which I had with You before the world was.

"I have manifested Your name to the men whom You have given Me out of the world. They were Yours, You gave them to Me, and they have kept Your word. Now they have known that all things which You have given Me are from You. For I have given to them the words which You have given Me; and they have received them, and have known surely that I came forth from You; and they have believed that You sent Me. I pray for them. I do not pray for the world but for those whom You have given Me, for they are Yours. And all Mine are Yours, and Yours are Mine, and I am glorified in them. Now I am no longer in the world, but these are in the world, and I come to You. Holy Father, keep through Your name those whom You have given Me, that they may be one as We are. While I was with them in the world, I kept them in Your name. Those whom You gave Me I have kept; and none of them is lost except the son of perdition,

that the Scripture might be fulfilled. But now I come to You, and these things I speak in the world, that they may have My joy fulfilled in themselves. I have given them Your word; and the world has hated them because they are not of the world, just as I am not of the world. I do not pray that You should take them out of the world, but that You should keep them from the evil one. They are not of the world, just as I am not of the world. Sanctify them by Your truth. Your word is truth. As You sent Me into the world, I also have sent them into the world. And for their sakes I sanctify Myself, that they also may be sanctified by the truth.

"I do not pray for these alone, but also for those who will believe in Me through their word; that they all may be one, as You, Father, are in Me, and I in You; that they also may be one in Us, that the world may believe that You sent Me. And the glory which You gave Me I have given them, that they may be one just as We are one: I in them, and You in Me; that they may be made perfect in one, and that the world may know that You have sent Me, and have loved them as You have loved Me. Father, I desire that they also whom You gave Me may be with Me where I am, that they may behold My glory which You have given Me; for You loved Me before the foundation of the world. O righteous Father! The world has not known You, but I have known You; and these have known that You sent Me. And I have declared to them Your name, and will declare it, that the love with which You loved Me may be in them, and I in them."

For my sake He was called a curse Who destroyed my curse, and sin Who takes away the sin of the world and became the New Adam to take the place of the old. So He makes my disobedience His own as head of the whole body. Then as long as I am disobedient and rebellious, both by denial of God and by my passions, so long as Christ also is called disobedient on my account...According to my view, this is the subjection of Christ to fulfill the Father's will. But as the Son subjects all to the Father, so does the Father to the Son, the One by His work, the Other by His good pleasure...making our condition His own. Of the same kind...is the expression, "My God, My God, why have You forsaken Me?" **It was not He who was forsaken either by the Father or by His own Godhead...but He was in His own person representing us. Before, we were the forsaken and despised; now, by His sufferings...we were taken up and saved...**For in His character of the Word He was neither obedient nor disobedient...But in the form of a servant, He condescends to His fellow servants, nay, to His servants, and takes upon Him a strange form, bearing all me and my in Himself, that in Himself He may exhaust the bad...by the art of His love for man He gauges our obedience, and measures all by comparison with His own sufferings, so that He may know our condition by His own, and how much is demanded of us, and how much we yield, taking into account, along with our environment, our weakness also…"Father, if it is possible, let this cup pass from Me"…It is not likely that He did not know whether it was possible or not, or that He would oppose will to will…this is the language of Him Who assumed our nature.

St. Gregory Nazianzen, *Fourth Theological Oration*, 5, 6, 12 (NPNF 2:7, p. 602)

THIRD HOUR: "THE GARDEN OF GETHSEMANE"

Ezek. 36:16-26; Psa. 108:1,2;
Matt. 26:30-35, Mk. 14:26-31, Lk. 22:31-39; Jn. 18:1, 2

Overview

Gethsemane is the Aramaic word for "oil press." It is a garden east of Jerusalem beyond the Kidron valley and near the Mount of Olives (Matt. 26:30). Christ often retreated with His disciples in the garden. It was the place where Christ met the Father, where man betrays God.

In the first garden, the Garden of Eden, Adam fell to temptation. But in the Second Garden (of Gethsemane), the Second Adam prevailed over temptation. Such power is only given through prayer and submission to God's will. The First Adam was cast out of the Garden and kept out by an angel; in Gethsemane God sent an angel to strengthen and comfort the Second Adam (Lk. 22:43-44).

As we chant in the Friday Theotokia of the Holy Psalmody, "He took what is ours and gave us what is His." And as St. Athanasius says, "He became like man so that man can become like God." So, He became human to take upon Himself our sin so that we could take for us His holiness.

During the first prophesy of Ezekiel we first read that the Lord will "pour out" His fury on the children of Israel for their bloodshed and defilement, and He shall "sprinkle" clean water upon them. Thus, blood and water are poured out to save His people. Consequently, He provides for us a new heart. Although the last two verses of this prophesy were read during the blessing of the water, in this hour we focus on the blood shed on the land.

As Christ and the disciples did not journey to Gethsemane before "singing a hymn," so too the Church does not progress without chanting the paschal hymns. Christ had warned the disciples they would betray Him and take offense to Him. Around the same time, Judas plotted with the Jews seeking to capture and kill Christ. In remembrance of such talk, a prophetic Psalm is read: "They have surrounded me with words of hatred, and fought against me without a cause" (Psa. 109:1,3). This Psalm is the most violent of the "cursing" psalms which explains the cruelty of the Lord's adversaries.

Readings and Patristic Meditations

EZEKIEL 36:16-26

*Moreover the word of the Lord came to me, saying: "Son of man, when the house of Israel dwelt in their own land, they defiled it by their own ways and deeds; to Me their way was like the uncleanness of a woman in her customary impurity. **Therefore I poured out My fury on them for the blood they had shed on the land, and for their idols with which they had defiled it.** So I scattered them among the nations, and they were dispersed throughout the countries; I judged them according to their ways and their deeds. When they came to the nations, wherever they went, they profaned My holy name—when they said of them, 'These are the people of the Lord, and yet they have gone out of His land.' But I had concern for My holy name, which the house of Israel had profaned among the nations wherever they went.*

*"Therefore say to the house of Israel, 'Thus says the Lord God: "I do not do this for your sake, O house of Israel, but for My holy name's sake, which you have profaned among the nations wherever you went. And I will sanctify My great name, which has been profaned among the nations, which you have profaned in their midst; and **the nations shall know that I am the Lord," says the Lord God, "when I am hallowed in you before their eyes.** For I will take you from among the nations, gather you out of all countries, and bring you into your own land. Then I will sprinkle clean water on you, and you shall be clean; I will cleanse you from all your filthiness and from all your idols. I will give you a new heart and put a new spirit within you; I will take the heart of stone out of your flesh and give you a heart of flesh.*

When Scripture, having up to a certain point been speaking about the species, makes a transition at that point from the species to the genus, the reader must then be carefully on his guard against seeking in the species what he can find much better and more surely in the genus.

Take, for example, what the prophet Ezekiel says: "When the house of Israel dwelt in their own land, they defiled it by their own way, and by their doings; their way was before me as the uncleanness of a woman. Therefore I poured My fury upon them for the blood that they had shed upon the land, and for their idols with which they had polluted it; and I scattered them among the heathen, and they were dispersed through the countries: according to their way, and according to their doings, I judged them." Now it is easy to understand that this applies to that house of Israel of which the apostle says, "Observe Israel after the flesh" (1 Cor. 10:18), because the people of Israel after the flesh did both perform and endure all that is here referred to.

What immediately follows, too, may be understood as applying to the same people. But when the prophet begins to say, "And I will sanctify My great Name, which was profaned among the heathen, which you have profaned in the midst of them; and the heathen shall know that I am the Lord" (Ezek. 36:23), the reader should now carefully observe the way in which the species is overstepped and the genus taken in. For he goes on to say: "And I shall be sanctified in you before their eyes. For I will take you from among the heathen, and gather you out of all countries, and will bring you into your own land. Then will I sprinkle clean water upon you, and you shall be clean from all your filthiness, and from all your idols, will I cleanse you. A new heart also will I give you, and a new spirit will I put within you; and I will take away the stony heart out of your flesh and I will give you a heart of flesh. And I will put My Spirit within you, and cause you to walk in My statutes, and you shall keep My commandments, and do them. And you shall dwell in the land that I gave to your fathers; and you shall be My people, and I will be your God. I will also save you from all your uncleannesses" (Ezek. 36:23-29).

Now that this is a prophecy of the New Testament, to which pertain not only the remnant of that one nation of which it is elsewhere said, "For though the number of the children of Israel be as the sand of the sea, yet a remnant of them shall be saved" (Isa. 10:22), but also the other nations which were promised to their fathers and our fathers; and that there is here a promise of that washing of regeneration which, as we see, is now imparted to all nations, no one who looks into the matter can doubt. And that saying of the apostle, when he is commending the grace of the New Testament and its excellence in comparison with the Old, "You are our epistle...written not with ink, but by the Spirit of the living God; not on tables of stone but on tablets of flesh, that is, of the heart" (2 Cor. 3:2-3), has an evident reference to this place where the prophet says, "A new heart also will I give you, and a new spirit will I put within you; and I will take away the stony heart out of your flesh, and I will give you an heart of flesh" (Ezek. 38:26). Now "the fleshy tables of the heart," is drawn, the prophet intended to point out as distinguished from the stony heart by the possession of sentient life; and by sentient he understood intelligent life. And thus the spiritual Israel is made up, not of one nation, but of all the nations which were promised to the fathers in their seed, that is, in Christ.

St. Augustine, *On Christian Doctrine*, 3 (NPNF 1:2)

PSALM 108:1,2

Do not keep silent, O God of my praise! For the mouth of the wicked and the mouth of the deceitful Have opened against me; they have spoken against me with a lying tongue.

He was betrayed by those whom He called His disciples...For he that betrayed Him gave to the multitude that came to apprehend Jesus, a sign, saying, "Whomever I shall kiss, it is He; seize Him,"—retaining still some element of respect for his Master; for unless he had done so, he would have betrayed Him, even publicly, without any pretense of affection. This circumstance, therefore, will satisfy all with regard to the purpose of Judas, that along with his covetous disposition, and his wicked design to betray his Master, he had still a feeling of a mixed character in his mind, produced in him by the words of Jesus, which had the appearance (so to speak) of some remnant of good. For it is related that, "then Judas, His betrayer, seeing that He had been condemned, was remorseful and brought back the thirty pieces of silver to the chief priest and elders, saying, 'I have sinned by betraying innocent blood.' And they said, 'What is that to us? You see to it!'" (Matt. 27:3-4)—and that, having thrown the money down in the temple, he departed, and went and hanged himself.

But if this covetous Judas, who also stole the money placed in the bag for the relief of the poor, repented, and brought back the thirty pieces of silver to the chief priests and elders, it is clear that the instructions of Jesus had been able to produce some feeling of repentance in his mind, and were not altogether despised and loathed by this traitor. No, the declaration, "I have sinned, in that I have betrayed the innocent blood," was a public acknowledgment of his crime. Observe, also, how exceedingly passionate was the sorrow for his sins that proceeded from that repentance, and which would not allow him any longer to live; and how, after he had cast the money down in the temple, he withdrew, and went away and hanged himself. For he passed sentence upon himself, showing what a power the teaching of Jesus had over this sinner Judas, this thief and traitor, who could not always treat with contempt what he had learned from Jesus...

Will Celsus[1] and his friends now say that those proofs which show that the apostasy of Judas was not a complete apostasy, even after his attempts

---

[1] A second century Greek philosopher who criticized Christianity to be a heretical deviation from Judaism.

against his Master, are inventions, and that this alone is true, viz., that one of His disciples betrayed Him; and will they add to the Scriptural account that he betrayed Him also with his whole heart? To act in this spirit of hostility with the same writings, both as to what we are to believe and what we are not to believe, is absurd. And if we must make a statement regarding Judas which may overwhelm our opponents with shame, we would say that, in the book of Psalms, **all of Psalm 108 contains a prophecy about Judas, the beginning of which is this: "O God, hold not Your peace before my praise; for the mouth of the sinner, and the mouth of the crafty man, are opened against me." And it is predicted in this psalm, both that Judas separated himself from the number of the apostles on account of his sins, and that another was selected in his place;** and this is shown by the words: "And his bishopric let another take" (Psa. 108:8). But suppose now that He had been betrayed by one of His disciples, who was possessed by a worse spirit than Judas, and who had completely poured out, as it were, all the words which he had heard from Jesus, what would this contribute to an accusation against Jesus or the Christian religion? And how will this demonstrate its doctrine to be false? We have replied in the preceding chapter to the statements which follow this, showing that Jesus was not taken prisoner when attempting to flee, but that He gave Himself up voluntarily for the sake of us all. From this it follows, that even if He were bound, He was bound agreeably to His own will; thus teaching us the lesson that we should undertake similar things for the sake of religion in no spirit of unwillingness.

The Scholar Origen, *Against Celsus*, 2.11 (ANF 4)

MATTHEW 26:30-35

And when they had sung a hymn, they went out to the Mount of Olives. Then Jesus said to them, "All of you will be made to stumble because of Me this night, for it is written: 'I will strike the Shepherd, and the sheep of the flock will be scattered.' But after I have been raised, I will go before you to Galilee." Peter answered and said to Him, "Even if all are made to stumble because of You, I will never be made to stumble." Jesus said to him, "Assuredly, I say to you that this night, before the rooster crows, you will deny Me three times." Peter said to Him, "Even if I have to die with You, I will not deny You!" And so said all the disciples.

MARK 14:26-31

And when they had sung a hymn, they went out to the Mount of Olives. Then Jesus said to them, "All of you will be made to stumble because of Me this night, for it is written: 'I will strike the Shepherd, and the sheep will be scattered.' "But after I have been raised, I will go before you to Galilee." Peter said to Him, "Even if all are made to stumble, yet I will not be." Jesus said to him, "Assuredly, I say to you that today, even this night, before the rooster crows twice, you will deny Me three times." But he spoke more vehemently, "If I have to die with You, I will not deny You!" And they all said likewise.

LUKE 22:31-39

And the Lord said, "Simon, Simon! Indeed, Satan has asked for you, that he may sift you as wheat. But I have prayed for you, that your faith should not fail; and when you have returned to Me, strengthen your brethren." But he said to Him, "Lord, I am ready to go with You, both to prison and to death." Then He said, "I tell you, Peter, the rooster shall not crow this day before you will deny three times that you know Me."

And He said to them, "When I sent you without money bag, knapsack, and sandals, did you lack anything?" So they said, "Nothing." Then He said to them, "But now, he who has a money bag, let him take it, and likewise a knapsack; and he who has no sword, let him sell his garment and buy one. For I say to you that this which is written must still be accomplished in Me: 'And He was numbered with the transgressors.' For the things concerning Me have an end." So they said, "Lord, look, here are two swords." And He said to them, "It is enough."

Coming out, He went to the Mount of Olives, as He was accustomed, and His disciples also followed Him.

JOHN 18:1,2

When Jesus had spoken these words, He went out with His disciples over the Brook Kidron, where there was a garden, which He and His disciples entered. And Judas, who betrayed Him, also knew the place; for Jesus often met there with His disciples.

He Prepares Them

And then He said to them, "you will all be made to stumble because of Me." After this He mentions a prophesy: "For it is written, 'I will strike the shepherd, and the sheep of the flock will be scattered.'" He was urging them to be attentive to what has been prophetically predicted of His death and Resurrection and at the same time He wanted to make it known that He was indeed crucified according to God's purpose. All of this was to show that He was no alien from the Old Covenant or from the God who preached it. What was done in the Old Testament was a dispensation. All of the prophets proclaimed all things beforehand from the beginning that are included in this salvific event. All this was to increase faith.

And [the Evangelist Matthew] teaches us to know what the disciples were before the crucifixion and what they did after the crucifixion. For indeed they who were not able so much as to stand their ground when He was crucified, after His death became mighty and stronger than adamant.

St. John Chrysostom, *Commentary on Matthew*, Homily 82.2 (NPNF 1:10)

Death is an awful thing, very full of terror, but not to those who have learned the true wisdom which is above. For he who knows nothing certain concerning things to come, but deems it to be a certain dissolution and end of life, with reason shudders and is afraid, as though he were passing into non-existence. But we who, by the grace of God, have learned the hidden and secret things of His wisdom, and deem the action to be a departure to another place, should have no reason to tremble, but rather to rejoice and be glad, that leaving this perishable life we go to one far better and brighter, and which has no end. Which Christ teaching by His actions, goes to His Passion, not by constraint and necessity, but willingly. "These things," it said, "Jesus spoke, and departed beyond the brook Kidron, where was a garden, into the which He entered, and His disciples.""...

He journeyed at midnight, crossed a river, and hastened to come to a place known to the traitor, lessening the labor to those who plotted against Him, and freeing them from all trouble; and showed to the disciples that He came willingly to the action, (a thing which was most of all sufficient to comfort them) and placed Himself in the garden as in a prison.

"These things Jesus spoke to them." What do you say? "Surely He was speaking with the Father, surely He was praying. Why then did it not say that, 'having ceased from the prayer,' He came there?" Because it was not prayer, but a speech made on account of the disciples.

"And the disciples entered into the garden." He had so freed them from fear that they no longer resisted, but entered with Him into the garden. But how came Judas there, or from where had he gained his information when he came? It is evident from this circumstance, that Jesus generally spent the night out of doors. For had He been in the habit of spending it at home, Judas would not have come to the desert, but to the house, expecting there to find Him asleep. And lest, hearing of a "garden," you should think that Jesus hid Himself, it adds, that "Judas knew the place"; and not simply so, but that He "often went there with His disciples." For He was often with them apart, conversing on necessary matters, and such as it was not permitted to others to hear. And He did this especially in mountains and gardens, seeking a place free from disturbance, that their attention might not be distracted from listening.

St. John Chrysostom, *Commentary on Matthew*, Homily 83 (NPNF 1:14)

Peter's Denial (Luke)

God teaches us that we must think humbly of ourselves, as being nothing, both as regards the nature of man and the readiness of our mind to fall away into sin, and strengthened and being what we are only through Him and of Him. If, therefore it is from Him that we borrow both our salvation and our seeming to be something in virtue and piety, what reason do we have for proud thoughts? For wall we have is from Him and of ourselves we have nothing. "For who makes you differ from another? And what do you have that you did not receive?" (1 Cor. 4:7). This is what the wise Paul said, and further the blessed David also at one time says, "Through God we will do valiantly," (Psa. 59:12) and "Our God is our refuge and strength," (Psa. 46:1) and the prophet Jeremiah has said, "O Lord, my strength and my fortress, my refuge in the day of affliction" (Jer. 16:19). And the blessed Paul also may be brought forward, who says with great clearness, "I can do all things through Christ who strengthens me" (Philip. 4:13). Yes, Christ Himself also somewhere says to us, "without Me you can do nothing" (Jn. 15:5).

Let us, then not glory in ourselves, but rather in His gifts. And if this is the state of anyone's mind, what place can the desire of being set above other men find in him, when thus we are all both partakers of the same one grace, and also have the same Lord of Hosts as the Giver of both of tendency to arrogance and to repress ambitious feelings, Christ shows that even he who seemed to be great is nothing and weak. Therefore, He passes by the other disciples and turns to him who is the foremost and sat at the head of the company, and says, "Satan has asked for you, that he may sift you as wheat"; that is to search and try you, and expose you to intolerable blows. For it is Satan's desire to attack men of more ordinary excellence, and, like some fierce and arrogant barbarian, he challenges to single combat those of chief repute in the ways of piety. So he challenged Job, but was defeated by his patience, and the boaster fell, being defeated by the endurance of that triumphant hero. But he makes human nature his prey, for it is weak and easy to be overcome. While he is harsh and pitiless and unappeasable in heart. For, as the sacred Scripture says of him, "His heart is as hard as stone, even as hard as the lower millstone" (Job 41:24). Yet he is placed under the feet of the saints by Christ's might; for He has said, "Behold, I give you the authority to trample on serpents and scorpions, and over all the power of the enemy, and nothing shall by any means hurt you" (Lk. 10:19). Therefore, He says, "Satan has asked for you, that he may sift you as wheat. But I have prayed for you, that your faith should not fail; and when you have returned to Me, strengthen your brethren."

See again, He humbles Himself unto us, and speaks according to the limits of man's estate, and yet He is God by nature, even though He became flesh. For though He is the power of the Father, by Whom all things are preserved, and from Whom they obtain the ability to continue in necessary, yes necessary, for Him Who, for the dispensation's sake became like us, to use also our words, when the occasion called Him thereto in accordance with what the dispensation itself required. Therefore, He says, "I have prayed for you, that your faith should not fail." Now by this then He shows that if [Simon Peter] had been yielded up to Satan to be tempted, he would have proved altogether unfaithful; since, even when not so yielded up, he proved weak from human feebleness, being unable to bear the fear of death. For he denied Christ, when a young girl troubled him in the high priest's palace by saying, "You are not also one of this Man's disciples, are you?" (Jn. 18:17).

The Savior then forewarned him what would have been the result if he was yielded over to Satan's temptation; but at the same time He offers him the word of consolation, and says, "and when you have returned to Me, strengthen your brethren," that is to be the support, and instructor and teacher of those who draw near unto Me by faith. Moreover, admire the beautiful skill of the passage, and the surpassing greatness of the divine gentleness! For, lest his impending fall should lead the disciples to desperation, as though he would be expelled from the glories of apostleship, and former following (of Christ) lose its reward, because of his proving unable to bear the fear of death, and denying Him, at once Christ fills him with good hope and grants him the blessings, and gather the fruits of steadfastness. For He says, "And when you have returned to Me, strengthen your brethren,"

O what great and incomparable kindness! The disciple had not yet been sickened with the malady of faithlessness and already he has received the medicine of forgiveness; not yet had the sin been committed, and he receives pardon; not yet had he fallen, and the saving hand is held out; not yet had he faltered, and he is confirmed; for He says, "when you have returned to Me, strengthen your brethren." [The authority to say this] belongs to One Who pardons, and restores him again to apostolic powers.

But Peter, in the passion of his zeal, made profession of steadfastness and endurance to the last extremity, saying that he would manfully resist the terrors of death, and count nothing of bonds; but in so doing he erred from what was right. When the Savior told him that he would prove weak, he should not have contradicted Him, loudly protesting the contrary; for the Truth could not lie; but rather he should have asked strength from Him, that either he might not suffer this, or be rescued immediately from harm. But, as I have already said, being fervent in spirit and warm in love towards Christ, and of unrestrainable zeal in rightly performing those duties which become a disciple in his attendance upon his Master, he declares that he will endure to the last extremity. But he was rebuked for foolishly speaking against what was foreknown and for his unreasonable haste in contradicting the Savior's words. For this reason He says, "I tell you, Peter, the rooster shall not crow this day before you will deny three times that you know Me." And this proved true. Therefore, let us not think highly of ourselves, even if we see ourselves greatly distinguished for our virtues; rather let us offer up the praises of our thanksgivings unto Christ Who redeems us, and Who also grants us even the desire to be able to act rightly; but Whom and with Whom to God the Father be praise and dominion, with the Holy Spirit, unto ages of ages. Amen.

St. Cyril of Alexandria, *Commentary on Luke*, Homily 145 (CS, pp. 575-577)

Out of twelve deserted; eleven remained loyal. The cross came; they fled; one remained—Peter, one with One. This one himself fled, and would that he had! He denied Christ. We may say, then, that the entire human race was lost. Because it had perished, the complaint of the Lord crucified is: "The wine press I have trodden alone, and of My people there was no one with Me" (Isa. 63:3). Then the Psalm was fulfilled, "Help, O Lord! For no one now is dutiful" (Psa. 12:1-2). "There is none who does good, no not even one" (Psa. 14:1-3; Rom. 3:12). He who has promised, "Even if I should have to die with You, or be imprisoned, I will not deny You" (Matt. 26:35; Mk. 14:31) denied Him.

St. Jerome, *Commentary on the Psalms*, Homily 54 (FC 48, p. 390)

Why do they have swords?

The swords were brought from the supper, and from the table. It was likely also there should be swords because of the lamb, and that the disciples, hearing that certain men were coming forth against Him, they took them for defense, as means to fight in behalf of their Master, which was of their thought only. Therefore, Peter is also rebuked for using it, and with a severe threat. For he was resisting the servant who came, warmly indeed, yet not defending himself, but doing this on behalf of his Master.

Christ however did not allow any harm to result. For He healed him, and showed forth a great miracle, enough to indicate at once both His forbearance and His power, and the affection and meekness of His disciple. For then he acted from affection, now with dutifulness. For when he heard, "Put your sword into its sheath," he immediately obeyed, and afterwards nowhere does this.

But another says, that they moreover asked, "Shall we smite?" but that He forbad it, and healed the man, and rebuked His disciple, and threatened, that He might move him to obedience. "For all they that take the sword," He said, "shall perish by the sword."

And He adds a reason, saying, "Do you not think that I cannot pray to my Father, and He shall presently give Me more than twelve legions of angels? But that the Scriptures might be fulfilled." By these words He quenched their anger, indicating that to the Scriptures also, this seemed good. Therefore there too He prayed, that they might take meekly what befell Him, when they had learned that this again is done according to God's will. By these two things, He comforted them, both by the punishment of them who are plotting against Him, "For all they," He said, "who take the sword shall perish with the sword;" and by His not undergoing these things against His will, "For I can pray," He said, "to My Father."

Therefore, He did not say, "Do you think that I cannot destroy them all?" Because He was more likely to be believed in saying what He did say; for not yet had they the right belief concerning Him. And a little while before He had said, "My soul is exceeding sorrowful even unto death," and, "Father, let the cup pass from me;" and He had appeared in an agony and sweating, and strengthened by an angel.

Since then He had shown forth many tokens of human nature, He did not seem likely to speak so as to be believed, if He had said, "Do you think that I cannot destroy them." Therefore, He says, "What, do you think that I cannot pray to my Father?" And again He speaks it humbly, in saying, "He will presently give Me twelve legions of angels." For if one angel slew one hundred and eighty-five thousand armed men, what need of twelve legions against a thousand men? But He frames His language with a view to their terror and weakness, for indeed they were dead with fear. Therefore also He brings against them the Scriptures, saying, "How then shall the Scriptures be fulfilled?" alarming them by this also. For if this is approved by the Scriptures, do you oppose and fight against them?...

So, why did they have swords? Because He had said to them, "Let him buy a sword." Yet this was not meant that they should arm themselves, far from it, but to indicate that He was going to be betrayed. The swords indicate that He was to be betrayed. The swords had a prophetic rather than a military purpose. They indicated Him being forcefully seized and betrayed.

St. John Chrysostom, Commentary on Matthew, Homily 84.1-2 (NPNF 1:10, pp. 501-503)

Why tell me to buy a sword?...a spiritual sword so that you may sell your inheritance, and purchase the Word (Matt. 13:44-46), by which the innermost parts of the mind are clothed. There is also the sword of offering, so that you may lay aside the body, and with the coverings of the sacrificed flesh, the crown of holy martyrdom may be brought for you. Finally, that you my know He spoke of suffering, lest He distress the spirits of His disciples, He offered an example concerning Himself (Lk. 22:37). Yet it is still inspired; and the disciples offered two swords, perhaps, indeed, one of the New, one of the Old Testament, with which were are armed against the deceits of the devil (Eph. 6:11). Then the Lord says, "It is enough." As if nothing is lacking to him whom the teaching of each Testament has fortified."

St. Ambrose, *Exposition*, 10.54-55 (ONT)

The Lord says this, not in fact so that they use weapons, but to hint to them of dangers and wars to come, and to teach them to prepare themselves for every eventuality.

The Blessed Theophylact (PG 123:473C, 1077; ONT 1)

"Lord, where are You going?"

This was the request of the disciples. Stay with us, Lord. I cannot stay with you for I am traveling today. Where are you going, Lord? I am going to the Cross, then to Hades to free man from sin. Then, I will return to you for a while, but I cannot stay. I will ascend to the right hand of the Father. But do not despair, I will send you the Comforter, until My Second Coming.

Even though, Lord You traveled to all these places on earth, in Hades, and in Heaven, O Lord You made it all a heaven, for in Your presence, we only dwell in the peace, love and joy in the heavenly places. For Lord, where You are, we are, for we are abiding in You. Where You go, we shall follow.

Ezek. 22:23-28; Psa. 58:1,68:18;

Matt. 26:36-46, Mk. 14:32-41, Lk. 22:40-46, Jn. 18:3-9

Overview

During this hour's **Gospel**, Christ asks the disciples to sit with Him and stay awake. He urges them three times to stay awake and pray, for His betrayers are at hand. Through such persistence, the Lord teaches us the importance of vigil in times of trouble.

The **Psalm** of the hour conjoins two prophetic psalms regarding the betrayal and capture of Christ by His enemies. When King Saul sent men to watch over David in order to kill him, David cries out to the Lord saying, "Deliver me from my enemies, O my God; defend me from those who rise up against me" (Psa. 59:1). This verse is part of a long prayer for comfort and deliverance from evil doers. The Church reads this psalm as a prayer for the deliverance of God from the hands of these evil men.

Readings and Patristic Meditations

EZEKIEL 22:23-28

And the Word of the Lord came to me, saying, "Son of man, say to her: 'You are a land that is not cleansed or rained on in the day of indignation.' The conspiracy of her prophets in her midst is like a roaring lion tearing the prey; they have devoured people; they have taken treasure and precious things; they have made many widows in her midst. Her priests have violated My law and profaned My holy things; they have not distinguished between the holy and unholy, nor have they made known the difference between the unclean and the clean; and they have hidden their eyes from My Sabbaths, so that I am profaned among them. Her princes in her midst are like wolves tearing the prey, to shed blood, to destroy people, and to get dishonest gain. Her prophets plastered them with untempered mortar, seeing false visions, and divining lies for them, saying, 'Thus says the Lord God,' when the Lord had not spoken.

Being the Logos of God, and above all, He alone had the natural worthiness to renew the creation of everything, to bear on behalf of all, and to intercede for all to the Father. It was necessary that no one except God Himself should incarnate; "For it was fitting for Him, for Whom are all things and by Whom are all things, in bringing many sons to glory, to make the captain of their salvation perfect through sufferings" (Heb. 2:10). By this [the Apostle Paul] means, that it was not for anyone else to save them, except for the Logos of God Who has created them from the beginning...By the sacrifice of His own Body, He put an end to the verdict against us, and made a new beginning of life for us.

St. Athanasius the Apostolic, *On the Incarnation*, 10.4-5

My inner Jerusalem became dross. So why should I blame the fire that consumed it?! My oppressing heart sheds the blood of the poor and needy; and my unclean thoughts profaned the temple of the Lord in me. A gap came to separate me from You, O God! Who would fill this gap?! Who would stand in this gap before You to intercede on my behalf — the foremost among sinners?! Who would pay my debt and renew my nature, to encounter with You?

I thank You, O My Savior; the incarnate Word of God; You alone bore my sins; You alone have been raised on the Cross; You have turned my earth into heaven! You provided me with Your Holy Spirit working in me; and lifted up my heart to the bosom of God Your Father! O, You the amazing and unique Intercessor, grant me to love sinners, pray for them, and be self-sacrificed for their love.

Fr. Tadros Malaty, *Patristic Commentary on Ezekiel 22*

PSALM 58:1, 68:18

Deliver me from my enemies, O my God; defend me from those who rise up against me. Draw near to my soul, and redeem it; deliver me because of my enemies.

In the Old Testament, Psalm 58 had referred to a time of bitter persecution, although the exact historic occasion it refers to is unknown. Some scholars believe it refers to the corruption of the justice warned about in Deut. 16:18-20. Nevertheless, this psalm was applied by the early Church to Jesus' trial before the Sanhedrin in Matt. 26:57-68—which is why it is included here as a preface to the gospel reading below.

Psalm 68 which is also chanted here was composed by someone hounded by persecutors, which blends sorrow and compunction with vigor and decisiveness. This psalm reveals a vulnerable man. The New Testament sees Christ prefigured in the singer's zeal for God's house and in His sufferings (9, 21). But the very juxtaposition of David cursing his tormentors and our Lord Jesus praying for His, brings out the gulf between type and antitype, and indeed between accepted attitudes among saints of the Old Testament and the New.

And when iniquity they speak, false things they speak; because deceitful is iniquity: and when justice they speak, false things they speak; because one thing with mouth they profess, another thing in heart they conceal...Alienated from what? From truth. Alienated from where? From the blessed country, from the blessed life...

St. Augustine, *Commentary on Psalm 59* (NPNF 1:8, p. 448)

This petition is evidently wonderful, neither briefly to be touched upon, nor hastily to be skipped over; truly wonderful...I see no reason for this petition, "Because of my enemies deliver me," unless we understand of it something else, which when I shall have spoken by the help of the Lord, He shall judge in you, Who dwells in you. There is a kind of secret deliverance of holy men, this for their own sakes is made. There is one public and evident: this is made because of their enemies, either for their punishment, or for their deliverance.

For truly God delivered not the brothers in the book of Maccabees from the fires of the persecutor...**But again the Three Children openly were delivered from the furnace of fire; because their body also was rescued, their safety was public.** The former were in secret crowned, the latter openly delivered, all however saved. ...There is then a secret deliverance, there is an open deliverance. Secret deliverance does belong to the soul, open deliverance to the body as well. For in secret the soul is delivered, openly the body.

Again, if this is the voice of the Lord in this Psalm, let us acknowledge that He speaks of secret deliverance when he said above, "Give heed to my soul, and redeem her." There remains the body's deliverance: for on His arising and ascending into the Heavens, and sending the Holy Spirit from above, there were converted to His faith they that at His death did rage, and out of enemies they were made friends through His grace, not through their righteousness. Therefore he has continued, "Because of my enemies deliver me. Give heed to my soul," but this in secret: but "because of my enemies deliver" even my body. For my enemies it will profit nothing if soul alone You shall have delivered; that they have done something, that they have accomplished something, they will believe. "What profit is there in my blood, while I go down into corruption?" Therefore "give heed to my soul, and redeem her," which You alone know: secondly also, "because of my enemies deliver me," that my flesh may not see corruption.

St. Augustine, *Commentary on Psalm 69* (NPNF 1:8, p. 448)

MATTHEW 26:36-46

Then Jesus came with them to a place called Gethsemane, and said to the disciples, "Sit here while I go and pray over there." And He took with Him Peter and the two sons of Zebedee, and He began to be sorrowful and deeply distressed. Then He said to them, "My soul is exceedingly sorrowful, even to death. Stay here and watch with Me." He went a little farther and fell on His face, and prayed, saying, "O My Father, if it is possible, let this cup pass from Me; nevertheless, not as I will, but as You will." Then He came to the disciples and found them asleep, and said to Peter, "What? Could you not watch with Me one hour? Watch and pray, lest you enter into temptation. The spirit indeed is willing, but the flesh is weak." Again, a second time, He went away and prayed, saying, "O My Father, if this cup cannot pass away from Me unless I drink it, Your will be done." And He came and found them asleep again, for their eyes were heavy. So He left them, went away again, and prayed the third time, saying the same words. Then He came to His disciples and said to them, "Are you still sleeping and resting? Behold, the hour is at hand, and the Son of Man is being betrayed into the hands of sinners. Rise, let us be going. See, My betrayer is at hand."

MARK 14:32-41

Then they came to a place which was named Gethsemane; and He said to His disciples, "Sit here while I pray." And He took Peter, James, and John with Him, and He began to be troubled and deeply distressed. Then He said to them, "My soul is exceedingly sorrowful, even to death. Stay here and watch." He went a little farther, and fell on the ground, and prayed that if it were possible, the hour might pass from Him. And He said, "Abba, Father, all things are possible for You. Take this cup away from Me; nevertheless, not what I will, but what You will." Then He came and found them sleeping, and said to Peter, "Simon, are you sleeping? Could you not watch one hour? Watch and pray, lest you enter into temptation. The spirit indeed is willing, but the flesh is weak." Again He went away and prayed, and spoke the same words. And when He returned, He found them asleep again, for their eyes were heavy; and they did not know what to answer Him. Then He came the third time and said to them, "Are you still sleeping and resting? It is enough! The hour has come; behold, the Son of Man is being betrayed into the hands of sinners.

LUKE 22:40-46

When He came to the place, He said to them, "Pray that you may not enter into temptation." And He was withdrawn from them about a stone's throw, and He knelt down and prayed, saying, "Father, if it is Your will, take this cup away from Me; nevertheless not My will, but Yours, be done." Then an angel appeared to Him from heaven, strengthening Him. And being in agony, He prayed more earnestly. **Then His sweat became like great drops of blood falling down to the ground.** *When He rose up from prayer, and had come to His disciples, He found them sleeping from sorrow. Then He said to them, "Why do you sleep? Rise and pray, lest you enter into temptation."*

JOHN 18:3-9

Then Judas, having received a detachment of troops, and officers from the chief priests and Pharisees, came there with lanterns, torches, and weapons. Jesus therefore, knowing all things that would come upon Him, went forward and said to them, "Whom are you seeking?" They answered Him, "Jesus of Nazareth." Jesus said to them, "I am He." And Judas, who betrayed Him, also stood with them. **Now when He said to them, "I am He," they drew back and fell to the ground.** *Then He asked them again, "Whom are you seeking?" And they said, "Jesus of Nazareth." Jesus answered, "I have told you that I am He. Therefore, if you seek Me, let these go their way," that the saying might be fulfilled which He spoke,* **"Of those whom You gave Me I have lost none."**

Gethsemane

Gethsemane is interpreted as the "very fertile valley" where the Lord ordered His disciples to sit down and wait for Him to return while He prayed alone for everyone.

St. Jerome, *Commentary on Matthew*, 4.26.37 (AACS 1b, p. 253)

Jesus brought His disciples from the Upper Room to a garden which was called Gethsemane because, after He was betrayed, He did not want to be arrested in the same place where He and His disciples had eaten the Passover. Even before He was betrayed, however, He thought it fitting to choose to pray in places devoted purely to prayer, for He knew that some locations are holier than others, as it is written, "The place where you are standing is holy ground" (Exod. 3:5, Acts 7:33).

The Scholar Origen, *Commentary on Matthew*, 89 (AACS, 1b, p. 254)

"Sit here while I pray"

His disciples were clinging to Him inseparably. So He said to His disciples, "'Sit here while I go pray over there'" (Matt. 26:36). For it was usual with Him to pray apart from them. He did this to teach us how to pray, how to use silence and solitude to pray for great matters. And taking with Him the three [disciples], He said to them, "My soul is exceedingly sorrowful, even to death. Stay here and watch with Me'" (Matt. 26:38). Why does He not take all of them with Him? So that they might not be more sorrowful. He took only those who had been spectators of His glory.

St. John Chrysostom, *Commentary on Matthew*, Homily 83.1 (NPNF 1:10, p. 497)

Not without reason does He inveigh against Peter most, although the others also had slept; but to make him feel by this also, for the cause which I mentioned before. Then because the others also said the same thing, for when Peter had said, "Though I must die with You, I will not deny You," the scriptures also adds, "likewise also said all the disciples"); He addresses Himself to all, convicting their weakness. For they who are desiring to die with Him, were not then able so much as to sorrow with Him wakefully, but sleep overcame them.

And He prays with earnestness, in order that the thing might not seem to be acting. And sweats flow over Him for the same reason again, even that the heretics might not say this, that He acts the agony. Therefore there is a sweat like drops of blood, and an angel appeared strengthening Him, and a thousand sure signs of fear, lest anyone should affirm the words to be feigned. For this reason also was this prayer. By saying then, "If it is possible, let this cup pass from Me," He showed His humanity; but by saying, "Nevertheless not as I will, but as You will," He showed His virtue and self-command, teaching us even when nature pulls us back, to follow God. For since it was not enough for the foolish to show His face only, He uses words also. Again, words sufficed not alone, but deeds likewise were needed; these also He joins with the words, that even they who are in a high degree contentious may believe, that He both became man and died. For if, even when these things are so, this is still disbelieved by some, much more, if these had not been. See by how many things He shows the reality of the Incarnation: by what He speaks, by what He suffers. After that He came and said to Peter, as it is said, "What, could you not watch one hour with Me?" All were sleeping, and He rebukes Peter, hinting at him, in what He spoke. And the words, "with Me," are not employed without reason; it is as though He had said, You could not watch with Me one hour, and You will lay down Your life for Me? And what follows also, intimates this self-same thing. For "Watch," He says, "and pray not to enter into temptation." See how He is again instructing them not to be self-confident, but contrite in mind, and to be humble, and to refer all to God.

St. John Chrysostom, *Homilies on Matthew* (26:36-38), Homily 83 (NPNF 1:10)

"Let this cup pass from Me. However not as I will..."

You have heard Christ say, "Father, if You will, remove this cup from Me." Was then His Passion an involuntary act? Was the need for Him to suffer or the voice of those who plotted against Him stronger than His own will? We say no. His passion was a voluntary act, although in another respect it was severe, because it implied the rejection and destruction of the synagogue of the Jews...Since it was impossible for Christ not to endure the passion, He submitted to it, because God the Father so willed it with Him.

St. Cyril of Alexandria, *Commentary on Luke*, Homily 147, p. 581

It is not clear to all that He said this as a lesson to us to ask help in our trials only from God, and to prefer God's will to our own, and as a proof that He did actually appropriate to Himself the attributes of our nature...[He also teaches] us to prefer God's will to our own. For that alone is impossible which is against God's will and permission. "However not as I will but as You will." For inasmuch as He is God, He is identical with the Father, while inasmuch as He is Man, He manifests the natural will of mankind. For it is this that naturally seeks escape from death.

John of Damascus, *Commentary on Matthew* (ONT 26, p. 125)

Let them quote in the seventh place that "The Son came down from Heaven, not to do His own Will, but the Will of Him Who sent Him." Well, if this had not been said by Himself Who came down, we should say that the phrase was modeled as issuing from the Human Nature, not from Him Who is conceived of in His character as the Savior, for His Human Will cannot be opposed to God, seeing it is altogether taken into God; but conceived of simply as in our nature, inasmuch as the human will does not completely follow the Divine, but for the most part struggles against and resists it. For we understand in the same way the words, "Father, if it is possible, let this cup pass from Me; nevertheless let not what I will but Your Will prevail" (Matt. 26:39; Lk. 22:42).

For it is not likely that He did not know whether it was possible or not, or that He would oppose will to will. But since, as this is the language of Him Who assumed our Nature (for it was He Who came down), and not of the Nature which He assumed, we must meet the objection in this way, that the passage does not mean that the Son has a special will of His own, besides that of the Father, but that He has not. So that the meaning would be, "not to do My own Will, for there is none of Mine apart from, but that which is common to Me and You; for as We have one Godhead, so We have one Will."

For many such expressions are used in common usage, and are expressed not positively but negatively; as, e.g., "God does not give the Spirit by measure" (Jn. 3:34), for as a matter of fact He does not give the Spirit to the Son, nor does He measure Him, for God is not measured by God; or again, "Not my transgression nor my sin" (Psa. 59:3). The words are not used because He has these things, but because He has them not. And again, "Not for our righteousness which we have done" (Tit. 3:5), for we have not done any.

And this meaning is evident also in the clauses which follow. For what, says He, is the Will of My Father? That everyone who believes in the Son should be saved, and obtain the final Resurrection. Now is this the Will of the Father, but not of the Son? Or does He preach the Gospel, and receive men's faith against His will? Who could believe that? Moreover, that passage, also, which says that the Word which is heard is not the Son's but the Father's has the same force (Jn. 14:24). For I cannot see how that which is common to two can be said to belong to one alone, however much I consider it, and I do not think anyone else can. If then you hold this opinion concerning the Will, you will be right and reverent in your opinion, as I think, and as every right-minded person thinks.

St. Gregory Nazianzen, *Oration* 30.12: On the Son (Library of Christian Classics, v. 3, p. 185)

He knew what He was saying to His Father, and was well aware that this chalice could pass from Him. But He had come to drink it for everyone, in order to acquit, through this chalice, the debt of everyone, [a debt] which the prophets and martyrs could not pray with their death...He assumed flesh. He clothed Himself with weakness eating when hungry; becoming tired after working, being overcome by sleep when weary. It was necessary, when the time for His death arrived, that all things that have to do with the flesh would be fulfilled then...Or it was to teach His disciples to confide their life and death to God. If He, Who is wise on account of the wisdom of God, asked for what was fitting for Him, how much more [should] ordinary people surrender their will to the One Who knows all things.

St. Ephrem the Syrian, *CTD* 20.11 (Oxford, pp. 292-296, AACS 2, pp. 210-211)

Why did Christ return the second time?

And why did He come the second time? In order to reprove them, for that they were so drowned in despondency, as not to have any sense even of His presence. He did not however reprove them, but stood apart from them a little, showing their unspeakable weakness, that not even when they had been rebuked, were they able to endure. But He did not awake and rebuke them again, lest He should smite them that were already smitten, but He went away and prayed, and when He came back again, He said, "Sleep on now, and take your rest." And yet then there was need to be wakeful, but to show that they will not bear so much as the sight of the dangers, but will be put to flight and desert Him from their terror, and that He had no need of their succor, and that He must by all means be delivered up, "Sleep on now," He said, "and take your rest; behold the hour is at hand, and the Son of Man is betrayed into the hands of sinners." He shows again that what is done belongs to a divine dispensation.

St. John Chrysostom, *Commentary on Matthew*, Homily 83.1 (NPNF 1:10)

"His sweat became like great drops of blood…" (Lk. 22:44)

He sweated to heal Adam who was sick. "It is by the sweat of your brow," God said, "that you will eat your bread" (Gen. 3:19). He remained in prayer in this garden to bring Adam back to his own garden again.

St. Ephrem the Syrian, *CTD*, 20.11 (Oxford, p. 297; AACS 3, p. 344)

The praying in Gethsemane was from His human nature…and this is declared by His sweat and by His agony which was so great that, as the saying goes, drops of blood fell from Him. For as the saying goes, as those who toil exceedingly, "sweat blood" and those who lament bitterly, "weep blood." This is why the evangelist uses the image of sweating drops of blood to show that the Lord was not merely damp, but perspired all around…In a more mystical sense, the Lord willed to suffer these things in order to heal human nature of cowardice…thus making cowardice obedient to divine will.

The Blessed Theophylact (PG 123:475BD, 1081; ONT, p. 395)

We must not indeed pass over the fact that in many manuscripts, both Latin and Greek, nothing is said of the angel's coming or the Bloody Sweat. But while we suspend judgment, whether this is an omission, where it is wanting, or an interpolation, where it is found (for the discordance of the copies leaves the question uncertain), let not the heretics encourage themselves that herein lies a confirmation of His weakness, that He needed the help and comfort of an angel. Let them remember the Creator of the angels needs not the support of His creatures. Moreover, His comforting must be explained in the same way as His sorrow. He was sorrowful for us, that is, on our account; He must also have been comforted for us, that is, on our account. If He sorrowed concerning us, He was comforted concerning us. The object of His comfort is the same as that of His sadness. Nor let anyone dare to impute the Sweat to a weakness, for it is contrary to nature to sweat blood. It was no infirmity, for His power reversed the law of nature. The bloody sweat does not for one moment support the heresy of weakness, while it establishes against the heresy which invents an apparent body, the reality all His body. Since, then, His fear was concerning us, and His prayer on our behalf, we are forced to the conclusion that all this happened on our account, for whom He feared, and for whom He prayed.

    St. Hilary of Poitiers, *On the Holy Trinity*, 10.40, 41 (NPNF 2:9)

    Moreover, the statement, "All my bones are poured out and dispersed like water; my heart has become like wax, melting in the midst of my belly," was a prediction of that which happened to Him on that night when men came out against Him to the Mount of Olives to seize Him. For in the memoirs which I say were drawn up by His apostles and those who followed them, [it is recorded] that His sweat fell down like drops of blood while He was praying, and saying, "If it is possible, let this cup pass." His heart and also His bones trembling; His heart being like wax melting in His belly, in order that we may perceive that the Father wished His Son really to undergo such sufferings for our sakes, and may not say that He, being the Son of God, did not feel what was happening to Him and inflicted on Him. Further, the expression, "My strength is dried up like a potsherd, and my tongue has cleaved to my throat," was a prophesy, as I previously remarked, of that silence, when He Who convicted all your teachers of being unwise returned no answer at all.

    St. Justin, *Dialogue with Trypho*, 103 (ANF 1)

    Those drops of sweat flowed from Him in a marvelous way like great drops of blood, in order that He might, as it were, drain off and empty the fountain of the fear which is proper to our nature. For unless this had been done with a mystical import, He certainly would not, even had He been the most fearful and lowly of men, have been sprayed in this unnatural way with drops of sweat like drops of blood under the mere force of His agony.

Of like import is also the sentence in the narrative which tells us that an angel stood by the Savior and strengthened Him. For this, too, bore also on the economy entered into on our behalf. For those who are appointed to engage in the sacred exertions of conflicts on account of piety, have the angels from heaven to assist them.

And the prayer, "Father, remove the cup," He uttered probably not as if He feared the death itself, but with the view of challenging the devil by these words to erect the cross for Him. With words of deceit that personality deluded Adam; with the words of divinity, then, let the deceiver himself now be deluded. However, assuredly the will of the Son is not one thing, and the will of the Father another. For He who wills what the Father wills, is found to have the Father's will. It is in a figure, therefore, that He says, "not My will, but Yours." For it is not that He wishes the cup to be removed, but that He refers to the Father's will the right issue of His passion, and honors by this the Father as the First...

St. Dionysius, *Exegetical Fragments* 2 (ANF 6)

"My Soul is Very Sorrowful"

What is meant by these words? The heretics think these words prove the consciousness of natural infirmity which made Christ begin to be sorrowful. Now I appeal to common intelligence. It cannot mean the same as to be sorrowful because of death, for where there is sorrow because of death, it is the death that is the cause of sadness. But a sadness even unto death implies that death is the completion, not the cause of sadness...it is not for Himself that the Lord is sorrowing and praying. It is for those whom He exhorts to watchfulness and prayer, lest the cup of suffering should be their lot, lest that cup which He prays may pass away from Him should rest with them.

St. Hilary of Poitiers, *On the Holy Trinity*, 10.36-37 (NPNF 2:9, p. 191)

The Lord, to test the fidelity of the human nature He had taken on, truly felt sorrowful. However, lest the suffering in His soul be overwhelming, He began to feel sorrowful over the events taking place just before His suffering. For it is one thing to feel sorrowful and another thing to begin to feel sorrowful. But He felt sorrowful, not because He feared the suffering that lay ahead and because He had scolded Peter for his timidity but because of the most unfortunate Judas, the falling away of all the apostles, the rejection by the Jewish people, and the overturning of woeful Jerusalem.

Jonah, too, became sad when the plant of ivy had withered, unwilling to have his booth disappear (Jonah 4:8).

St. Jerome, *Commentary on Matthew*, 4.26.37 (AACS 1b, p. 255)

The passion of grief, or affliction or sore distress, as we may call it, cannot have reference to the divine nature of the Word, which is not able to suffer. That is impossible since it transcends all passion. We say that the incarnate Word also willed to submit Himself to the measure of human nature by suffering what belongs to it. He is said to have hungered although He is life, the cause of life and the living Bread. He was also weary from a long journey although He is the Lord of Powers. It is also said that He was grieved and seemed to be capable of anguish. It would not have been fitting for Him Who submitted Himself to emptiness and stood in the measure of human nature to have seemed unwilling to endure human things. The Word of God the Father, therefore, is altogether free from all passion. For the appointed time's sake, He wisely submitted Himself to the weakness of humankind in order that He might not seem to refuse that which the time required. He even obeyed human customs and laws. He still did not bear this in His own [divine] nature.

St. Cyril of Alexandria, *Commentary on Luke*, Homily 146, p. 583

It is proposed now, however, that we explain how, in respect to the previously mentioned words, "when Jesus had said these things He was troubled," not His soul, nor in His soul, nor even of the spirit, but "in the spirit." That our observation concerning the spirit, then may not be useless, we must say that in the statement, "Now My soul is troubled" (Jn. 12:27), the experience of trouble belonged to the soul, but in the statement, "Jesus was troubled in spirit," which is the human spirit, the experience had come to the realm of the spirit.

For just as the saint lives in the spirit, which is he origin, while he lives, of every act and prayer and hymn to God, so everything he does, whatever it may be, he does in the spirit, even to the extent that he suffers, he suffers in the spirit.

And if the saint does this, by how much more must we say these things of Jesus, the leader of the saints, whose human spirit in Him, that He has taken up the whole man stirred up the other human elements in Him?

And so He "was troubled in Spirit," that He might testify and say with a divine oath, as it were, the "truly" in respect to the statement, "I say to you that one of you will betray Me."

For I think, when the spirit beheld the devil had already put into the heart of Judas Iscariot, the son of Simon, to betray the Teacher; Jesus having been enlightened on what was to be, was troubled, and since the trouble had come from knowledge in the spirit, which was also in a state of disturbance, "Jesus," it is said, "was troubled in spirit."

But perhaps the flesh was troubled too according to one interpretation of the saying, "the flesh is weak" (Matt. 26:41, Mk. 14:38). Now, Jesus was these things, of whom Gabriel had said to Mary, "And behold, you shall conceive in your womb and bring forth a Son, and shall call His Name Jesus. He will be great, and will be called Son of the Highest" (Lk. 1:31-32).

The Scholar Origen, *Commentary on John*, 32 (FC 89, pp. 383-384)

When we read that the Lord was sad, we must examine everything that was said to find out why He was sad. He previously warned that they would all fall away. Brimming with confidence, Peter responded that even though all the others might be alarmed, he would not be moved (Matt. 26:33)—he who the Lord predicted would deny knowing Him three times (Matt. 26:34). In fact, Peter and all the other disciples promised that even in the face of death they would not deny Him (Matt. 26:35). He then proceeded on and ordered His disciples to sit down while He prayed (Matt. 26:36)

Having brought with Him Peter, James and John, He began to grieve. Before He brought them along with Him, He did not feel sad. It was only after they had accompanied Him that He grew exceedingly sad. His sadness thus arose not from Himself but from those whom He had taken with Him. It must be realized that the Son of Man brought with Him none but those whom he showed that He would come into His kingdom at that time when, in the presence of Moses and Elijah on the mountain, He was surrounded by all the splendor of His eternal glory. But the reason for bringing them with Him both then and now was the same.

St. Hilary of Poitiers, *Commentary on Matthew*, 31.4 (AACS 1b, p. 254)

"Behold the hour is at hand"

Whatever is written concerning our Savior in His human nature, should be considered as applying to the whole race of mankind; because He took our body and exhibited Himself human infirmity. Now for this reason John has written thus, "They sought to take Him; but no one laid a hand on Him, because His hour had not yet come" (Jn. 7:30). And before it came, He Himself said to His Mother, "My hour has not yet come" (Jn. 2:4). and to them who were called His brethren, "My time has not yet come" (Jn. 7:6).

And again, when His time was come, He said to the disciples, "'Are you still sleeping and resting? Behold, the hour is at hand, and the Son of Man is being betrayed into the hands of sinners'" (Matt. 26:45).

St. Athanasius, *In Defense of His Flight*, 13 (NPNF 2:4, p. 259)

We may conclude that...after addressing these words to them, "Sleep on now, and take your rest," the Lord was silent for a space, so that what He had thus given them permission to do might be [seen to be] really acted upon; and that thereafter He made the other declaration "Behold the hour has come" Thus it is that in Mark's Gospel we find those words [regarding the sleeping] followed immediately by the phrase, "It is enough;" that is to say, "the rest which you have had is enough now." But as no distinct notice is introduced of this silence on the Lord's part which intervened then, the passage comes to be understood in a forced manner, and it is supposed that a peculiar pronunciation must be given to these words.

St. Augustine, *Harmony of the Gospels*, 3.4.11 (NPNF 1:6)

Ninth Hour: "The Arrest"

Jer. 9:7-11, Ezek. 21:28-32, Psa. 27:3,4; 34:4;

Matt. 26:47-58, Mk. 14:43-54, Lk. 22:47-55, Jn. 18:10-14

Overview

In this hour, we read of the capture of our Lord in the garden of Gethsemane. Judas signals to the others by kissing Him as a friend and calling Him Master, although he betrayed Him in word and in deed. The first prophesy of **Jeremiah** and the **Psalm** speak about the deceit of the tongue, and although one may speak good words, he waits to attack and destroy his Friend and Lord.

Also in this hour, Simon Peter draws his sword and cuts the ear of the servant Malchus, yet the Lord tells him to return the sword to its sheath, as prophesied in the second prophesy of **Ezekiel**.

Readings and Patristic Meditations

JEREMIAH 9:7-15

Therefore thus says the Lord of hosts: "Behold, I will refine them and try them; for how shall I deal with the daughter of My people? Their tongue is an arrow shot out; jt speaks deceit; one speaks peaceably to his neighbor with his mouth, but in his heart he lies in wait. Shall I not punish them for these things?" says the Lord. "Shall I not avenge Myself on such a nation as this?"

I will take up a weeping and wailing for the mountains, and for the dwelling places of the wilderness a lamentation, because they are burned up, so that no one can pass through; Nor can men hear the voice of the cattle. Both the birds of the heavens and the beasts have fled; they are gone.

"I will make Jerusalem a heap of ruins, a den of jackals. I will make the cities of Judah desolate, without an inhabitant."

The mouth is the source of every evil. Yet, it is not the mouth, but rather those who misuse it. From it come insults, blasphemies, provocations of lusts, murder, adultery, and stealing; all of which result from misusing the mouth.

St. John Chrysostom[2]

---

[2] See Fr. Tadros Malaty's *Patristic Commentary on Jeremiah.*

41

If you control your mouth, O brother, it will give you contrition of heart that makes you look deep into yourself; and thus enter into the spiritual joy. Whereas if your mouth controls you - believe me - you will not be able to escape from the darkness.

Mar Isaac the Syrian

EZEKIEL 21:28-32

"And you, son of man, prophesy and say, 'Thus says the Lord God concerning the Ammonites and concerning their reproach,' and say:

'A sword, a sword is drawn, polished for slaughter, for consuming, for flashing—While they see false visions for you, while they divise a lie to you, to bring you on the necks of the wicked, the slain Whose day has come, Whose iniquity shall end.

'Return it to its sheath. I will judge you in the place where you were created, in the land of your nativity. I will pour out My indignation on you; I will blow against you with the fire of My wrath, and deliver you into the hands of brutal men who are skillful to destroy.

You shall be fuel for the fire; your blood shall be in the midst of the land. You shall not be remembered, for I the Lord have spoken.'"

The prophesy here points to the drawing of the polished sword that is ready for the slaughter. The Lord permitted the sword to be drawn against Him by Judas and His adversaries, but He did not permit the sword to be drawn by St. Peter and the disciples. Instead, He told St. Peter to return it to its sheath, as mentioned in Ezek. 21:30.

PSALM 27:3,4; 34:4

Who speak peace to their neighbors, but evil is in their hearts. Give them according to their deeds, and according to the wickedness of their endeavors; Give them according to the work of their hands; Render to them what they deserve.

Let those be put to shame and brought to dishonor who seek after my life; Let those be turned back and brought to confusion who plot my hurt.

The first part of the psalm prophesies of the evil nature of Judas who spoke in peace and even kissed the Savior, but had evil in His heart to betray His Master (Psa. 27:3,4). In the second part, David declares the punishment of those who seek to kill him, "Let those bet put to shame and brought to dishonor who seek after my life, let those be turned back and brought to confusion who plot my hurt" (Psa. 35:4). A later verse from Psalm 35 is read during the first hour of Great Friday. Thus, Psalm 35 is known as a Passion psalm for it introduces the persecutors who speedily seek destruction.

Christ, who spoke no guile from His mouth, and who exhibited all righteousness and humility, not only...was not exposed to that kind of death for his own deserts, but (was so exposed) in order that what was predicted by the prophets as destined to come upon Him through your means might be fulfilled; just as, in the Psalms, the Spirit Himself of Christ was already singing, saying, "They were repaying me evil for good" (Psa. 34); and, "What I had not seized I was then paying in full" (Psa. 69:4)...all which He, actually and thoroughly suffering, suffered not for any evil action of His own, but "that the Scriptures from the mouth of the prophets might be fulfilled."

The Scholar Tertullian, *An Answer to the Jews*, 10 (ANF 3)

MATTHEW 26:47-58

And while He was still speaking, behold, Judas, one of the twelve, with a great multitude with swords and clubs, came from the chief priests and elders of the people. Now His betrayer had given them a sign, saying, "Whomever I kiss, He is the One; seize Him." Immediately he went up to Jesus and said, "Greetings, Rabbi!" and kissed Him. But Jesus said to him, "Friend, why have you come?" Then they came and laid hands on Jesus and took Him. And suddenly, one of those who were with Jesus stretched out his hand and drew his sword, struck the servant of the high priest, and cut off his ear. But Jesus said to him, "Put your sword in its place, for all who take the sword will perish by the sword. Or do you think that I cannot now pray to My Father, and He will provide Me with more than twelve legions of angels? How then could the Scriptures be fulfilled, that it must happen thus?" In that hour Jesus said to the multitudes, "Have you come out, as against a robber, with swords and clubs to take Me? I sat daily with you, teaching in the temple, and you did not seize Me. But all this was done that the Scriptures of the prophets might be fulfilled." Then all the disciples forsook Him and fled.

And those who had laid hold of Jesus led Him away to Caiaphas the high priest, where the scribes and the elders were assembled. But Peter followed Him at a distance to the high priest's courtyard. And he went in and sat with the servants to see the end.

MARK 14:43-54

And immediately, while He was still speaking, Judas, one of the twelve, with a great multitude with swords and clubs, came from the chief priests and the scribes and the elders. Now His betrayer had given them a signal, saying, "Whomever I kiss, He is the One; seize Him and lead Him away safely." As soon as He had come, immediately he went up to Him and said to Him, "Rabbi,

Rabbi!" and kissed Him. Then they laid their hands on Him and took Him. And one of those who stood by drew his sword and struck the servant of the high priest, and cut off his ear. Then Jesus answered and said to them, "Have you come out, as against a robber, with swords and clubs to take Me? I was daily with you in the temple teaching, and you did not seize Me. But the Scriptures must be fulfilled." Then they all forsook Him and fled.

Now a certain young man followed Him, having a linen cloth thrown around his naked body. And the young men laid hold of him, and he left the linen cloth and fled from them naked.

And they led Jesus away to the high priest; and with him were assembled all the chief priests, the elders, and the scribes. But Peter followed Him at a distance, right into the courtyard of the high priest. And he sat with the servants and warmed himself at the fire.

LUKE 22:47-55

And while He was still speaking, behold, a multitude; and he who was called Judas, one of the twelve, went before them and drew near to Jesus to kiss Him. But Jesus said to him, "Judas, are you betraying the Son of Man with a kiss?" When those around Him saw what was going to happen, they said to Him, "Lord, shall we strike with the sword?" And one of them struck the servant of the high priest and cut off his right ear. But Jesus answered and said, "Permit even this." And He touched his ear and healed him. Then Jesus said to the chief priests, captains of the temple, and the elders who had come to Him, "Have you come out, as against a robber, with swords and clubs? When I was with you daily in the temple, you did not try to seize Me. But this is your hour, and the power of darkness."

Having arrested Him, they led Him and brought Him into the high priest's house. But Peter followed at a distance. Now when they had kindled a fire in the midst of the courtyard and sat down together, Peter sat among them.

JOHN 18:10-14

Then Simon Peter, having a sword, drew it and struck the high priest's servant, and cut off his right ear. The servant's name was Malchus. So Jesus said to Peter, "Put your sword into the sheath. Shall I not drink the cup which My Father has given Me?"

Then the detachment of troops and the captain and the officers of the Jews arrested Jesus and bound Him. And they led Him away to Annas first, for he was the father-in-law of Caiaphas who was high priest that year. Now it was Caiaphas who advised the Jews that it was expedient that one man should die for the people.

Why didn't He escape from the Jews?

As it was not fitting for the Word of God, being the Life, to inflict death Himself on His own body, so neither was it suitable to fly from death offered by others, but rather to follow it up unto destruction, for which reason He naturally neither laid aside His body of His own accord, nor, again, fled from the Jews when they took counsel against Him.

But this did not show weakness on the Word's part, but, on the contrary, showed Him to be Savior and Life; in that He both awaited death to destroy it, and hasted to accomplish the death offered Him for the salvation of all. And besides, the Savior came to accomplish not His own death, but the death of men; whence He did not lay aside His body by a death of His own — for He was Life and had none—but received that death which came from men, in order perfectly to do away with this when it met Him in His own body.

Again, from the following also one might see the reasonableness of the Lord's body meeting this end. The Lord was especially concerned for the resurrection of the body which He was set to accomplish. For what He was to do was to manifest it as a monument of victory over death, and to assure all of His having effected the blotting out of corruption, and of the incorruption of their bodies from thenceforward; as a gage of which and a proof of the resurrection in store for all, He has preserved His own body incorrupt.

If, then, once more, His body had fallen sick, and the word had been sundered from it in the sight of all, it would have been unbecoming that He who healed the diseases of others should suffer His own instrument to waste in sickness. For how could His driving out the diseases of others have been believed in if His own temple fell sick in Him? For either He had been mocked as unable to drive away diseases, or if He could, but did not, He would be thought insensible toward others also.

St. Athanasius, *On the Incarnation*, 22 (SVS Press)

Jesus was not taken prisoner; for at the fitting time He did not prevent Himself falling into the hands of men, as the Lamb of God, that He might take away the sin of the world. For, knowing all things that were to come upon Him, He went forth, and said to them, "Whom do you seek? "and they answered, "Jesus of Nazareth," and He said to them, "I am He." Judas also, who betrayed Him, was standing with them. When, therefore, He had said to them, "I am He," they went backwards and fell to the ground. Again He asked them, "Whom do you seek?" and they said again, "Jesus of Nazareth."

Jesus said to them, "I told you I am He, if then you seek Me, let these go away." No, even to Him who wished to help Him, and who smote the high priest's servant, and cut off his ear, He said: "Put up your sword into its sheath...

And if any one imagines these statements to be inventions of the writers of the Gospels, why should not those statements rather be regarded as inventions which proceeded from a spirit of hatred and hostility against Jesus and the Christians? And these the truth, which proceed from those who manifest the sincerity of their feelings towards Jesus, by enduring everything, whatever it may be, for the sake of His words? For the reception by the disciples of such power of endurance and resolution continued even to death, with a disposition of mind that would not invent regarding their Teacher what was not true, is a very evident proof to all candid judges that they were fully persuaded of the truth of what they wrote, seeing they submitted to trials so numerous and so severe, for the sake of Him whom they believed to be the Son of God.

The Scholar Origen, *Against Celsus*, 2.10 (ANF 4)

The Kiss

How magnificent is the endurance of evil by the Lord who was even kissed His own traitor, and then spoke words even softer than a kiss! For He did not say, "O you abominable one, or traitor, is this what you do in return for great kindness?" He simply says, "Judas" using his first name (Lk. 22:48). This is in the voice of One commiserating with another or who wished another to come back to Him, not the voice of anger.

(Pseudo-) Dionysius of Alexandria, Exegetical Fragments (ANF 6, p. 116)

You are offering a kiss, you who do not know the mystery of a kiss. What is wanted is not the kiss of lips, but rather the kiss of the heart and the soul.

St. Ambrose of Milan

There is a certain order to the different facets of Christ's suffering. But the reason for Judas's kiss was that we might discern all our enemies and those who we know would delight in raging against us. The Lord does not resist his kiss.

St. Hilary of Poitiers, *Commentary on Matthew*, 32.2 (AACS 1b, pp. 260-261)

And the traitor said to Jesus, "Master." Indeed, all heretics, like Judas, address Jesus in the same way, "Master." They kiss Him even as Judas did. Jesus speaks peacefully to them all, since they are all Judases who betray Him: "Judas, is it with a kiss that you betray the Son of Man?" As for Judas, he is approached by Christ for his false friendship. "Friend, why are you here?" We hear of no one who is good called by that name in the Scriptures. Moreover, to the wicked and the one not wearing a garment he says, "Friend, how did you come in here without a wedding garment?'" (Matt. 22:12). Wicked too is that man in the parable of the denarius who hears the words, "'Friend, I am doing you no wrong. Did you not agree with me for a denarius? Take what is yours and go your way. I wish to give to this last man the same as I give to you" (Matt. 20:13-14).

The Scholar Origen, *Commentary on Matthew*, 100 (AACS 1b, p. 261)

Look at the hypocrisy! I think it is exposed through the question that accuses the traitor with the compassion of love: "Judas do you betray the Son of Man with a kiss?" That is like saying, "Do you wound the pledge of love, shed blood in the duty of charity, and give death with the instrument of peace? Do you, a servant, betray your Lord, a disciple his master, a chosen one the Creator?" In other words, "the wounds of a friend are more useful than the voluntary kisses of an enemy" (Prov. 27:6). He says this to a traitor. What does Christ say to a peacemaker? "Let him kiss me with the kisses of his mouth" (Song 1:2). He kissed Judas, not that Christ should teach us to pretend but that He should not appear to flee from betrayal. Hence He did not deprive Judas of the dues of love (Matt. 26:49). It is written, "It was peaceful among those that hate peace" (Psa. 119:6).

St. Ambrose of Milan, *Exposition of the Gospel of Luke* (10:63-64)

For indeed [Judas] was afraid of the multitude, and desired to seize Him alone. Oh madness! How did covetousness altogether blind him! For he that had often seen Him when He went through the midst, and was not seized, and when He afforded many demonstrations of His Godhead and power, looked to lay hold on Him; and this while He was using like a charm for him so many, both awful and soothing words, to put an end to this evil thought. For not even at the supper did He forbear from this care of him. But unto the last day talked to him of these things. But he profited nothing. But the Lord never ceased to do His part.

Knowing this, then, let us also not intermit to do all things unto them that sin and are remiss, warning, teaching, exhorting, admonishing, advising, though we profit nothing. For Christ indeed foreknew that the traitor was incorrigible, yet nevertheless He ceased not to supply what could be done by Himself, as well admonishing, threatening and bewailing over him, and nowhere plainly, nor openly, but in a concealed way. And at the very time of the betrayal, He allowed him even to kiss Him, but this benefited him nothing. So great an evil is covetousness, this made him both a traitor, and a sacrilegious robber.

Listen, all you covetous, you who have the disease of Judas. Listen and beware of the calamity! For if he who was with Christ, and performed miracles, and had the benefit of so much instruction—but because he was not freed from this disease and was sunk into such a gulf—how much more shall you, who do not so much as listen to the Scripture, who are constantly riveted to the things present, become an easy prey to this calamity, unless you have the advantage of constant care?! Every day was that man with Him, who had not where to lay His head, and every day was he instructed by deeds, and by words, not to have gold, nor silver, nor two coats; and yet he was not taught self-restraint; and how do you expect to escape the disease [of covetousness], if you have not the benefit of earnest attention, and do not use much diligence?

For terrible, terrible is the monster [of covetousness], yet nevertheless, if you are willing, you will easily get the better of it. For the desire is not natural; and this is manifest from those who are free from it. For natural things are common to all; but this desire has its origin from remissness alone; hence it takes its birth, hence it derives its increase, and when it has seized upon those who look greedily after it, it makes them live contrary to nature. For when they regard not their fellow countrymen, their friends, their brethren, in a word all men, and with these even themselves, this is to live against nature. From this it is evident that the vice and disease of covetousness, with which Judas, being entangled, became a traitor, is contrary to nature. And how did he become such a one, you may say, having been called by Christ? Because God's call is not compulsory, neither does it force the will of those who are not minded to choose virtue, but admonishes indeed, and advises, and does and manages all things, so as to persuade men to become good; but if some endure not, it does not compel. But if you would learn from what reason he became such as he was, you will find him to have been ruined by covetousness.

St. John Chrysostom, *Commentary on Matthew*, Homily 80 (NPNF 1:10)

Why did He chose [Judas], and...make him a steward? To show His perfect love and His perfect mercy. [It was] also that our Lord might teach

His Church that, even if there are false teachers in it, it is nevertheless the true seat [of authority]...It was also [to] teach that even if there are evil stewards, the stewardship itself is true. He therefore washed his feet (cf. Jn. 13:5)...Jesus kissed the mouth which gave the signal for death to those who apprehended Him. He reached out and gave bread into the hand that reached out and took his price, and sold Him unto slaughter...**The tribe of Judah marked the beginning of the kingdom (cf. Gen. 49:10), and the apostle Judas marked its extinction...the Lord called animosity friendship and He turned toward Judas.** The deceitful disciple approached the true Master to kiss Him. The Lord withdrew from him the Spirit that He breathed into him. He removed It from him, not wanting the corrupting wolf to be among His sheep. He said, "even what he has will be taken away from him" (Matt. 13:12)...

St. Ephrem the Syrian, *CTD*, 20.12 (ACS 2-3, pp. 216, 346)

He does not escape, but protects the disciples from harm.

[In the garden], the wolf, clad in a sheep's skin, and tolerated among the sheep by the profound counsel of the Father of the family, learned where he might opportunely scatter the slender flock, and lay his coveted snares for the Shepherd. "Judas then," he adds, "having received a cohort, and officers from the chief men and the Pharisees, came there with lanterns, and torches, and weapons." It was a cohort, not of Jews, but of soldiers.

Therefore, we are to understand it as having been received from the governor, as if for the purpose of securing the person of a criminal, and by preserving the forms of legal power, to deter any from venturing to resist His captors: although at the same time so great a band had been assembled, and came armed in such a way as either to terrify or even attack any ne who should dare to make a stand in Christ's defense. For only in so far was His power concealed and prominence given to His weakness, that these very measures were deemed necessary by His enemies to be taken against Him, for whose hurt nothing would have sufficed but what was pleasing to Himself; in His own goodness making a good use of the wicked, and doing what was good in regard to the wicked, that He might transform the evil into the good, and distinguish between the good and the evil.

St. Augustine, *Tractates on John*, Tractate 112 (NPNF 1:12)

Here He declares Himself to be Master even as the Father. If so, He is the Shepherd, and the sheep are His...Oh! what depravity had the traitor's soul received. For with what kind of eyes did he then look at his Master?

With what mouth did he kiss Him? Oh! accursed purpose; what did he devise? What did he dare? What sort of sign of betrayal did he give? "Whomever I shall kiss," he said. He was encouraged by his Master's gentleness, which more than all was sufficient to shame him, and to deprive him of all excuse for that he was betraying one so meek...

"Aren't you ashamed even of the form of the betrayal?", He said. Even this did not stop him. He submitted to be kissed, and gave Himself up willingly. So they laid their hands on Him, and seized Him that night on which they ate the Passover, to such a degree they boiled with rage, and were mad. However, they would have had no strength, unless He had Himself allowed it. Yet this delivers not Judas from intolerable punishment, but even more exceedingly condemns him, for that though he had received such proof of His power, lenity, meekness, and gentleness, he became fiercer than any wild beast. Knowing then these things, let us flee from covetousness...

St. John Chrysostom, *Commentary on Matthew*, Homily 83 (NPNF 1:10)

Cutting the Ear

The Apostle cuts off the ear of the slave of the high priest. That is, a disciple of Christ cuts of a disobedient ear from a man in the priesthood. What was once incapable of hearing the truth is now cut off.

St. Hilary of Poitiers, *Commentary on Matthew* 32.2 (AACS 1b, p. 261)

Perhaps what Peter did was a mystery, for the right ear of the Jewish people had to be cut off because of their malice toward Jesus. Though they seem to hear the law, they now hear with their left ear the shadowy tradition of the law, but not the truth, since they are enslaved by the words that profess the service of God but do not serve Him in truth. They mystery of these words against Christ is found in the person of Christ's adversary, the high priest Caiaphas. Now it seems to me, since all the Gentile believers were made one people in Christ, the very fact that they believed in Christ was the reason why the right ear of the Jews was cut off, according to what had been prophesied about them, "Make the heart of this people dull, and their ears heavy, and shut their eyes; lest they see with their eyes, and hear with their ears, and understand with their heart, and return and be healed" (Isa. 6:10).

The Scholar Origen, *Commentary on Matthew*, 101 (AACS 1b, p. 261)

The wounds increase in their bitterness because they came wrapped up in the covering of false love, and tender words that carry under the poisonous evil. We, too, when we unite with the Lord Jesus, we are encountered by one of our own 'household', as Judas. He cuts short the Spirit of truth in us, for he says that man's enemies are of his own household. The Lord gave Judas the last chance, even at the last moments when He was being arrested. He blamed him in gentle words, "Friend, why have you come?'" (Matt. 26:50). With a kiss, Judas betrayed his Master.

Fr. Tadros Malaty, *Patristic Commentary on Matthew*

Saint Peter cut the right ear of the servant of the chief priest. This act was a sign of the inability of the Jews to good listening, for they did not listen well to the words of Jesus. They have rather honored the left ear, that is, they obeyed their impulses that sprung up from their fanaticism. They have thus become "deceiving and being deceived" (2 Tim. 3:13). As the Book says "And in vain they worship Me, teaching as…the commandments of men…" (Matt. 15:19). It is as if St. Peter has revealed what is in their depths that the spiritual right ear has been cut off, since they paid more attention to the left ear and listened to falsehood. But the Lord has come to heal the right ear and to make it listen to spiritualities.

St. Cyril of Alexandria

Put Your Sword Away

He said to Peter, "Put your sword back into its place" (which is one of patience). After restoring the amputated ear, as the other Evangelist says (Lk. 22:51), (which was a sign of both supreme kindness and divine power), He spoke these words that they might ring true to what He had said and done before. Although they might not remember the good things done in the past, they might acknowledge the good things done in the present.

The Scholar Origen, *Commentary on Matthew*, 103 (AACS 1b, pp. 261-262)

But perhaps He may be thought to have feared to the extent that He prayed that the cup might be removed from Him: "Abba, Father, all things are possible unto You: remove this cup from Me." To take the narrowest ground of argument, might you not have refuted for yourself this dull impiety by your own reading of the words, "Put up your sword into its sheath": the cup which My Father has given Me, shall I not drink it? Could fear induce Him to pray for the removal from Him of that which, in His zeal for the Divine Plan, He was hastening to fulfill? To say He shrank from the suffering He desired is not consistent. You allow that He suffered willingly: would it not be more reverent to confess that you had misunderstood this passage, than to rush with blasphemous and headlong folly to the assertion that He prayed to escape suffering, though you allow that He suffered willingly?

St. Hilary of Poitiers, *On the Holy Trinity*, 10.30 (NPNF 2:9)

The Disciples Fled

Up until the time He was seized, they remained. But when He had said these things to the multitudes, they fled. For from then on they could see that escape was no longer possible. So He gave Himself up to them voluntarily saying that this was done according to the scriptures.

St. John Chrysostom, *Commentary on Matthew*, Homily 84.2 (NPNF 1:10, p. 503)

Eleventh Hour: "The Trials Begin"

Isa. 27:11-28:15, Psa. 2:1-2; 4-5;
Matt. 26:59-75; Mk. 14:55-72; Lk. 22:56-65; Jn. 18:15-27

Overview

Isaiah here speaks of the crown of pride on the heads of the enemy (28:1), yet the Lord wears a crown of glory and beauty (28:5). This is the crown of suffering. God also promises to gather His children together, as is mentioned in the gospels as well.

We read during this hour four verses from **Psalm 2**, which is considered Messianic by both Jewish and Christian traditions. Here, believers from all nations are renewed and sanctified by His Holy Spirit. This psalm is frequently quoted in the New Testament, where it is applied to Christ as the King, the great Son of David and God's Anointed (Acts 4:25ff; 13:33; Heb. 1:5; 5:5). In other Orthodox services, this chapter is read during Christmas Eve, as the refrain for one of the hymns; and on Great Friday, where the entire psalm is sung in the First Hour prayer.

The **Gospels** show the Lord's example of the "temple" and St. Peter's three denials.

The **Exposition** of the hour explains further how this psalm is a prophesy that the kings of the earth would condemn Him with false testimony.

Readings and Patristic Meditations

ISAIAH 27:11-28:15

When its boughs are withered, they will be broken off; the women come and set them on fire. For it is a people of no understanding; Therefore He who made them will not have mercy on them, and He who formed them will show them no favor.

*And it shall come to pass in that day that the Lord will thresh, from the channel of the River to the Brook of Egypt; **And you will be gathered one by one**, O you children of Israel.*

So it shall be in that day: The great trumpet will be blown; They will come, who are about to perish in the land of Assyria, and they who are outcasts in the land of Egypt, and shall worship the Lord in the holy mount at Jerusalem.

Woe to the crown of pride, to the drunkards of Ephraim, whose glorious beauty is a fading flower Which is at the head of the verdant valleys, to those who are overcome with wine! Behold, the Lord has a mighty and strong one, like a tempest of hail and a destroying storm, Like a flood of mighty waters overflowing, Who will bring them down to the earth with His hand. The crown of pride, the drunkards of Ephraim, will be trampled underfoot; And the glorious beauty is a fading flower which is at the head of the verdant valley, Like the first fruit before the summer, which an observer sees; He eats it up while it is still in his hand.

*In that day the Lord of hosts will be for a **crown of glory and a diadem of beauty to the remnant of His people**, For a spirit of justice to him who sits in judgment, and for strength to those who turn back the battle at the gate.*

*But they also have erred through wine, and through intoxicating drink are out of the way; **The priest and the prophet have erred through intoxicating drink**, they are swallowed up by wine, They are out of the way through intoxicating drink; They err in vision, they stumble in judgment. For all tables are full of vomit and filth; No place is clean.*

*"Whom will he teach knowledge? And whom will he make to understand the message? Those just weaned from milk? Those just drawn from the breasts? For **precept must be upon precept, precept upon precept, line upon line, line upon line, here a little, there a little.***"

For with stammering lips and another tongue He will speak to this people, To whom He said, "This is the rest with which You may cause the weary to rest," and, "This is the refreshing;" Yet they would not hear.

But the Word of the Lord was to them, "Precept upon precept, precept upon precept, Line upon line, line upon line, here a little, there a little," That they might go and fall backward, and be broken And snared and caught.

*Therefore hear the word of the Lord, you scornful men, who rule this people who are in Jerusalem, Because you have said, "**We have made a covenant with death**, and with Sheol we are in agreement. When the overflowing scourge passes through, It will not come to us, For we have made lies our refuge, **and under falsehood we have hidden ourselves.***"

Some see in this a prophecy about gathering the children of Israel at the end of time, when they receive faith in Christ, while others see in it a portrait of God's work along the ages, as He brought His people out of the land of Egypt, then saved them from the Babylonian captivity. Or it may, likewise refer to the new Israel, the Church that gathered nations and peoples to enjoy the risen life.

Fr. Tadros Malaty, *Patristic Commentary on Isaiah*, p. 276.

PSALM 2:1-2, 4-5

*Why do the nations rage, and the people plot a vain thing? The kings of the earth set themselves, and the rulers take counsel together, **Against the Lord and against His Anointed, saying,** He who sits in the heavens shall laugh; The Lord shall hold them in derision. Then He shall speak to them in His wrath, and distress them in His deep displeasure.*

This psalm originated in a political setting and was related to the coronation ceremony of new kings at Jerusalem temple and the royal palace. It declares how the pagan kings are against the new anointed and coronated king who is a symbol of the Messianic King.

Fr. Tadros Malaty, *Patristic Commentary on the Psalms (2)*

"He who dwells in the heavens shall laugh at them." If by "heaven" we understand holy souls, God (who dwells in His saints), foreknows what is to come, and "shall laugh at them, and shall hold them in derision."

St. Augustine

He who dwells in the heaven shall laugh at them, because the Lord indeed, being the Son, and Heir since He is in essence one with the Father and enjoys the authority of God the Father, having become Man, called those who believe in Him unto communion and participation of His heavenly kingdom and of His eternal glories. But the wicked in their pride, refused, thinking that they could reign without Him.

St. Cyril of Alexandria, *Commentary on John*, Homily 53

Christ Himself declares, "See! Your house is left to you desolate" (Matt. 23:38). And His parables declare the same thing when He says, "What will he do to those vinedressers? He will destroy those wicked men miserably" (Matt. 21:40,41).

St. John Chrysostom, *Homilies on John*, 53.2 (NPNF 1:14), p. 122

MATTHEW 26:59-75

Now the chief priests, the elders, and all the council sought false testimony against Jesus to put Him to death, but found none. Even though many false witnesses came forward, they found none. But at last two false witnesses came forward and said, "This fellow said, 'I am able to destroy the temple of God and to build it in three days.' And the high priest arose and said to Him, "Do You answer nothing? What is it these men testify against You?" But Jesus kept silent. And the high priest answered and said to Him, "I put You under oath by the living God: Tell us if You are the Christ, the Son of God!" Jesus said to him,

"It is as you said. Nevertheless, I say to you, hereafter you will see the Son of Man sitting at the right hand of the Power, and coming on the clouds of heaven." Then the high priest tore his clothes, saying, "He has spoken blasphemy! What further need do we have of witnesses? Look, now you have heard His blasphemy! What do you think?" They answered and said, "He is deserving of death." Then they spat in His face and beat Him; and others struck Him with the palms of their hands, saying, "Prophesy to us, Christ! Who is the one who struck You?"

Now Peter sat outside in the courtyard. And a servant girl came to him, saying, "You also were with Jesus of Galilee." But he denied it before them all, saying, "I do not know what you are saying." And when he had gone out to the gateway, another girl saw him and said to those who were there, "This fellow also was with Jesus of Nazareth." But again he denied with an oath, "I do not know the Man!" And a little later those who stood by came up and said to Peter, "Surely you also are one of them, for your speech betrays you." Then he began to curse and swear, saying, "I do not know the Man!" Immediately a rooster crowed. And Peter remembered the word of Jesus who had said to him, "Before the rooster crows, you will deny Me three times." So he went out and wept bitterly.

MARK 14:55-72

Now the chief priests and all the council sought testimony against Jesus to put Him to death, but found none. For many bore false witness against Him, but their testimonies did not agree. Then some rose up and bore false witness against Him, saying, "We heard Him say, 'I will destroy this temple made with hands, and within three days I will build another made without hands.'" But not even then did their testimony agree. And the high priest stood up in the midst and asked Jesus, saying, "Do You answer nothing? What is it these men testify against You?" But He kept silent and answered nothing. Again the high priest asked Him, saying to Him, "Are You the Christ, the Son of the Blessed?" Jesus said, "I am. And you will see the Son of Man sitting at the right hand of the Power, and coming with the clouds of heaven." Then the high priest tore his clothes and said, "What further need do we have of witnesses? You have heard the blasphemy! What do you think?" And they all condemned Him to be deserving of death. Then some began to spit on Him, and to blindfold Him, and to beat Him, and to say to Him, "Prophesy!" And the officers struck Him with the palms of their hands.

Now as Peter was below in the courtyard, one of the servant girls of the high priest came. And when she saw Peter warming himself, she looked at him and said, "You also were with Jesus of Nazareth." But he denied it, saying, "I neither know nor understand what you are saying." And he went out on the porch, and a rooster crowed. And the servant girl saw him again, and began to say to those who stood by, "This is one of them." But he denied it again. And a little later those who stood by said to Peter again, "Surely you are one of them; for you are a Galilean, and your speech shows it." Then he began to curse and swear, "I do not know this Man of whom you speak!" A second time the rooster crowed. Then Peter called to mind the word that Jesus had said to him, "Before the rooster crows twice, you will deny Me three times." **And when he thought about it, he wept.**

LUKE 22:56-65

And a certain servant girl, seeing him as he sat by the fire, looked intently at him and said, "This man was also with Him." But he denied Him, saying, "Woman, I do not know Him." And after a little while another saw him and said, "You also are of them." But Peter said, "Man, I am not!" Then after about an hour had passed, another confidently affirmed, saying, "Surely this fellow also was with Him, for he is a Galilean." But Peter said, "Man, I do not know what you are saying!" Immediately, while he was still speaking, the rooster crowed. And the Lord turned and looked at Peter. And Peter remembered the word of the Lord, how He had said to him, "Before the rooster crows, you will deny Me three times." So Peter went out and wept bitterly.

Now the men who held Jesus mocked Him and beat Him. And having blindfolded Him, they struck Him on the face and asked Him, saying, "Prophesy! Who is the one who struck You?" And many other things they blasphemously spoke against Him.

JOHN 18:15-27

And Simon Peter followed Jesus, and so did another disciple. Now that disciple was known to the high priest, and went with Jesus into the courtyard of the high priest. But Peter stood at the door outside. Then the other disciple, who was known to the high priest, went out and spoke to her who kept the door, and brought Peter in. Then the servant girl who kept the door said to Peter, "You are not also one of this Man's disciples, are you?" He said, "I am not." Now the servants and officers who had made a fire of coals stood there, for it was cold, and they warmed themselves. And Peter stood with them and warmed himself.

The high priest then asked Jesus about His disciples and His doctrine. Jesus answered him, "I spoke openly to the world. I always taught in synagogues and in the temple, where the Jews always meet, and in secret I have said nothing. Why do you ask Me? Ask those who have heard Me what I said to them. Indeed they know what I said." And when He had said these things, one of the officers who stood by struck Jesus with the palm of his hand, saying, "Do You answer the high priest like that?" Jesus answered him, "If I have spoken evil, bear witness of the evil; but if well, why do you strike Me?" Then Annas sent Him bound to Caiaphas the high priest.

Now Simon Peter stood and warmed himself. Therefore they said to him, "You are not also one of His disciples, are you?" He denied it and said, "I am not!" One of the servants of the high priest, a relative of him whose ear Peter cut off, said, "Did I not see you in the garden with Him?" Peter then denied again; and immediately a rooster crowed.

Why did our Lord keep silent?

We find in the law several cases of swearing. Here, the priest commands Jesus to swear "by the living God." In this regard, I believe it is improper for one who wants to live by the gospel to command someone to swear. Therefore it is clear that the high priest unlawfully ordered Jesus to swear, even though he may have ordered him to swear "by the living God."...

It was not fitting for our Lord to respond to the high priest's command to swear...For this reason, He neither denied that He was Christ, the Son of God, nor did He openly declare it. Instead, as though accepting to be a swearing witness...He replied, "You have said so."

And since everyone who commits sin is "of the devil" (1 Jn. 3:8), the high priest also committed a sin in plotting against Jesus. Therefore, he was of the devil, and being of the devil as it were, he imitated his very father, who doubtingly asked the Savior twice, "If You are the Son of God," as it is written concerning his temptations. Similar in fact are the words, "If You are the Son of God" and "If You are the Christ, the Son of God" (Matt. 4:3,6). Someone may rightly say in this regard that to doubt whether Christ is the Son of God is the work of the devil and of the high priest who plotted against the Lord.

The Scholar Origen, *Commentary on Matthew*, 110 (AACS 1b, pp. 265-266)

Blind anger and impatience, bereft of grounds for a false accusation, dislodged the high priest from his seat and he displayed the extreme state of his mind with a violent bodily gesture. The more Jesus kept silent over the false witnesses and dishonorable priests indignant at His response, all the more did the high priest, overcome with rage, provoke him to give an incriminating reply. Still Jesus kept quiet, because as God He knew that whatever He replied would be twisted into grounds for accusation.

St. Jerome, *Commentary on Matthew*, 4.26.43 (AACS 1b, p. 266)

It was not in vain that the prophesy had preceded Him, "Yet He opened not His mouth; He was led as a lamb to the slaughter, and as a sheep before its shearers is silent, so He opened not His mouth" (Isa. 53:7). When

He did not open His mouth it was reminiscent of the figure of a lamb. It was not as one of bad conscience convicted of sins, but as one who in His meekness was being sacrificed for the sins of others.

St. Augustine, *Tractates on John*, Tractate 116.45 (NPNF 1:7, p. 426)

When Pilate debated with the religious leaders, the Lord Jesus was silent, realizing what the prophet said: "He opened not His mouth and in His humility there was wisdom" (Isa. 53: 7, 8).

St. John Chrysostom, *Commentary on Matthew* (NPNF 1:10)

It was fitting for Him to be silent during His passion; but He would not be so in His judgment, when He who, in great humility, was sentenced, comes to judge all...The Lord Christ kept silent during the ordeal of His trial, in order to conceal His Deity, to let them consummate what they intended to do. But at His ultimate coming, He "Shall not keep silent" (Psa. 50:3), as He will be proclaiming His Deity.

St. Augustine, *Commentary on Psalm 38* (NPNF 1:8)

Why did Caiaphas tear his garments?

The high priest rent his clothes, saying, "He has spoken blasphemy." He did this to add force to the accusation and to aggravate what He said by symbolic action. What had been said moved the hearers to fear. They did in this case what they would later do in the case of Stephen: they stopped their ears (Acts 7:57). The high priest does the same thing.

St. John Chrysostom, *Commentary on Matthew*, Homily 84, 2-3 (NPNF 1:10, p. 514)

The one whom fury had lifted out of his priestly throne was impelled by that same fury to tear his garments. When Caiaphas tore his robes, he demonstrated that the Jews had lost the glory of the priesthood and that the seat of the high priest was now vacant. But it is the custom of the Jews to tear their clothes when they hear any blasphemy against God. We read that Paul and Barnabas did this when they were honored and worshipped as gods in Lyaconia.

St. Jerome, *Commentary on Matthew*, 2.46.65 (AACS 1b, p. 267)

His Sufferings

This is clearly a reflection of the holy prophet's words, "Be astonished, O heavens, at this, and be horribly afraid; be very desolate," says the Lord"

(Jer. 2:12). The one true God, the King of kings and Lord of lords. He was dishonored by us: first He endured blows, and then he endured laughter from the sinful, demonstrating the highest patience yet presented to us. How can the One who "examines the heart and mind" the One who illuminates the prophets, not know "who strikes You"?

St. Cyril of Alexandria, Fragment 301 (AACS 1b, p. 267)

Who is this strange One who says that He had been silent before, but would not always be silent? Who is He Who was led as a sheep to the slaughter and Who, like a lamb without making a sound before its shearer, did not open His mouth? (Isa. 53:7) Who is He who did not cry out and Whose voice was not heard in the streets? Surely it was He Who was not stubborn and Who did not murmur when He offered His back to the scourges and His cheeks to the blows. He did not turn His face away from their filthy spittle (Isa. 50:5-6, Mat. 26:67, Mk. 14:65, Lk. 22:63). When accused by the priests and elders, He answered nothing (Matt. 26:63, Mk. 14:61) and, to the amazement of Pilate, kept a most patient silence (Matt. 27:14, Mk. 15:5).

St. Cyprian, *The Good of Patience*, 23 (FC 36, p. 286)

By suffering these things in our place, He would deliver us (as I believe) who were worthy to suffer all that disgrace. Truly He did not "die for us" (Rom. 5:8) that we might not die, but that we might not die for ourselves. And He was spit upon and beaten for us, so that we who were worthy of all these things because of our sins might not just suffer them but, suffering them for the sake of justice, we might gratefully accept them. Paul makes it clear that the Savior, "And being found in appearance as a man, He humbled Himself and became obedient to the point of death, even the death of the cross" (Philip. 2:8). On account of all this, "God also has exalted Him..." (Philip. 2:9). God not only exalted Him because of the death He underwent for our sake but also because of the beating, the spitting, and all the rest.

Christ did not turn His face away from "insult and spitting" (Isa. 50:6) so His face might be glorified more than the face of Moses (Exod. 34:29)—with so much glory that comparatively the glorification of Moses' face was outshone, even as the light of a lamp is outshone by that of the sun and even as knowledge, which knows in part, is outshone "when that which is perfect has come" (1 Cor. 13:10), but they also buffeted the holy head of the Church. Because of this, they will be beaten by Satan...as just punishment for the sin they omitted in beating Jesus.

Not content with spitting in His face and buffeting Him, they even struck His face with the palms of their hands, and mocking Him, they said, "Prophesy to us, O Christ! Who is it that struck You?" on account of this...they have been struck and punished. Yet they were unwilling to accept any discipline, as Jeremiah had prophesied about them: "You have stricken them, but they have not grieved; You have consumed them, but they have refused to receive correction" (Jer. 5:3). And now whoever harms anyone in the Church and does these things to him spits on the very face of Christ, and buffeting Christ, they slap Him with the palms of their hands."

The Scholar Origen, *Commentary on Matthew*, 113 (AACS 1b, p. 268)

The Three Denials

I believe that the first servant girl who caused Christ's disciples to deny Him symbolizes the synagogue of the Jews, "according to the flesh," who have frequently coerced the faithful to deny Him. The second maidservant stands for the assembly of Gentiles who also in persecuting Christians has forced them to deny the Lord. And third were the bystanders in the courtyard, who are ministers of the different heresies who compel others top deny the truth of Christ.

The Scholar Origen, *Commentary on Matthew*, 114 (AACS 1b, pp. 270-271)

We do not say that the denial took place in order that Christ's words might come true. We say, rather, that His purpose was to forewarn the disciple, inasmuch as what was about to happen did not escape Christ's knowledge. The misfortune, therefore, happened to the disciple from the cowardice of human nature. Since Christ had not risen from the dead, He had not yet abolished death and wiped corruption away. The fear of undergoing death was something beyond human endurance...The miserable act arose from the affliction of human cowardice. The disciple's conscience condemned him...for he grieved immediately afterwards and his tears of repentance that fell from his eyes as for a serious sin. It says, "having gone out, he wept bitterly" after Christ had looked at him and reminded him of what He had said to him.

St. Cyril of Alexandria, *Commentary on Luke*, Homily 149

What difference does it make that the maid is the first to give Peter away? The men could have recognized him instead. Perhaps this happened so that we may see that the female gender also sinned by killing the Lord, so that His Passion should also redeem womankind. A woman therefore was the first to receive the mystery of the Resurrection and to obey the commands (Jn. 20:11-18), so that she abolished the old error of her sin.

St. Ambrose of Milan, *Exposition of Luke*, 10.73 (AACS 2, pp. 348-349)

Oh strange and wonderful acts! When indeed he saw his Master seized, Peter was so fervent as both to draw his sword, and to cut off the man's ear. But when it was natural for him to be more indignant, and to be inflamed and to burn, hearing such insults, then he becomes a denier. For who would not have been inflamed to madness by the things that were then done? Yet the great disciple, overcome by fears, so far from showing indignation, even denies, and endures not the threat of a tiny and lowly servant girl.

This happens not once only, but he denies His Lord for a second and third time. In a short period, and not so much as before judges, for it was without for "when he had gone out into the porch," they asked him, and he did not even readily come to a sense of his fall. And this Luke said, namely, that Christ looked at him showing that he not only denied Him, but was not even brought to remembrance from within, and this though the cock had crowed; but he needed a further remembrance from his master, and His look was to him instead of a voice; so exceedingly was he full of fear...

But Mark says, that when he had once denied, then first the cock crew, but when thrice, then for the second time; for he declares more particularly the weakness of the disciple, and that he was utterly dead with fear; having learnt these things of his masters himself, for he was a follower of Peter. In which respect one would most marvel at him, that so far from hiding his Teacher's faults, he declared it more distinctly than the rest. on this very account, that he was His disciple.

How then is what is said true, when Matthew affirms that Christ said, "Verily I say to you, that before the cock crow you will deny Me three times;" and Mark declares after the third denial, that "The cock crew the second time?" No, most certainly is it both true and in harmony. For because at each crowing the cock is wont to crow both a third and a fourth time, Mark, to show that not even the sound checked him, and brought him to recollection said this. So that both things are true. For before the cock had finished the one crowing, he had denied a third time. And not even when reminded of his sin by Christ did he dare to weep openly, lest he should be betrayed by his tears, but "he went out, and wept bitterly."

St. John Chrysostom, *Commentary on Matthew*, Homily 85.1-2 (NPNF 1:10 p. 507)

The second time he denied not simply but with an oath; the third time also with cursing. By this we are instructed never to promise without consideration anything above our human ability.

The Scholar Origen, *Commentary on Matthew*, 86 (AACS 1b, p. 220)

Why did Peter weep?

Peter also wept bitterly. He wept so that he could purge his sin with tears. If you want to deserve pardon, you should wash away your guilt with tears. At that same moment and time, Christ looks at you. If you perhaps fall into some sin, because He is a witness to your secrets, He looks at you so that you may recall and confess your error. Imitate Peter, when he says, in another place for the third time, "Yes, Lord; you know that I love you" (Jn. 21:15). since he denied Him a third time, he confesses Him a third time. He denied at night, but he confesses by day.

These words are written that we should know that no one must boast of himself. If Peter fell because he said, "Even if all are made to stumble because of You, I will never be made to made to stumble," what other person can rightly take himself for granted? Since David also said, "I said in my prosperity, 'I shall never be moved'" he admitted that his boasting had harmed him, saying, "You turned away Your face, and I was troubled" (Psa. 30:6-7).

Why did Peter weep? **Guilt took him by surprise.** I am accustomed to weep if I lack guilt, if I do not avenge myself, or do not get what I wickedly desire. **Peter grieved and wept because he went astray as a man.** I do not learn why he spoke, but I learn that he wept. I read of his tears, but I do to read of his explanation. What cannot be defended can be purged. Tears may wash away the offense that is a shame to confess aloud. Tears deal with pardon and shame. Tears speak of guilt without fear and confess sin without the obstacle of shame. Tears do not demand pardon and deserve it. I learn why Peter was silent, lest a swift petition for pardon might offend even more. **First he must weep, and then he must pray.**

St. Ambrose of Milan, *Exposition of Luke*, 10.73,88, 90, 91 (AACS 2, pp. 348-350)

Remembrance of his denial was necessarily bitter, so that the grace of redemption might be even more sweet. If Christ had not left him to himself, he would not have denied. If Christ had not looked at him, he would not have wept. God hates people relying presumptuously on their own powers. Like a doctor, he lances this swollen tumor in those whom He loves. By lancing it, of course, He inflicts pain, but He also ensures health later. When He rises again, the Lord entrusts His sheep to Peter, to that one who denied him. Peter denied Him because he relied on himself, but later Peter would feed His flock as a pastor, because he loved Him. After all, why does He ask him three times about his love, if not to prick his conscience about his threefold denial?

St. Augustine, *Exposition of Luke*, 10.73,88, 90, 91 (AACS 2, pp. 348-350)

To wash away the sin of denial, Peter needed the baptism of tears. From where would he get this, unless the Lord gave him this too? That is why the apostle Paul gave this advice to his people concerning deviant opinions and about how they should deal with them. He said they must be "in humility correcting those who are in opposition, if God perhaps will grant them repentance, so that they may know the truth" (2 Tim. 2:25). So even repentance is a gift from God. The heart of the proud is hard ground. It is softened for repentance only if it is rained on by God's grace.

St. Augustine, Sermon 290.1 (AACS 3, pp. 350)

II

GREAT FRIDAY

"This is He who offered Himself up as an acceptable sacrifice…"

Overview

By far, the one day of the entire Church year in which the Church prays together is Great Friday. More prayers are prayed, more readings read, more hymns chanted than any other time. All because of the perfect sacrifice of Christ on the Cross for the life of the world. Through such meditations and hymns, truly all time passes by.

On this day, we meditate upon the Holy Cross, which is the joy of every Christian soul; the path to salvation; the road to eternal victory; the weapon against pain, sorrow, and death; the doorway to the heavenly kingdom.

This atmosphere the Church created for us of prayer and worship make us feel as if we are witnessing the events transpire before our eyes. We not only are witnesses to the Holy Passion of our Good Savior, but we become participants in the story of salvation. We find ourselves at the end of the Twelfth Hour, and feel that it was just a few moments ago that we began this holy day.

Through this Holy Pascha Week, the Church has revealed to us the great mysteries of our Lord Jesus Christ. On Lazarus Saturday, He is the meaning and purpose of our Life, who declared to us, "I am the Way, the Truth and the Life." On Palm Sunday, He is revealed as the King of kings, riding on the donkey into our hearts to become enthroned on the Cross. On Monday, He is the Gardener that seeks to implant in us the seeds of truth, so that we may yield the fruit of the Holy Spirit. On Tuesday, He is our beloved Bridegroom—He takes us from this world, into a new home so that we may spend eternity with Him in perfect love and the fullness of joy. On Wednesday He is the aroma of life to those who are being saved (as the woman at His feet); and the aroma of death to those who are perishing (as Judas, who betrays Him on this day). On Holy Thursday, He is the humble Servant who washes our feet as well as the Bread of Life Who offers us His Body and Blood to be one with Him and dine with Him. Finally, on Great Friday He appears as the Lamb of God Who takes away the sins of the world.

The Lamb of God appears throughout each hour in a different form. During the First hour, He is tried and convicted under false accusations and testimony. During the Third hour, He was bruised and suffered Lamb—whipped, spat upon, and mocked for our sakes. During the Sixth Hour, He was crucified for our sakes. In the Ninth Hour, He gave His soul to the

Father. In the Eleventh, He was taken down from the Cross. Finally, in the Twelfth, He was buried in the tomb.

First Hour: "The Trial"

Deut. 8:19-24; Isa.1:2-9, 2:10-21, Jer. 22:29-23:6; 3:1-6;
Zech. 11:11-14; Wisdom 2:12-22; Job 12:18-13:1; Micah 1:16-2:3;
Psa. 26:12,34:11,12;
Matt. 27:1-14; Mk. 15:1-5; Lk. 22:66-23:12; Jn. 18:28-40

Overview

The First Hour focuses on the Trial of God with man, and that of man with God. In the Old Testament, God often put man on trial because of his many sins, and sought condemnation for his rebellion and stubbornness. Thus, the first two prophesies focus on the rebellion against God by the Israelites. First, in **Deuteronomy**, Moses tells the Jews how they sinned against God while he was on the mountain, and how he interceded before God not to destroy them. Despite their sin, the Lord tells them, "You are to cross over the Jordan today…" Thus, the Lord does not prevent us from the baptism or the cross due to our sin.

In the second prophesy of **Isaiah**, the Lord tells His people, "You have rebelled against Me." He calls them a sinful nation, who work iniquity, vipers, corrupt ones, stiffed-necked, who provoked God to anger. Their trouble increases because of their sin (Isa. 1:4), the natural consequence of sin. Despite their sin, the Lord has not left them to be like Sodom and Gomorrah.

The third prophesy of **Jeremiah** speaks of the Cross, the Throne of God upon which He is glorified throughout the nations. Although the shepherds have destroyed and scattered the sheep, the Lord promises us, "But I will gather the remnant of My flock out of all countries where I have driven them, and bring them back to their folds; and they shall be fruitful and increase." Thus, through the Cross, the Lord converts sin into repentance; desolation to fruitfulness; sorrow into joy. In the second passage of Jeremiah, God accuses us, as His bride, of being unfaithful by having many lovers. Despite our unfaithfulness, He still leaves the door open to return, "'But you have played the harlot with many lovers; yet return to Me,' says the Lord."

The **Wisdom** of Solomon shows how the Jews will spitefully examine and torture Him, but He will be saved. We see many accusers, not just one, as the Lord is brought to Pilate, Caiphas, and stood before many accusers. They tested His patience, teachings, and divinity. The passage assures us, however, that if He is truly the "Son of God, He will help Him and deliver

Him from the hand of His adversaries" (Wisdom 2:18). Truly, He is God and truly He conquered His adversaries through His resurrection.

The passage of **Job**, though not included in some books, also refers to the Lord's victory over His enemies. He "loosens the bonds of kings...leads princes away plundered,... overthrows the mighty...He disarms the mighty...and brings the shadow of death the light."

Micah the prophet also clearly reassures us of His resurrection proclaims, "for I have fallen yet shall arise; for though I should sit in darkness, the Lord shall be a light to me."

The remaining prophesies foretell the trials in which the Jews falsely condemned our Lord Jesus Christ. The chief priests took the silver and bought a potter's field with it to bury strangers in. This itself was the fulfillment of two prophesies (Zec. 11:12-13; Jer. 19:1-13, 32:9). Judas hung himself, unable to acknowledge the forgiveness of God, and unwilling to depend on Christ. Instead of repentance, Judas turned a transgression into another transgression. The "fierce witnesses" mentioned in **Psalm** 35:11 specifically refers to these false witnesses at the trial of Christ.

In the **Gospels**, our Lord began to be judged in front of a series of councils. The chief priests convened together and condemned the Savior so that they might deliver Him to Pilate to kill Him (Exposition). False witnesses came forth to falsely accuse Him. When Judas saw that He was condemned, he brought the thirty pieces of silver to the chief priests and elders to avoid the responsibility for innocent blood (Matt. 23:34-35; Deut. 21:9, 27:25).

Then, they had bound Jesus and delivered Him to Pontius Pilate, the governor. A set of charges is presented to Pilate. When Pilate discovers that our Lord was from Galilee, he sent Him to Herod, who questioned and mocked Him. Then the Accused is then returned back to Pilate to without being found guilty. When Christ is returned to Pilate, he tries twice to release Him, even offering a lesser penalty of whipping. Finally, Pilate gives in to the "will" of the Jews. It was a custom to release one of the prisoners at the time of the feast, but the people chose to release Barabbas instead of Jesus. Then Pilate washed His hands in front of them, denying any responsibility for the Innocent One.

Judas' love of money led to his demise, as explained in the homily of St. John Chrysostom, Ironically, Judas has the same name as Judah, one of the twelve sons of Jacob, who rather than shedding his brother Joseph's blood, sold him for twenty (or thirty) pieces of silver (Gen. 37:26-28).

At the end of this hour, the Icon of the Crucifixion is placed on an icon holder in the chorus of deacons. Candles, lamps, crosses, gospels, and censor(s) and rose petals are placed before the icon of Crucifixion. The rose petals remind us of life which springs forth from the earth, which will happen for us through Christ, who is now condemned to His death.

My Lord Jesus when we enter the Church this morning and stand before Your Cross, may we be joyful because we took this free gift and You bought us with Your Blood while we are worth dust. This was not because of any merit or any righteousness from our part. It is Your love, O Master, that made You undress and raised You on the Cross to take us from death to life.

Fr. Pishoy Kamel, *JTG*, p. 66

Readings and Patristic Meditations

DEUTERONOMY 8:19-9:24

Then it shall be, if you by any means forget the Lord your God, and follow other gods, and serve them and worship them, I testify against you this day that you shall surely perish. As the nations which the Lord destroys before you, so you shall perish, because you would not be obedient to the voice of the Lord your God.

"Hear, O Israel: You are to cross over the Jordan today, and go in to dispossess nations greater and mightier than yourself, cities great and fortified up to heaven, a people great and tall, the descendants of the Anakim, whom you know, and of whom you heard it said, 'Who can stand before the descendants of Anak?' Therefore understand today that the Lord your God is He who goes over before you as a consuming fire. He will destroy them and bring them down before you; so you shall drive them out and destroy them quickly, as the Lord has said to you. Do not think in your heart, after the Lord your God has cast them out before you, saying, 'Because of my righteousness the Lord has brought me in to possess this land'; but it is because of the wickedness of these nations that the Lord is driving them out from before you. It is not because of your righteousness or the uprightness of your heart that you go in to possess their land, but because of the wickedness of these nations that the Lord your God drives them out from before you, and that He may fulfill the word which the Lord swore to your fathers, to Abraham, Isaac, and Jacob. Therefore understand that the Lord your God is not giving you this good land to possess because of your righteousness, for you are a stiff-necked people.

"Remember. Do not forget how you provoked the Lord your God to wrath in the wilderness. From the day that you departed from the land of Egypt until you came to this place, you have been rebellious against the Lord. Also in Horeb you

provoked the Lord to wrath, so that the Lord was angry enough with you to have destroyed you. When I went up into the mountain to receive the tablets of stone, the tablets of the covenant which the Lord made with you, then I stayed on the mountain forty days and forty nights. I neither ate bread nor drank water. Then the Lord delivered to me two tablets of stone written with the finger of God, and on them were all the words which the Lord had spoken to you on the mountain from the midst of the fire in the day of the assembly. And it came to pass, at the end of forty days and forty nights, that the Lord gave me the two tablets of stone, the tablets of the covenant. Then the Lord said to me, 'Arise, go down quickly from here, for your people whom you brought out of Egypt have acted corruptly; they have quickly turned aside from the way which I commanded them; they have made themselves a molded image.'

*"Furthermore the Lord spoke to me, saying, 'I have seen this people, and indeed they are a stiff-necked people. **Let Me alone, that I may destroy them and blot out their name from under heaven; and I will make of you a nation mightier and greater than they.**' So I turned and came down from the mountain, and the mountain burned with fire; and the two tablets of the covenant were in my two hands. And I looked, and behold, you had sinned against the Lord your God—had made for yourselves a molded calf! You had turned aside quickly from the way which the Lord had commanded you. Then I took the two tablets and threw them out of my two hands and broke them before your eyes. And I fell down before the Lord, as at the first, forty days and forty nights; I neither ate bread nor drank water, because of all your sin which you committed in doing wickedly in the sight of the Lord, to provoke Him to anger. For I was afraid of the anger and hot displeasure with which the Lord was angry with you, to destroy you. But the Lord listened to me at that time also. And the Lord was very angry with Aaron and would have destroyed him; **so I prayed for Aaron also at the same time.** Then I took your sin, the calf which you had made, and burned it with fire and crushed it and ground it very small, until it was as fine as dust; and I threw its dust into the brook that descended from the mountain.*

*"Also at Taberah and Massah and Kibroth Hattaavah you provoked the Lord to wrath. Likewise, when the Lord sent you from Kadesh Barnea, saying, 'Go up and possess the land which I have given you,' then you rebelled against the commandment of the Lord your God, and you did not believe Him nor obey His voice. **You have been rebellious against the Lord from the day that I knew you.***

In the previous days, we read about the Lord's enemies who were plotting His death; today we begin reading of His victory over His enemies, which begins through the salvation on the Cross. In the first reading, we see the Lord "is a consuming fire" destroying His enemies and the nations. This also reminds us of our fasting, after the example of the Lord who fasted as Moses did, for he drank no water and ate no bread on account of the people's sins.

In like manner He points to the cross of Christ...in Moses, when Israel was attacked by strangers. And that He might remind them, when assailed, that it was on account of their sins they were delivered to death, the Spirit speaks to the heart of Moses, that he should make a figure of the cross, and of Him about to suffer thereon; for unless they put their trust in Him, they shall be overcome forever. Moses therefore placed one weapon above another in the midst of the hill, and standing upon it, so as to be higher than all the people, he stretched forth his hands, and thus again Israel acquired the mastery. But when again he let down his hands, they were again destroyed. For what reason? That they might know that they could not be saved unless they put their trust in Him. And in another prophet He declares, "All day long I have stretched forth My hands to an unbelieving people, and one that denys My righteous way."

Epistle of Barnabas, 12 (ANF 1)

ISAIAH 1:2-9

Hear, O heavens, and give ear, O earth! For the Lord has spoken: "I have nourished and brought up children, and they have rebelled against Me;

The ox knows its owner and the donkey its master's crib; but Israel does not know, My people do not consider."

Alas, sinful nation, a people laden with iniquity, a brood of evildoers, children who are corrupters! They have forsaken the Lord, they have provoked to anger the Holy One of Israel, they have turned away backward.

Why should you be stricken again? You will revolt more and more. The whole head is sick, and the whole heart faints. From the sole of the foot even to the head, there is no soundness in it, but wounds and bruises and putrefying sores; They have not been closed or bound up, or soothed with ointment.

Your country is desolate, your cities are burned with fire; strangers devour your land in your presence; And it is desolate, as overthrown by strangers. So the daughter of Zion is left as a booth in a vineyard, as a hut in a garden of cucumbers, as a besieged city. Unless the Lord of hosts Had left to us a very small remnant, we would have become like Sodom, we would have been made like Gomorrah.

According to nature - to creation - we are said to be the children of God, being all His creation. But, as far as obedience and discipline are concerned, we are not all, children of God. Only those who believe in Him, and who consummate His will, are His children. Those who do otherwise are the children of the devil and his angels, as they are doing his works.

St. Irenaeus, *Against the Heresies*, 4.41.2 (ANF 1)

When the Pharisees prosecuted our Lord and Savior, He wept for their coming destruction. They mistreated Him; yet, He did not do the same to them, not even under threat; and not even when they killed Him. On the contrary, He felt sorry for their behavior... All these things were actually written before their eyes in the Holy Scripture; as Isaiah prophesied: "I have nourished and brought up children, and they rebelled against Me" (Isa. 1:2). They are no longer the people of God, nor a holy nation, but have become: "Rulers of Sodom... and people of Gomorrah" (Isa. 1:10). They even surpassed the transgressions of Sodom, as the prophet prophesied: "Neither... Sodom, nor... (Gomorrah) have done as you... have done" (Ezek. 16: 48). The people of Sodom opposed angels; but those people attacked God, Lord of all, and their King. They killed the King of angels, not realizing that Christ they killed is still living up to this day.

St. Athanasius, *Paschal Epistle 8* (NPNF 2:4)

ISAIAH 2:10-21

Enter into the rock, and hide in the dust, from the terror of the Lord and the glory of His majesty. The lofty looks of man shall be humbled, the haughtiness of men shall be bowed down, and the Lord alone shall be exalted in that day.

For the Day of the Lord of hosts shall come upon everything proud and lofty, upon everything lifted up—and it shall be brought low— upon all the cedars of Lebanon that are high and lifted up, and upon all the oaks of Bashan; upon all the high mountains, and upon all the hills that are lifted up; upon every high tower, and upon every fortified wall; Upon all the ships of Tarshish, and upon all the beautiful sloops. The loftiness of man shall be bowed down, and the haughtiness of men shall be brought low; the Lord alone will be exalted in that day, but the idols He shall utterly abolish.

*They shall go into the holes of the rocks, and into the caves of the earth, From the terror of the Lord and the glory of His majesty, **when He arises to shake the earth mightily.***

In that day a man will cast away his idols of silver and his idols of gold, which they made, each for himself to worship, to the moles and bats,

*To go into the clefts of the rocks, and into the crags of the rugged rocks, from the terror of the Lord **and the glory of His majesty, when He arises to shake the earth mightily.***

"The glory of His majesty" is mentioned twice in this passage—in the very first and very last verses of this passage. The first verse refers to the glory of His Cross, for the rock mentioned here is Christ, just as Moses hit the Rock and hid in the rock to see the glory of God (Exod. 33:20,21). As St. Paul says, "and that Rock was Christ" (1 Cor. 10:4) The very last verse refers to the glory of His resurrection, especially in the earthquake. Then, He arose "to shake the earth mightily."

What is the rock in which we hide before the divine splendor, but the Lord Christ? And in Him we find for ourselves a refuge before divine justice. That is why, when the prophet Moses desired to behold the divine glory, he was told: "You cannot see My face, for no man shall see My face and live... Here is a place by Me: you shall stand on the rock (Christ is our rock). So it shall be, while My glory passes by, that I will put you in the cleft of the rock, and will cover you with My hand while I pass by" (Exod. 33:20,21,22). As long as we lean on our Christ, the true Rock, and abide in Him, and He puts us as though in a cleft within Him, we shall be able to behold the divine glory. But if we lean on ourselves, or on a human arm, we shall perish and be denied beholding God.

Fr. Tadros Malaty, *Patristic Commentary on Isaiah*, 71-72

The sacred books acknowledge with regard to Christ, that as He is the Son of man, so is the same Being not a [mere] man; and as He is flesh, so is He also spirit, and the Word of God, and God. And as He was born of Mary in the last times, so did He also proceed from God as the First-begotten of every creature; and as He hungered, so did He satisfy [others]; and as He thirsted, so did He of old cause the Jews to drink, for the "Rock was Christ" Himself. Thus does Jesus now give to His believing people power to drink spiritual waters, which spring up to life eternal. And as He was the son of David, so was He also the Lord of David. And as He was from Abraham, so did He also exist before Abraham. And as He was the servant of God, so is He the Son of God, and Lord of the universe. And as He was spit upon ignominiously, so also did He breathe the Holy Spirit into His disciples. And as He was saddened, so also did He give joy to His people. And as He was capable of being handled and touched, so again did He, in a non-apprehensible form, pass through the midst of those who sought to injure Him, and entered without impediment through closed doors. And as He slept, so did He also rule the sea, the winds, and the storms. And as He suffered, so also is He alive, and life-giving, and healing all our infirmity. And as He died, so is He also the Resurrection of the dead. He suffered shame on earth, while He is higher than all glory and praise in heaven; Who, "though He was crucified through weakness, yet He lives by divine power;" Who "descended into the lower parts of the earth," and Who "ascended up above the heavens;" for whom a manger sufficed, yet who filled all things; who was dead, yet who lives forever and ever. Amen.

St. Irenaeus, Fragment 52 (ANF 1)

JEREMIAH 22:29-23:6

O earth, earth, earth, hear the word of the Lord! Thus says the Lord: 'Write this man down as childless, a man who shall not prosper in his days; For none of his descendants shall prosper, sitting on the throne of David, and ruling anymore in Judah.'"

"Woe to the shepherds who destroy and scatter the sheep of My pasture!" says the Lord. Therefore thus says the Lord God of Israel against the shepherds who feed My people: "You have scattered My flock, driven them away, and not attended to them. Behold, I will attend to you for the evil of your doings," says the Lord. "But I will gather the remnant of My flock out of all countries where I have driven them, and bring them back to their folds; and they shall be fruitful and increase. I will set up shepherds over them who will feed them; and they shall fear no more, nor be dismayed, nor shall they be lacking," says the Lord.

"Behold, the days are coming," says the Lord, "That I will raise to David a Branch of righteousness; a King shall reign and prosper, and execute judgment and righteousness in the earth. In His days Judah will be saved, and Israel will dwell safely; now this is His name by which He will be called: THE LORD OUR RIGHTEOUSNESS.

JEREMIAH 3:1-6

Now "They say, 'If a man divorces his wife, and she goes from him and becomes another man's, may he return to her again?' Would not that land be greatly polluted? But you have played the harlot with many lovers; yet return to Me," says the Lord.

"Lift up your eyes to the desolate heights and see: Where have you not lain with men? By the road you have sat for them like an Arabian in the wilderness; And you have polluted the land with your harlotries and your wickedness. Therefore the showers have been withheld, and there has been no latter rain. You have had a harlot's forehead; you refuse to be ashamed. Will you not from this time cry to Me, 'My father, You are the guide of my youth? Will He remain angry forever? Will He keep it to the end?' Behold, you have spoken and done evil things, as you were able."

The Lord said also to me in the days of Josiah the king: "Have you seen what backsliding Israel has done? She has gone up on every high mountain and under every green tree, and there played the harlot.

Here, He reveals the essence of marital life, clarifying that marriage is supposed to be an unbreakable secret union; yet, if a third party got in between, that union is dissolved for good. No man would remarry his harlot divorcee, lest the "land", namely his body, would get defiled! God, on the other hand, is not like any human husband, to expel His betrayer wife. But, in His limitless love, although He sees that the soul has voided her union with Him through her union with His enemies—the Devil and his hosts with their evil works, counting them as her friends... yet He calls her again, saying, "Return to Me."

Fr. Tadros Malaty, *Patristic Commentary on Jeremiah*

This is a new kind of goodness; God receives the soul, even after harlotry, if she returns and repents from her whole heart...Here God appears as jealous; He seeks your soul, and wishes that you attach to Him. He is indeed not pleased; He is angry; and revealing some kind of jealousy; to let you know that He longs for your salvation.

The Scholar Origen

He speaks of that who presents herself to harlotry with a multitude, who came to corrupt her; those who are related to Satan and his angels, who plot to defile and corrupt the beauty of our rational mind and sound insight; through dialogue, and corrupting every soul that is betrothed to the Lord.

Father Methodius

WISDOM OF SOLOMON 2:12-22

"Let us lie in wait for the righteous man, because He is inconvenient to us and opposes our actions; he reproaches us for sins against the law, and accuses us of sins against our training. He professes to have knowledge of God, and calls Himself the Son of God. He became to us a reproof of our thoughts; the very sight of Him is a burden to us, because His manner of life is unlike that of others, and His ways are strange. We are considered by Him as something base, and He avoids our ways as unclean; He calls the last end of the righteous happy, and boasts that God is His Father.

Let us see if His words are true, and let us test what will happen at the end of His life; for if the righteous man is the Son of God, He will help Him, and will deliver Him from the hand of his adversaries. Let us test Him with insult and torture, that we may find out how gentle He is, and make trial of His forbearance. Let us condemn Him to a shameful death, for, according to what He says, He will be protected." Thus they reasoned, but they were led astray, for their wickedness blinded them, and they did not know the secret purposes of God, nor hope for the wages of holiness, nor discern the prize for blameless souls.

This passage contains the cry of the wicked, when Pilate examined Him with the Roman soldiers, they said, "let us see if his works are true…Let us examine him with despite and torture, that we may know His meekness and prove His patience." Finally, they declared, "Let us condemn Him with a shameful death." Truly, they were blind, as the prophet declares, they did not know the mysteries of God, that they had the Messiah the Son of God before them. Many interpret this passage as direct prophesies of Matthew 27:41-44.

This passage also prophesies of the resurrection of the Lord as well, when the accusers say, for if the righteous man is the Son of God, "He will help Him, and will deliver Him from the hand of his adversaries." This is precisely what had happened, despite all of Satan's trickeries and deceit.

ZECHARIAH 11:11-14

So it was broken on that day. Thus the poor of the flock, who were watching me, knew that it was the word of the Lord. Then I said to them, "If it is agreeable to you, give me my wages; and if not, refrain." So they weighed out for my wages thirty pieces of silver. And the Lord said to me, "Throw it to the potter"—that princely price they set on me. So I took the thirty pieces of silver and threw them into the house of the Lord for the potter. Then I cut in two my other staff, bonds, that I might break the brotherhood between Judah and Israel.

Hear now in regard to the thirty pieces of silver: "And I will say to them, 'If it seems good to you, give me my wages, or refuse.'" One recompense is due me for curing the blind and the lame, and I receive another; instead of thanksgiving, dishonor, and instead of worship, insult. Do you see how Scripture foresaw all this? "And they counted out my wages, thirty pieces of silver." O prophetic accuracy! A great and unerring wisdom of the Holy Spirit! For he did not say ten or twenty but thirty, exactly the right amount. Tell also what happened to this payment, O prophet! Does he who received it keep it, or does he give it back? And after its return what becomes of it? The prophet says, "So I took thirty pieces of silver, and I cast them into the house of the Lord, into the foundry." Compare this to the prophesy of the Gospel, which says, "Judas repented and flung the pieces of silver into the temple and withdrew."

St. Cyril of Jerusalem, *Catechetical Lectures*, 13.10 (FC 64, pp. 11-12)

MICAH 7:1-8

Woe is me! For I am like those who gather summer fruits, like those who glean vintage grapes; There is no cluster to eat of the first-ripe fruit which my soul desires. The faithful man has perished from the earth, and there is no one upright among men. **They all lie in wait for blood; every man hunts his brother with a net.**

That they may successfully do evil with both hands— **The prince asks for gifts, the judge seeks a bribe,** *and the great man utters his evil desire; So they scheme together. The best of them is like a brier; The most upright is sharper than a thorn hedge; The day of your watchman and your punishment comes; Now shall be their perplexity.*

Do not trust in a friend; Do not put your confidence in a companion; Guard the doors of your mouth from her who lies in your bosom. For son dishonors father, daughter rises against her mother, daughter-in-law against her mother-in-law; a man's enemies are the men of his own household. Therefore I will look to the Lord; I will wait for the God of my salvation; My God will hear me.

Do not rejoice over me, my enemy; when I fall, I will arise; when I sit in darkness, the Lord will be a light to me.

Malice is a dreadful thing and full of hypocrisy. It has filled the world with ten thousand evils; through this malady the law courts are filled, from this comes the desire of fame and wealth, from this the love of rule, and insolence, through this the roads have wicked robbers and the sea pirates, from this proceed the murders through the world, through this our race is rent asunder, and whatever evil you may see, you will perceive to arise from this. This has even burst into the Churches, this has caused ten thousand dreadful things from the beginning, this is the mother of greed, this malady has turned all things upside down, and corrupted justice...

For "gifts, blind the eyes of the wise, and as a muzzle on the mouth turn away reproofs" (Eccles. 20:29). This makes slaves of freemen, concerning this we talk every day, and no good comes of it, we become worse than wild beasts; we plunder orphans, strip widows, do wrong to the poor, join woe to woe. "Alas! that the righteous has perished from the earth!" (Micah 7:1, 2). It is our part too henceforth to mourn, or rather we have need to say this every day. We profit nothing by our prayers, nothing by our advice and exhortation, it remains therefore that we weep.

Thus, after repeatedly exhorting those in Jerusalem, when they profiled nothing, Christ wept at their hardness. This also do the Prophets, and this let us do now. Henceforth is the season for mourning and tears and wailing;

it is seasonable for us also to say now, "Call for the mourning women, and send for the cunning women, that they may cry aloud" (Jer. 9:17); perhaps thus we shall be able to cast out the malady of those who build splendid houses, of those who surround themselves with lands gotten by rapine. It is seasonable to mourn; but do you take part with me in mourning, you who have been stripped and injured, by your mournings bring down my tears. But while mourning we will mourn, not for ourselves but for them; they have not injured you, but they have destroyed themselves; for you have the Kingdom of Heaven in return for the injustice done you, they have hell in return for their gain.

On this account it is better to be injured than to injure. Let us bewail them with a lamentation not of man's making, but that from the Holy Scriptures with which the Prophets also wailed. With Isaiah let us wail bitterly, and say, "Woe, they that add house to house, that lay field to field, that they may take somewhat from their neighbor; will you dwell alone upon the earth? Great houses and fair, and there shall be no inhabitants in them" (Isa. 5:8, 9).

St. John Chrysostom, *Commentary on Matthew*, Homily 64 (NPNF 1:14)

JOB 12:18-13:1

*He loosens the bonds of kings, and binds their waist with a belt. **He leads princes away plundered, and overthrows the mighty.** He deprives the trusted ones of speech, and takes away the discernment of the elders. **He pours contempt on princes, and disarms the mighty.** He uncovers deep things out of darkness, and brings the shadow of death to light. He makes nations great, and destroys them; He enlarges nations, and guides them. He takes away the understanding of the chiefs of the people of the earth, and makes them wander in a pathless wilderness. They grope in the dark without light, and He makes them stagger like a drunken man. "Behold, my eye has seen all this, my ear has heard and understood it.*

PSALM 26:12, 34:11,12

For false witnesses have risen against me, and such as breathe out violence. Fierce witnesses rise up; they ask me things that I do not know. They reward me evil for good, to the sorrow of my soul.

Again, there were others who had their hands full of iniquity, and accusing these he said, "Iniquities are in their hands, and their right hand is filled with gifts." But He Himself had hands practiced in nothing but in being stretched out towards heaven. Therefore he said of these also, "the lifting up of My hands [let it be] an evening sacrifice."

St. John Chrysostom, *On the Statues*, Homily 4.11 (NPNF 1:9)

MATTHEW 27:1-14

When morning came, all the chief priests and elders of the people plotted against Jesus to put Him to death. And when they had bound Him, they led Him away and delivered Him to Pontius Pilate the governor.

Then Judas, His betrayer, seeing that He had been condemned, was remorseful and brought back the thirty pieces of silver to the chief priests and elders, saying, "I have sinned by betraying innocent blood." And they said, "What is that to us? You see to it!" Then he threw down the pieces of silver in the temple and departed, and went and hanged himself. But the chief priests took the silver pieces and said, "It is not lawful to put them into the treasury, because they are the price of blood." And they consulted together and bought with them the potter's field, to bury strangers in. Therefore that field has been called the Field of Blood to this day. Then was fulfilled what was spoken by Jeremiah the prophet, saying, "And they took the thirty pieces of silver, the value of Him who was priced, whom they of the children of Israel priced, and gave them for the potter's field, as the Lord directed me."

Now Jesus stood before the governor. And the governor asked Him, saying, "Are You the King of the Jews?" So Jesus said to him, "It is as you say." And while He was being accused by the chief priests and elders, He answered nothing. Then Pilate said to Him, "Do You not hear how many things they testify against You?" **But He answered him not one word, so that the governor marveled greatly.**

MARK 15:1-5

Immediately, in the morning, the chief priests held a consultation with the elders and scribes and the whole council; and they bound Jesus, led Him away, and delivered Him to Pilate. Then Pilate asked Him, "Are You the King of the Jews?" He answered and said to him, "It is as you say." And the chief priests accused Him of many things, but He answered nothing. Then Pilate asked Him again, saying, "Do You answer nothing? See how many things they testify against You!" But Jesus still answered nothing, so that Pilate marveled.

LUKE 22:66-23:12

As soon as it was day, the elders of the people, both chief priests and scribes, came together and led Him into their council, saying, "If You are the Christ, tell us." But He said to them, "If I tell you, you will by no means believe. And if I also ask you, you will by no means answer Me or let Me go. Hereafter the Son of Man will sit on the right hand of the power of God." Then they all said, "Are You then the Son of God?" So He said to them, "You rightly say that I am." And they said, "What further testimony do we need? For we have heard it ourselves from His own mouth."

Then the whole multitude of them arose and led Him to Pilate. And they began to accuse Him, saying, "We found this fellow perverting the nation, and forbidding to pay taxes to Caesar, saying that He Himself is Christ, a King."

Then Pilate asked Him, saying, "Are You the King of the Jews?" He answered him and said, "It is as you say." So Pilate said to the chief priests and the crowd, "I find no fault in this Man." But they were the more fierce, saying, "He stirs up the people, teaching throughout all Judea, beginning from Galilee to this place."

When Pilate heard of Galilee, he asked if the Man were a Galilean. And as soon as he knew that He belonged to Herod's jurisdiction, he sent Him to Herod, who was also in Jerusalem at that time. Now when Herod saw Jesus, he was exceedingly glad; for he had desired for a long time to see Him, because he had heard many things about Him, and he hoped to see some miracle done by Him. Then he questioned Him with many words, but He answered him nothing. And the chief priests and scribes stood and vehemently accused Him. Then Herod, with his men of war, treated Him with contempt and mocked Him, arrayed Him in a gorgeous robe, and sent Him back to Pilate. That very day Pilate and Herod became friends with each other, for previously they had been at enmity with each other.

JOHN 18:28-40

Then they led Jesus from Caiaphas to the Praetorium, and it was early morning. But they themselves did not go into the Praetorium, lest they should be defiled, but that they might eat the Passover. Pilate then went out to them and said, "What accusation do you bring against this Man?" They answered and said to him, "If He were not an evildoer, we would not have delivered Him up to you." Then Pilate said to them, "You take Him and judge Him according to your law." Therefore the Jews said to him, "It is not lawful for us to put anyone to death," that the saying of Jesus might be fulfilled which He spoke, signifying by what death He would die. Then Pilate entered the Praetorium again, called Jesus, and said to Him, "Are You the King of the Jews?" Jesus answered him, "Are you speaking for yourself about this, or did others tell you this concerning Me?" Pilate answered, "Am I a Jew? Your own nation and the chief priests have delivered You to me. What have You done?" Jesus answered, "My kingdom is not of this world. If My kingdom were of this world, My servants would fight, so that I should not be delivered to the Jews; but now My kingdom is not from here." Pilate therefore said to Him, "Are You a king then?" Jesus answered, "You say rightly that I am a king. For this cause I was born, and for this cause I have come into the world, that I should bear witness to the truth. Everyone who is of the truth hears My voice." Pilate said to Him, "What is truth?" And when he had said this, he went out again to the Jews, and said to them, "I find no fault in Him at all.

"But you have a custom that I should release someone to you at the Passover. Do you therefore want me to release to you the King of the Jews?" Then they all cried again, saying, "Not this Man, but Barabbas!" Now Barabbas was a robber.

Judas and the Field of Blood

If they had put the blood money into the treasury, their deed might have remained relatively more hidden. But the religious leaders make clear their guilt to all subsequent generations by buying the piece of land for burial. They thereby unconsciously declare their guilt.

So do not imagine that someone might do a good work through murder and use the reward for some supposed good purpose. Such alms are satanic. Such reasoning is twisted. Do not be naive about this. There are still many who imagine that they are permitted to violently take countless things that belong to others. Then they make an excuse for their violence if they give some ten or a hundred gold pieces to charity. Of these the prophet has said, "You have covered my altar with tears" (Mal. 2:13). Christ is not willing to be fed by covetousness. He does not accept these gifts. Why do you insult your Lord by offering these unclean things? It is better to leave people to pine with hunger than to feed them from these polluted sources....

Once again they are self-condemned by their own conscience. Don't you see this? They knew that they had been paying straightaway for a murder. They even bought a field for the burial of strangers. They did not even put the silver into a treasury. So this directness itself became a witness against them and a proof of their treason...

They did not make these decisions randomly but took counsel together. This indicates that no one is innocent of the deed. All are guilty. So it is in cases of conspiracy... Even the very name of the place proclaims more sharply than a trumpet their guilt of murder.

All these things had been foretold from ancient times by prophecy. It was not the apostles alone but the prophets who were also declaring these events precisely as they occurred. Don't you see how they foresaw in every way the suffering of Christ? How they knew of its chastisement beforehand?

St. John Chrysostom, *Commentary on Matthew*, Homily 85.3 (NPNF 1:10 pp. 508-509)

Because the quality of resting places for the dead varies (for many are buried in their ancestral tombs which were secured by a pledge, but those who suffer misfortune are often buried in the graves of the homeless), those who received payment in exchange for the blood of Jesus used it to acquire a potter's field for the purpose of having a place in which to bury those foreigners who could not supply a pledge to secure a proper tomb. If it is suitable to interpret these foreigners typologically, we can consider those persons to be foreigners who remained strangers to God until the end and alien to his covenants. Vagabonds such as these meet their end buried in a potter's field, acquired with blood money. The righteous are able to say, "We are buried with Christ in a new tomb cut from the rock in which no dead body had yet been laid," but those foreigners who remain finally estranged from Christ and alien to God will have to say, "We are buried with strangers in the field which is called the 'Field of Blood.'"

The Scholar Origen, *Commentary on Matthew*, 117 (AACS 1b, p. 274)

This is amazing! The killers say "what is that to us?" they ask of him who received the price for the crime to see for himself. As for them, His killers, they did not have to see. They then tell themselves "It is not lawful to put it in the treasury is considered sinful," how much more would the shedding of blood be? And if you see a pretext for crucifying Christ, then why do you refuse to accept the price?

St. Cyril of Jerusalem[3]

Why have they bought it? So as to use it as a graveyard for strangers. We are the ones making use of it, for it was bought for our sake with the blood of Jesus for its price."

St. Jerome

The field according to the divine words, is the entire present world (Matt 13:36). The price of the blood is the price for the Lord's suffering, who has bought the world with the price of His blood so as to save it, (Jn. 3:17). He came to keep those who are buried with Christ and have died with Him in baptism (Rom. 6:4,8; Col.2:12) so as to obtain eternal blessings. Instead of living as strangers under the law, they have become close by means of the blood of Jesus (Eph. 2:11-13).

St. Ambrose of Milan

---

[3] The following excerpts are from Fr. Tadros's *Patristic Commentary on Matthew*.

Are You King of the Jews?

Do you see what He is first asked? Is this the same charge that they had been continually bringing forward at every circumstance? Since they saw Pilate making no account of the matters of the law, they direct their accusation to the state charges. So likewise did they in the case of the apostles, ever bringing forward these things, and saying that they were going about proclaiming king one Jesus, speaking as of a mere man, and investing them with a suspicion of usurpation.

From this it is manifest, that both the rending the garment and the amazement were a pretense. But all things they got up, and plied, in order to bring Him to death.

This at any rate Pilate then asked. What then did Christ say? "You have said." He confessed that He was a king, but a heavenly king, which elsewhere also He spoke more dearly, replying to Pilate, "My Kingdom is not of this world" (Jn. 18:36) that neither they nor this man should have an excuse for accusing Him of such things. And He gives a reason that cannot be denied, saying, "If I were of this world, my servants would fight, that I should not be delivered." For this purpose I say, in order to refute this suspicion, He both paid tribute [to Cesar], and commanded others to pay it, and when they would make Him a king, He fled.

St. John Chrysostom, *Commentary on Matthew*, Homily 86.1 (NPNF 1:10, p. 511)

The False Charges

They say, "We no longer need any testimony," as begin the hearers of Christ's words. What had they heard Him say? O vile and senseless people, you wanted to learn if He was the Christ! He taught you that by nature and in truth He is the Son of God the Father and He shares the throne of Deity with Him. As you confessed, you now have no need of testimony, because you have heard Him speak. You might now have learned best that He is the Christ. This would have proved for you the pathway to faith, had you only been one of those who would know the truth. Making even the pathway of salvation an occasion for their soul's ruin, they do not understand...

You say, "We found this Man perverting our people." Tell us in what this perversion consisted? Christ taught repentance; where did He forbid giving tribute to Caesar? He said, "Give to Caesar the things that are Caesar's and to God the things that are God's" (Matt. 22:17). Where then did He forbid giving tribute to Caesar? Their only purpose was to bring down to death the One who was raising them to life. This was the goal of their strategy, the shameful deeds they planned, of the falsehood they invented, and the bitter words running from their wicked tongues. The law still loudly proclaims to you, "You shall not bear false witness against your neighbor" (Exod. 20:16) and "Do not kill the innocent and righteous" (Exod. 23:7).

St. Cyril of Alexandria, *Commentary on Luke*, Homily 150, pp. 597, 602.

Why didn't Christ defend Himself, but remained silent?

As Lamb, He is silent (Isa. 53:7)—yet He is the "Word" proclaimed by the "voice of one crying in the wilderness" (Mat. 3:3). He is weakened, wounded (Isa. 53:5)—yet He cures every disease and every weakness (Mat. 9:35). He is brought up to the tree (1 Pet. 2:4) and nailed to it (Jn. 19:17-18)—yet by the Tree of Life He restores us (Gen. 2:9, 3:22; Rev. 2:7).

St. Gregory Nazianzen, *Oration 29 on the Son*, 20 (AACS 1b, p. 223)

The Lord became defender of truth, and came in silence before Pilate, on behalf of truth which had been oppressed (Jn. 18:37-38). Others gain victory through making defenses, but our Lord gained victory through His silence, because the recompense of His death through divine silence was the victory of true teaching. He spoke in order to teach, but kept silent in the tribunal. He was not silent over that which was exalting us, but He did not struggle against those who were provoking Him. The words of His accusers, like a crown on His head, were a source of redemption. He kept silent so that His silence would make them shout even louder, and so that His crown would be made more beautiful through all this clamor.

St. Ephrem the Syrian, *CTD* 2, p. 301 (AACS 2, p. 223)

He is the One Who, although He was silent in His passion, will not be silent finally in the day of reckoning. He is our God, even if unrecognized. He is already known among the faithful and all who believe. When He comes manifesting Himself in His Second Coming, He will not be silent. For although he was formerly hidden in humility, He will come manifested in power.

St. Cyprian, *The Good of Patience* (FC 36, p. 286; AACS 2, p. 334)

Why then did He not bring forward these things, it may be said, at that time, when accused of usurpation? Because having the proofs from His acts, of His power, His meekness, His gentleness, beyond number, they were willfully blind, and dealt unfairly, and the tribunal was corrupt. For these reasons then He replies to nothing, but holds His peace, yet answering briefly (so as not to get the reputation of arrogance from continual silence) when the high priest adjured Him, when the governor asked, but in reply to their accusations He no longer says anything; for He was now not likely to persuade them. Even as the prophet declaring this self-same thing from of old, said, "In His humiliation His judgment was taken away."

St. John Chrysostom, *Commentary on Matthew*, Homily 86.1 (NPNF 1:10, p. 511)

He was silent, and quietly endured everything...to teach us all meekness and long-suffering. Let us now imitate Him. For not only did He now hold His peace, but even came among them again, and being questioned answered and showed the things relating to His foreknowledge. Although He was called "demon-possessed" and "a madman," by men who had received from Him ten thousand benefits many times, not only did He refrain from avenging Himself, but even He did not cease to benefit them...[for] He laid down His life for them, and while being crucified spoke in their behalf to His Father. This then let us also imitate, for to be a disciple of Christ, is the being gentle and kind. But how can this gentleness come to us? If we continually ponder our sins, if we mourn, if we weep.

St. John Chrysostom, *Commentary on John*, Homily 60 (NPNF 1:14)

It might seem remarkable, I say, brothers, that the Savior should be accused and should remain silent. Silence is occasionally understood as avowal, of when a person does not wish to respond to what is asked of him he appears to confirm what is raised against him. Does the Lord then confirm his accusation by not speaking? Clearly He does not confirm His accusation by not speaking; rather He despises it by not refuting it. For one who needs no defense does well to keep silent, but let one who fears to be overcome defend himself and one who is afraid of being defeated hasten to speak. When Christ is condemned, however, He also overcomes, and when He is judged He also defeats, as the prophet says, "That You may be found just when You speak, and blameless when You judge" (Psa. 51:4, 50:6). Why was it necessary for Him therefore to speak before being judged, when for Him judgment was a complete victory?

Maximus of Turin, *Sermons*, 57.1 (AACS 1b, pp. 277-278)

They accuse the Lord and He stands mute (Matt. 27:12, 14). The One that does not lack a defense is suitably mute. Let those who fear to being overcome seek a defense. By remaining silent, He does not confirm the accusation. By not refuting it, He despises it. A special attribute of Christ is that among wicked judges He seemed to have been unwilling rather than unable to be defended. The Lord explained why He would remain silent, saying, "If I should tell you, you will not believe Me; and if I should also ask you, you will not answer Me" (cf. Jn. 5:46-47) it is extraordinary that He chose to prove Himself a king, rather than speak, so that those who confess what they taunt would have no grounds for condemnation...

When Herod wanted to see Him work wonders, He was silent and performed none because Herod's cruelty did not merit to behold the divine and the Lord shunned boasting. Perhaps Herod prefigures all the impious, who if they did not believe in the law and the prophets cannot see the miraculous works of Christ in the gospel either.

St. Ambrose of Milan, *Exposition on the Gospel of Luke*, 10.97-99 (AACS 2, pp. 353-354)

Pilate Amazed

At these things the governor marveled, and indeed it was worthy of admiration to see Him showing such great patience, and holding His peace, Him that had countless things to say. For neither did they accuse Him from knowing of any evil thing in Him, but from jealousy and envy only. At least when they had set false witness, why, having nothing to say, did they still urge their point? And when they saw Judas was dead, and that Pilate had washed his hands of it, why were they not pricked with remorse. For indeed He did many things even at the very time, that they might recover themselves, but by none were they amended.

St. John Chrysostom, *Commentary on Matthew*, Homily 86.1 (NPNF 1:10, p. 511)

Why was our Lord wearing white?

It is significant that Jesus is clothed in a white garment by Herod. It denotes His sinless passion, because the Lamb of God without stain and with glory accepted the sins of the world (Jn. 1:29). Herod and Pilate, who became friends instead of enemies through Jesus Christ, symbolize the peoples of Israel and the Gentiles, since the future harmony of both follows from the Lord's passion (Eph. 2:13). First the people of the nations capture the Word of God and bring it to the people of the Jews, through the devotion of their faith. They clothe with glory the body of Christ, Whom they had previously despised.

St. Ambrose of Milan, *Exposition on the Gospel of Luke*, 10.103 (AACS 2, p. 354)

Now our Lord is wearing the white garments, but in the next hour, they shall be crimson, reddened by our sins and stained by our iniquities.

HOMILY OF ST. JOHN
CHRYSOSTOM[4]

For the love of money is a dreadful, dreadful thing. It disables both eyes and ears; makes men worse to deal with than a wild beast; and allows a man to consider neither conscience, nor friendship, nor fellowship, nor the salvation of his own soul. But having withdrawn them at once from all these things, like some harsh mistress, it makes those captured by it its slaves. And the dreadful part of so bitter a slavery is, that it persuades them even to be grateful for it; and the more they become enslaved, the more does their pleasure increase; and in this way especially the malady becomes incurable, in this way the monster becomes hard to conquer.

This made Gehazi a leper instead of a disciple and a prophet; this destroyed Ananias and his wife; this made Judas a traitor; this corrupted the rulers of the Jews, who received gifts, and became the partners of thieves. This has brought in ten thousand wars, filling the ways with blood, the cities with wailings and lamentations. This has made meals to become impure, and tables accursed, and has filled food with transgression.

Therefore, Paul has called it "idolatry" (Col. 3:5), and not even so has he deterred men from it. And why does he call it "idolatry"? Many possess wealth, and dare not use it, but consecrate it, handing it down untouched, not daring to touch it, as though it were some dedicated thing. And if at any time they are forced to do so, they feel as though they had done something unlawful. Besides, as the Greek carefully tends his graven image, so you entrust your gold to doors and bars; providing a chest instead of a shrine, and laying it up in silver vessels. But you do not bow down to it as he to the image? Yet you show all kind of attention to it.

Again, he would rather give up his eyes or his life than his graven image. So also would those who love gold. "But," one says, "I do not worship the gold." Neither does he, he says, worship the image, but the devil that dwells in it; and in like manner you, though you do not worship the gold, yet you worship that devil who springs on your soul, from the sight of the gold and you lust for it. For more grievous than an evil spirit is the lust of money-loving, and many obey it more than others do idols. For these last in many things disobey, but in this case

---

[4] St. John Chrysostom, Homily 65 on John (NPNF 1:14). Although only an excerpt of this homily was chosen as the homily of this hour, we have included all in this passage for the benefit of the reader.

they yield everything, and whatever it tells them to do, they obey. What does it say? "Be at war with all," it says, "at enmity with all, know not nature, despise God, sacrifice to me yourself," and in all they obey. To the graven images they sacrifice oxen and sheep, but avarice says, sacrifice to me your own soul, and the man obeys. See what kind of altars it has, what kind of sacrifices it receives? The covetous shall not inherit the Kingdom of God, but not even so do they fear (1 Cor. 6:10). Yet this desire is weaker than all the others, it is not inborn, nor natural (for then it would have been placed in us at the beginning). But there was no gold at the beginning, and no man desired gold. But if you will, I will tell you from where the mischief entered.

By each man's envying the one before him, men have increased the disease, and he who has gotten in advance provokes him who had no desire. For when men see splendid houses, and extensive lands, and troops of slaves, and silver vessels, and great heaps of apparel, they use every means to outdo them; so that the first set of men are causes of the second, and these of those who come after. Now if they would be sober-minded, they would not be teachers (of evil) to others; yet neither have these any excuse. For others there are also who despise riches. "And who," says one, "despises them?"

For the terrible thing is, that, because wickedness is so general, this seems to have become impossible, and it is not even believed that one can act aright. Shall I then mention many both in cities and in the mountains? And what would it avail? You will not from their example become better. Besides, our discourse has not now this purpose, that you should empty yourselves of your substance: I would that you could do so; however, since the burden is too heavy for you, I constrain you not; only I advise you that you desire not what belongs to others, that you impart somewhat of your own. Many such we shall find, contented with what belongs to them, taking care of their own, and living on honest labor. Why do we not rival and imitate these?

Let us think of those who have gone before us. Do not their possessions stand, preserving nothing but their name; such a one's bath, such a one's suburban seat and lodging? Do we not, when we behold them, straightway groan, when we consider what toil he endured, what rapine committed? And now he is nowhere seen, but others luxuriate in his possessions, men whom he never expected would do so, perhaps even his enemies, while he is suffering extreme punishment. These things await us also; for we shall certainly die, and shall certainly have to submit to the same end. How much wrath, tell me, how much expense, how many enmities these men incurred; and what is the gain? Deathless punishment, and having no consolation; and this being not only while alive, but when gone, accused by all. What? When we see the images of the many laid up in their houses, shall we not weep the more? Of a truth well said the Prophet, "Verily, every man living disquiets himself in vain" (Psa. 39:11); for anxiety about such things is indeed disquiet, disquiet and superfluous trouble. But it is not so in the everlasting mansions, not so in those tabernacles. Here one has labored, and another enjoys; but there each shall possess his own labors, and shall receive a manifold reward. Let us press forward to get that possession, there let us prepare for ourselves houses, that we may rest in Christ Jesus our Lord, with whom to the Father and the Holy Spirit be glory, for ever and ever. Amen.

THIRD HOUR:
"*VIA DOLOROSA*: THE WAY OF SUFFERING"

Gen. 48:1-19; Isa. 50:4-9, 3:9-15, 63:1-7; Job 29:21-30:10;

Psa. 37:17, 21:16;

Matt. 27:15-26; Mk. 15:6-25; Lk. 23:13-25; Jn. 19:1-12

Overview

The Third Hour begins the painful torment of Lamb. After Pilate washes His hands, the soldiers took Him into the common hall, paraded around Him, stripped Him and divided His garments. All of this was prophesied about in Psalm 22:17, "They look and stare at Me. They divide My garments among them, and for My clothing they cast lots." They dressed Him in a scarlet robe, platted a crown of thorns, and placed a reed in His hand.

Great Friday is a day of pain and sorrows. But St. Paul reminds us of the need for a Christian to "...not only to believe in Him, but also to suffer for His sake" (Philip.1:29). By actively participating in the Holy Pascha Week, through fasting, prayer and repentance we suffer for His sake. Suffering is a gift from God, bestowed upon us so that we can experience inner joy and strength in the death of Christ, thereby capturing the quiet endurance of the saints. Through meditation of the Cross, we witness His Divine Love for us. "Greater love has no man than this, that a man lay down His life for His friends." There are various early Christian hymns which proclaim the meaning of Christ's death on the Cross for the life of the world.

This hour contains five main prophesies (and one prophesy of Amos that is in some Pascha books). The remaining prophesies directly predict the sufferings of our Lord in this hour.

Old Testament Prophesy	New Testament Fulfillment
Gen. 48:1-19—Jacob blesses Joseph's sons, Ephraim and Manasseh.	The Mystery of the Cross and its blessing upon the Jews and the Christians.
Isa. 50—"I gave My back to those who struck Me, And My cheeks to those who plucked out the beard; I did not hide My face from shame and spitting."	Mk. 15:15—"and he delivered Jesus, after he had scourged Him, to be crucified." Jn. 19:3—"Then they said, 'Hail, King of the Jews!' And they struck Him with their hands."
Isa. 3—"And they declare their sin as Sodom; They do not hide it. Woe to their soul! For they have brought evil upon themselves."	Matt. 27:24-25—"'I am innocent of the blood of this just Person. You see to it.' And all the people answered and said, 'His blood be on us and on our children.'"
Isa. 63—"I have trodden the winepress alone, and from the peoples no one was with Me. For I have trodden them in My anger, and trampled them in My fury; Their blood is sprinkled upon My garments, and I have stained all My robes."	Matt. 27:23,25—"'Why, what evil has He done?' But they cried out all the more, saying, 'Let Him be crucified!' And all the people answered and said, 'His blood be on us and on our children.'"
Job 29—"But now they mock at me…They abhor me, they keep far from me; They do not hesitate to spit in my face."	Mk. 15:17-19—"And they clothed Him with purple; and they twisted a crown of thorns, put it on His head…Then they struck Him on the head with a reed and spat on Him; and bowing the knee, they worshiped Him."
Psa. 21—"The congregation of the wicked has enclosed Me. They pierced My hands and My feet."	Jn. 19:17-37—"And He, bearing His cross, went out to a place called the Place of a Skull, which is called in Hebrew, Golgotha, where they crucified Him…But one of the soldiers pierced His side with a spear…For these things were done that the Scripture should be fulfilled, "Not one of His bones shall be broken." And again another Scripture says, "They shall look on Him whom they pierced.""

Readings and Patristic Meditations

GENESIS 48:1-19

Now it came to pass after these things that Joseph was told, "Indeed your father is sick"; and he took with him his two sons, Manasseh and Ephraim, and went to Jacob. Thus Jacob was told, "Look, your son Joseph is coming to you"; and Israel strengthened himself and sat up on the bed. Then Jacob said to Joseph: "My God appeared to me at Luz in the land of Canaan and blessed me and said to me, 'Behold, I will increase and multiply you, and I will make of you a gathering of nations, and give this land to your seed after you as an everlasting possession.' Now therefore, your two sons, Ephraim and Manasseh, who were born to you in the land of Egypt before I came to you in Egypt, are mine; as Reuben and Simeon, they shall be mine. Your offspring whom you beget after them shall take possession of their inheritances within the tribes of their brothers. But as for me, when I came from Mesopotamia of Syria, Rachel died beside me in the land of Canaan on the way, when there was but a little distance to go to Ephrath; and I buried her there on the way to Ephrath" (that is, Bethlehem).

*Then Israel saw Joseph's sons, and said, "Who are these with you?" So Joseph said to his father, "They are my sons God gave me here." Jacob then said, "Bring them to me here." Now the eyes of Israel were dim by reason of his old age, and he could not see. Then Joseph brought them near him, and he kissed them and embraced them. Then Israel said to Joseph, "I had not thought to see your face; but in fact, God has also shown me your seed." **So Joseph brought them from beside his knees, and they bowed down with their face to the ground. Then Joseph took them both, Ephraim with his right hand toward Israel's left hand, and Manasseh with his left hand toward Israel's right hand, and brought them near him.** Thus Israel stretched out his right hand and laid it on Ephraim's head, who was the younger, and his left hand on Manasseh's head, guiding his hands knowingly, for Manasseh was the firstborn. Then he blessed them and said:*

"God, before whom my fathers Abraham and Isaac were well pleasing, The God who has fed me all my life long to this day, The Angel who has redeemed me from all evil, Bless the lads; Let my name be named upon them, and the name of my fathers Abraham and Isaac; And let them grow into a multitude in the midst of the earth."

Now when Joseph saw his father put his right hand on the head of Ephraim, it displeased him; so he took hold of his father's hand to remove it from Ephraim's head to Manasseh's head. So Joseph said to his father, "Not so, my father, for this one is the firstborn; put your right hand on his head." But his father refused and said, "I know, my son, I know. He also shall become a people, and he also shall be exalted; but truly, his younger brother shall be greater than he, and his seed shall become a multitude of nations."

Now, as Isaac's two sons, Esau and Jacob, furnished a type of the two people, the Jews and the Christians, although as pertains to carnal descent it was not the Jews but the Idumeans who came of the seed of Esau, nor the Christian nations but rather the Jews who came of Jacob's; for the type holds only as regards the saying, "The elder shall serve the younger" (Gen. 25:23), so the same thing happened in Joseph's two sons; for the elder was a type of the Jews, and the younger of the Christians...

The blessing of Jacob is a proclamation of Christ to all nations. It is this which has come to pass, and is now being fulfilled. Isaac is the law and the prophecy: even by the mouth of the Jews, Christ is blessed by prophecy as by one who knows not, because it is itself not understood. The world like a field is filled with the aroma of Christ's Name: His is the blessing of the dew of heaven, that is, of the showers of divine words; and of the fruitfulness of the earth, that is, of the gathering together of the peoples.

St. Augustine, *City of God*, 16.42, 16.38

O You Light, which Tobias saw, when, his eyes being closed, he taught his son the way of life; himself going before with the feet of charity, never going astray (Tobit 4). Or that which Isaac saw, when his fleshly "eyes were dim, so that he could not see" by reason of old age; it was permitted him, not knowingly to bless his sons, but in blessing them to know them. Or that which Jacob saw, when he too, blind through great age, with an enlightened heart, in the persons of his own sons, threw light upon the races of the future people, pre-signified in them; and laid his hands, mystically crossed, upon his grandchildren by Joseph, not as their father, looking outwardly, corrected them, but as he himself distinguished them (Gen. 48:13-19).

St. Augustine, *Confessions*, 10.34 (NPNF 2:1)

Here also the Cross is clearly symbolized to depict that mystery with which Israel the firstborn departed, just as Manasseh the firstborn, and the peoples increase in the manner of Ephraim the younger.

St. Ephrem the Syrian, *Commentary on Genesis*, 41.4 (FC 91, p. 199; AACS OT 2, p. 316)

When this very Jacob was about to bless Manasseh and Ephraim, the sons of Joseph, with his hands placed across on the heads of the lads...he had called [on] God...to "bless these lads." ...[Jacob placed] his hands crossed upon the lads, as if their father was Christ, and showing, from thus placing his hands, the figure and future form of the passion. Let no one, therefore, who does not shrink from speaking of Christ as an Angel, thus shrink from pronouncing Him God also, when he perceives that He Himself was invoked in the blessing of these lads, by the sacrament of the passion, intimated in the type of the crossed hands, as both God and Angel.

Novatian, *Treatise on the Trinity*, 19 (ANF 5)

[Jacob's] vision became so dim that he could not see Ephraim and Manasseh, although with the inner eye and the prophetic spirit he could foresee the distant future and the Christ that was to come of his royal line.

St. Jerome, *Epistle 68.1* (NPNF 2:6)

All that have been raised were not first born; for our Lord is the First-born of Sheol. How can any that is dead go before Him, that power whereby He was raised? There are last that are first, and younger that have become first-born. For though Manasseh was first-born, how could it be that Ephraim should take the birthright? And if the second born was set before him, how much rather shall the Lord and Creator prevent all in His Resurrection!

St. Ephrem the Syrian, *The Nisebene Hymns*, 38.7 (NPNF 2:18)

ISAIAH 50:4-9

"The Lord God has given Me the tongue of the learned, that I should know how to speak a word in season to him who is weary. He awakens Me morning by morning, He awakens My ear to hear as the learned. The Lord God has opened My ear; and I was not rebellious, nor did I turn away.

I gave My back to those who struck Me, and My cheeks to those who plucked out the beard; I did not hide My face from shame and spitting.

*"For the Lord God will help Me; therefore I will not be disgraced; therefore I have set My face like a flint, and I know that I will not be ashamed. He is near who justifies Me; who will contend with Me? Let us stand together. **Who is My adversary? Let him come near Me.** Surely the Lord God will help Me; who is he who will condemn Me? Indeed they will all grow old like a garment; the moth will eat them up.*

Our Lord and Savior Jesus Christ is an example to teach us how to bear sufferance. By His own will He allowed them to lead Him - the all goodness - to death. Following His example, we can trample over serpents, scorpions, and all powers of the enemy.

St. Athanasius the Apostolic, *Paschal Epistle*, 8 (NPNF 2:4)

You may say, "The enemy is horrible and dangerous; he cannot be opposed..." Look at him again, and compare him with another image, to learn how to despise him. All accusations, insults, rebukes, ridicules, and plans of the enemies are like a garment eaten by the moths (Isa. 50: 9)... Now, do not let any of this trouble you; stop seeking help from this or that; do not chase shadows. But insistently seek Jesus Whom you serve; with a little bow of His head, all evils will come to an end.

St. John Chrysostom, *Letter to Olympias*, 1:2 (NPNF 2:9)

O my Master, You did not hide Your face from the shame of spitting... You came to slaughter like a Lamb, even to the Cross...

The Liturgy of St. Gregory

You ignorant, how did you dare to spit on His face? How did your tongue dare? How did the earth bear to watch that scene? How horrible and amazing for man to see the wax spits on flame! That also happened because of Adam, who was worthy of being spat on. Instead of the slave who sinned, the Master Himself bore all that shame! He offered His face to receive spitting, as He promised in the book of Isaiah not to hide His face from shame of spitting!

St. Jacob of Sarug, *Divine Love*, p. 424

As to saying, "to demonstrate His righteousness," He means, not only being righteous, but to make of those covered by soars of the filthy sin righteous. Therefore do not doubt... Do not reject the righteousness of God, which is not through works [of Law], but through the [living] faith, that is easy and open to all.

St. John Chrysostom, *Oration on the Holy Baptism* 40:36 (NPNF 2:9)

I wish we do not walk in the light of our own fire (Isa. 50: 11), and in the sparks we have kindled. I know of a purified fire, sent by Christ on the earth (Lk. 12: 49). He Himself symbolically seemed as a fire that would consume all our bad habits; that fire He wishes to kindle swiftly, yearning to hasten us to do goodness.

St. Gregory Nazianzen, *Divine Love*, pp. 424-425

ISAIAH 3:9-15

The look on their countenance witnesses against them, **and they declare their sin**
as Sodom; *they do not hide it. Woe to their soul! For they have brought evil*
upon themselves.

"Say to the righteous that it shall be well with them, For they shall eat the fruit
of their doings. Woe to the wicked! It shall be ill with him, For the reward of his
hands shall be given him.

As for My people, children are their oppressors, and women rule over them. O
My people! Those who lead you cause you to err, and destroy the way of your
paths."

The Lord stands up to plead, and stands to judge the people. The Lord will
enter into judgment with the elders of His people and His princes: "For you
have eaten up the vineyard; The plunder of the poor is in your houses. What do
you mean by crushing My people and grinding the faces of the poor?" Says the
Lord God of hosts.

Indeed your hand is raised to do evil. You have killed Christ and did
not repent. You steal as much as you can, hate and kill those who believe in
Him, and in God the Father of all; and still curse us, and those who take our
side for no reason. As for us, we pray for your sake, and for the sake of all
mankind, as we were taught by Christ, the Lord, who instructed us to pray
even for our enemies, and to love those who hate and curse us.

St. Justin Martyr, *Dialogue with Trypho*, 133 (ANF 1)

They tied up Jesus, and brought Him to the Hall of the high priest. Do
you want to know that this had been written and prophesied? Of which
Isaiah says, "Woe to their soul, for they have brought evil upon themselves,
saying, let us tie up the righteous for he causes us trouble."

St. Cyril of Jerusalem, *Catechetical Lectures*, 13:12 (FC 61)

ISAIAH 63:1-7

Who is this who comes from Edom, With dyed garments from Bozrah, This One
Who is glorious in His apparel, Traveling in the greatness of His strength?—"I
who speak in righteousness, mighty to save."

Why is Your apparel red, and Your garments like one who treads in the
winepress?

"I have trodden the winepress alone, and from the peoples no one was with
Me. For I have trodden them in My anger, and trampled them in My fury;
their blood is sprinkled upon My garments, and I have stained all My robes.

For the day of vengeance is in My heart, and the year of My redeemed has come. I looked, but there was no one to help, and I wondered That there was no one to uphold; therefore My own arm brought salvation for Me; and My own fury, it sustained Me. I have trodden down the peoples in My anger, Made them drunk in My fury, and brought down their strength to the earth."

I will mention the loving-kindnesses of the Lord and the praises of the Lord, According to all that the Lord has bestowed on us, and the great goodness toward the house of Israel, Which He has bestowed on them according to His mercies, According to the multitude of His loving-kindnesses.

He did a marvelous ordinance for the suffering body that was adorned with passion and glorified with Deity. There is nothing more sweet and beautiful.

St. Gregory Nazianzen, *Oration On Easter*, 35. NPNF, s. 2, v. 7.

In Isaiah also the Holy Spirit testifies this same thing concerning the Lord's passion, saying, "Why are Your garments red, and Your apparel as from the treading of the wine-press full and well trodden?" Can water make garments red? Or is it water in the wine-press which is trodden by the feet, or pressed out by the press? Assuredly, therefore, mention is made of wine, that the Lord's blood may be understood, and that which was afterwards manifested in the cup of the Lord might be foretold by the prophets who announced it. The treading also, and pressure of the wine-press, is repeatedly dwelt on; because just as the drinking of wine cannot be attained to unless the bunch of grapes be first trodden and pressed, so neither could we drink the blood of Christ unless Christ had first been trampled upon and pressed, and had first drunk the cup of which He should also give believers to drink.

St. Cyprian, *Epistle 62.7* (ANF 5)

Next turning to the right [Paula] passed from Bethzur to Eshcol which means "a cluster of grapes." It was hence that the spies brought back that marvelous cluster which was the proof of the fertility of the land and a type of Him who says of Himself: "I have trodden the wine press alone; and of the people there was none with Me."

St. Jerome, *Epistle 108.11* [About Paula] (NPNF 2:6)

I am baffled with this great prophet Isaiah. He has seen by inspiration the passions of the Savior who is the Logos of God. He said, "Who is He who comes from Adam, His clothes are red, and He is dressed in a magnificent robe; His mantle is from red blood as one Who comes up from the press, and His clothes are stained by the blood of its vines." Truly these are the words of this prophet who revealed this before these days. Truly, He is the Logos of God, our Savior, Jesus. He wore the old flesh of Adam, the first creation. The sublime Divinity united with humanity (without mixing nor change). An immutable mantle united with God the Logos. He inflicted His wrath on the Hebrews and trampled over them in the press of His anger. He granted His mercy and grace to the Gentiles whom He made a new people. As for Israel, his foolishness will prevail on him forever.

Exposition of the Third Hour of Great Friday

JOB 29:21-30:10

"Men listened to me and waited, and kept silence for my counsel. After my words they did not speak again, and my speech settled on them as dew. They waited for me as for the rain, and they opened their mouth wide as for the spring rain. If I mocked at them, they did not believe it, and the light of my countenance they did not cast down. I chose the way for them, and sat as chief; So I dwelt as a king in the army, as one who comforts mourners.

"But now they mock at me, men younger than I, whose fathers I disdained to put with the dogs of my flock. Indeed, what profit is the strength of their hands to me? Their vigor has perished. They are gaunt from want and famine, fleeing late to the wilderness, desolate and waste, Who pluck mallow by the bushes, and broom tree roots for their food. They were driven out from among men, they shouted at them as at a thief. They had to live in the clefts of the valleys, in caves of the earth and the rocks. Among the bushes they brayed, under the nettles they nestled. They were sons of fools, yes, sons of vile men; They were scourged from the land.

"And now I am their taunting song; yes, I am their byword. They abhor me, they keep far from me; They do not hesitate to spit in my face.

PSALM 37:17, 21:16

For I am ready to fall, and my sorrow is continually before me. For dogs have surrounded Me; The congregation of the wicked has enclosed Me. They pierced My hands and My feet.

Quite a magnificent expression; as if He were saying, "It was even for this that I was born; that I might suffer." For He was not to be born, but from Adam, to whom the scourge is due. But sinners are in this life sometimes not scourged at all, or are scourged less than what they deserve, because the wickedness of their heart is given over as already desperate. Those, however, for whom eternal life is prepared, must be scourged in this life, for that sentence is true: "My son, do not despise the chastening of the Lord, neither be weary when you are rebuked by Him." "For whom the Lord loves He chastens, and scourges every son whom He receives." Let not my enemies therefore insult over me; let "them not magnify themselves;" and if my Father scourges me, "I am prepared for the scourge;" because there is an inheritance in store for me. You will not submit to the scourge: the inheritance is not bestowed upon you. For "every son" must needs be scourged. So true it is that "every son" is scourged, that He spared not even Him who had no sin. For "I am prepared for the scourges."

St. Augustine, *Commentary on the Psalms* (NPNF 2:8)

But, perhaps, having heard the prophecy of His death, you ask to learn also what is set forth concerning the Cross. For not even this is passed over; it is displayed by the holy men with great clarity. First Moses predicts [His death]...then, the prophets after him witness of this..."They pierced My hands and My feet, they numbered all My bones, they parted My garments among them, and for My vesture they cast lots."

Now a death raised on high and that takes place on a tree, could be none other than the Cross: and again, in no other death are the hands and feet pierced, except on the Cross only...[for] who among those recorded in Scripture was pierced in the hands and feet, or hung at all upon a tree, and was sacrificed on a cross for the salvation of all? For Abraham died, ending his life on a bed; Isaac and Jacob also died with their feet raised on a bed; Moses and Aaron died on the mountain; David in his house, without being the object of any conspiracy at the hands of the people; true, he was pursued by Saul, but he was preserved unhurt. Isaiah was sawn asunder, but not hung on a tree. Jeremiah was shamefully treated, but did not die under condemnation; Ezekiel suffered, not however for the people, but to indicate what was to come upon the people.

St. Athanasius, *On the Incarnation*, 35, 37 (NPNF 2:4)

"But He was wounded for our iniquities" (Isa.53:5), and in the Psalm it says, "They have pierced My hands and feet," so that He might cure our wounds by His own wound; and "He was bruised," or enfeebled, "for our crimes" (Isa. 53:5), so that, having been reviled for us, He might spare us from being reviled.

St. Jerome, *Commentary on Isaiah*, Homily 114:53:5.

If you require still further prediction of the Lord's cross, the twenty-first Psalm is sufficiently able to afford it to you, containing as it does the entire passion of Christ, who was even then prophetically declaring His glory. **"They pierced my hands and my feet,"** which is the special cruelty of the Cross. And again, when He implores His Father's help, He says, "Save me from the lion's mouth," that is, the jaws of death, "and my humiliation from the horns of the unicorns;" in other words, from the extremities of the cross, as we have shown above. Now, **David himself did not suffer this cross, nor did any other king of the Jews; so that you cannot suppose that this is the prophecy of any other's passion than His who alone was so notably crucified by the nation.**

The Scholar Tertullian, *Against Marcion*, 3.19 (ANF 3)

So also in that where Christ utters through prophecy the humiliation of His passion, saying, "They pierced my hands and feet; they counted all my bones. Yea, they looked and stared at me." By which words he certainly meant His body stretched out on the Cross, with the hands and feet pierced and perforated by the striking through of the nails, and that He had in that way made Himself a spectacle to those who looked and stared. And he adds, "They parted my garments among them, and over my vesture they cast lots." How this prophecy has been fulfilled the Gospel history narrates...we do not consider that these events are in the past, but consider them as present, are beheld by the whole world, being now exhibited just as they are read of in this very psalm as predicted so long before. As it is said a little after, "All the ends of the earth shall remember, and turn unto the Lord, and all the kindreds of the nations shall worship before Him; for the kingdom is the Lord's, and He shall rule the nations."

St. Augustine, *City of God*, 17.17 (NPNF 2:2)

Zechariah also thus wrote: "And they shall look on me, whom they pierced" (Zech. 12:10). Also David in the twenty-first Psalm: "They pierced my hands and my feet; they numbered all my bones; they themselves looked and stared upon me; they divided my garments among them; and upon my vesture they did cast lots."

It is evident that the prophet did not speak these things concerning himself. For he was a king, and never endured these sufferings; but the Spirit of God, Who was about to suffer these things, after ten hundred and fifty years, spoke by him. For this is the number of years from the reign of David to the crucifixion of Christ.

Lactantius, *Divine Institutes*, 4.8 (NPNF 2:7)

What a marvelous and magnificent thing that our Lord Jesus Christ, the Son of God, and also the Son of man, granted to us by…combated unto salvation…even the combatants themselves, **for He also was made a spectacle Himself.** He has told us Himself, and foretold it before He was made a spectacle, and in the words of prophecy announced beforehand what was to come to pass, as if it were already done, saying in the Psalms, "They pierced My hands and My feet, they told all My bones." Behold! how He was made a spectacle, for His bones to be told! And this spectacle He expresses more plainly, "they observed and looked upon Me." He was made a spectacle and an object of derision, made a spectacle by them who were to show Him no favor indeed in that spectacle, but who were to be furious against Him, just as at first He made His martyrs spectacles; as the Apostle says, "…we have been made a spectacle to the world, both to angels and to men" (1 Cor. 4:9).

When these things are read of in the Church, you [should] behold them with pleasure with these eyes of the heart. If you were to behold nothing, you would hear nothing; so you see you have not neglected the spectacles today, but have made a choice of spectacles.

May God then be with you, and give you grace…**and may you, love God, of whom none who love Him can ever be ashamed, for that they love Him who cannot be overcome…** love Christ, Who when He seemed to be overcome, overcame the whole world. For He has overcome the whole world as we see, my brethren…. [so] overcome in Him who said, "Be of good cheer, I have overcome the world." For the Captain suffered Himself to be tried, only that He might teach His soldier to fight.

St. Augustine, *Sermon 1.2* (NPNF 2:6)

MATTHEW 27:15-26

Now at the feast the governor was accustomed to releasing to the multitude one prisoner whom they wished. And at that time they had a notorious prisoner called Barabbas. Therefore, when they had gathered together, Pilate said to them, "Whom do you want me to release to you? Barabbas, or Jesus who is called Christ?" For he knew that they had handed Him over because of envy. While he was sitting on the judgment seat, his wife sent to him, saying, "Have nothing to do with that just Man, for I have suffered many things today in a dream because of Him." But the chief priests and elders persuaded the multitudes that they should ask for Barabbas and destroy Jesus. The governor answered and said to them, "Which of the two do you want me to release to you?" They said, "Barabbas!" Pilate said to them, "What then shall I do with Jesus who is called Christ?" They all said to him, "Let Him be crucified!" Then the governor said, "Why, what evil has He done?" But they cried out all the more, saying, "Let

Him be crucified!" When Pilate saw that he could not prevail at all, but rather that a tumult was rising, he took water and washed his hands before the multitude, saying, "I am innocent of the blood of this just Person. You see to it." And all the people answered and said, "His blood be on us and on our children." Then he released Barabbas to them; and when he had scourged Jesus, he delivered Him to be crucified.

MARK 15:6-25

Now at the feast he was accustomed to releasing one prisoner to them, whomever they requested. And there was one named Barabbas, who was chained with his fellow rebels; they had committed murder in the rebellion. Then the multitude, crying aloud, began to ask him to do just as he had always done for them. But Pilate answered them, saying, "Do you want me to release to you the King of the Jews?" For he knew that the chief priests had handed Him over because of envy. But the chief priests stirred up the crowd, so that he should rather release Barabbas to them. Pilate answered and said to them again, "What then do you want me to do with Him whom you call the King of the Jews?" So they cried out again, "Crucify Him!" Then Pilate said to them, "Why, what evil has He done?" But they cried out all the more, "Crucify Him!" So Pilate, wanting to gratify the crowd, released Barabbas to them; and he delivered Jesus, after he had scourged Him, to be crucified.

Then the soldiers led Him away into the hall called Praetorium, and they called together the whole garrison. **And they clothed Him with purple; and they twisted a crown of thorns, put it on His head, and began to salute Him, "Hail, King of the Jews!"** *Then they struck Him on the head with a reed and spat on Him; and bowing the knee, they worshiped Him.* **And when they had mocked Him, they took the purple off Him, put His own clothes on Him, and led Him out to crucify Him.**

Then they compelled a certain man, Simon a Cyrenian, the father of Alexander and Rufus, as he was coming out of the country and passing by, to bear His cross. And they brought Him to the place Golgotha, which is translated, Place of a Skull. Then they gave Him wine mingled with myrrh to drink, but He did not take it. And when they crucified Him, they divided His garments, casting lots for them to determine what every man should take. Now it was the third hour, and they crucified Him.

LUKE 23:13-25

Then Pilate, when he had called together the chief priests, the rulers, and the people, said to them, **"You have brought this Man to me, as one who misleads the people. And indeed, having examined Him in your presence, I have found no fault in this Man concerning those things of which you accuse Him; no, neither did Herod, for I sent you back to him; and indeed nothing deserving of** *death has been done by Him. I will therefore chastise Him and release Him" (for it was necessary for him to release one to them at the feast). And they all cried out at once, saying, "Away with this Man, and release to us Barabbas"— who had been thrown into prison for a certain rebellion made in the city, and for murder. Pilate, therefore, wishing to release Jesus, again called out to them. But they shouted, saying, "Crucify Him, crucify Him!" Then he said to them the third time, "Why, what evil has He done? I have found no reason for death in Him. I will therefore chastise Him and let Him go."* **But they were insistent, demanding with loud voices that He be crucified. And the voices of these men and of the chief priests prevailed. So Pilate gave sentence that it should be as** *they requested. And he released to them the one they requested, who for rebellion and murder had been thrown into prison; but he delivered Jesus to their will.*

JOHN 19:1-12

So then Pilate took Jesus and scourged Him. And the soldiers twisted a crown of thorns and put it on His head, and they put on Him a purple robe. Then they said, "Hail, King of the Jews!" And they struck Him with their hands. Pilate then went out again, and said to them, "Behold, I am bringing Him out to you, that you may know that I find no fault in Him."

Then Jesus came out, wearing the crown of thorns and the purple robe. And Pilate said to them, "Behold the Man!" Therefore, when the chief priests and officers saw Him, they cried out, saying, "Crucify Him, crucify Him!" Pilate said to them, "You take Him and crucify Him, for I find no fault in Him." The Jews answered him, "We have a law, and according to our law He should to die, because He made Himself the Son of God." Therefore, when Pilate heard that saying, he was the more afraid, and went again into the Praetorium, and said to Jesus, "Where are You from?" But Jesus gave him no answer. Then Pilate said to Him, "Are You not speaking to me? Do You not know that I have power to crucify You, and power to release You?" Jesus answered, **"You could have no power at all against Me unless it had been given you from above. Therefore the one who delivered Me to you has the greater sin."** *From then on Pilate sought to release Him, but the Jews cried out, saying, "If you let this Man go, you are not Caesar's friend. Whoever makes himself a king speaks against Caesar."*

Barabbas or Jesus?

Barabbas represents the one who enacts dissension, war and murder in human souls; but Jesus is the Son of God who works peace, reason, wisdom, and everything good. When the two of them were bound humanly and bodily, the people requested that Barabbas be released. Because of this act, they suffer continual dissention, murder and robbery. Such things afflict the pagans from without, but the Jews, who do not believe in Jesus, from within their very souls. Where Jesus is absent, there is dissention, strife, and war. Where Jesus is present, however, in such a way that the people can say, "And if Christ is in you, the body is dead because of sin, but the Spirit is alive because of righteousness" (Rom. 8:10). [With Him], everything is good, spiritual riches beyond measure and peace, for "He Himself is our peace, Who has made us both one" (Eph. 2:14). Anything contrary to this should be recognized as the mark of Barabbas struggling to be set free form his bondage within human souls, that is, not only in the historically sinful Israel, considered according to the flesh, but in all who teach like it and live like it. Within everyone who does evil, then, Barabbas is set free and Christ is bound. Within everyone who does good, however, Christ is set free and Barabbas is bound... The crowd—truly sizable crowd walking, as it were, on the "broad is the way that leads to destruction" (Matt. 7:13) sought to keep crying out to have Barabbas released to them.

The Scholar Origen, *Commentary on Matthew*, 121, 123 (AACS 1b, pp. 279, 280)

Here was their choice: let an acknowledged criminal go free, or free one whose guilt was still disputed. If they should choose to let the known offender go free, would it not be even more fitting to allow the innocent to go free? For surely Jesus did not seem to them morally worse than acknowledged murderers. But they instead chose a robber. This was not just any robber but one who was infamous for wickedness in many murders.

St. John Chrysostom, *Commentary on Matthew*, Homily 86.2 (NPNF 2:10, p. 512)

The mystery of [the Jews'] future infidelity is contained in Barabbas' very name, which means, "son of the father." They preferred this "son of the father" to Christ. At the instigation of their leaders, they chose the Antichrist, a man of sin and son of the devil (2 Thess. 2:3). They chose the one elected for damnation over the Author of life.

St. Hilary of Poitiers, *Commentary on Matthew*, 33.2 (AACS 1b, p. 280)

Barabbas means "son of the father"—"bar" meaning son and "abbas" meaning "father". These Jews, therefore, demanded the son of their spiritual father, the devil, but Jesus they crucified. And to this day, there are those like them who have chosen Antichrist, the substitute messiah, the son of their father, and have rejected Christ, the true Messiah.

The Blessed Theophylact, *TGM*, p. 242.

What kind of people crucified the Lord of glory! Those that violently demand the death of an innocent Man fittingly seek the release of a murderer. Wickedness has such laws as to hate innocence and love guilt. The interpretation of the name gives the likeness of the image, because *Barabbas* means "Son of the father." He belongs to those top whom it is said, "You are of your father the devil" (Jn. 8:44). They were about to choose the Antichrist as son of their father, rather than the Son of God.

St. Ambrose of Milan, *Exposition of the Gospel of Luke*, 10.101-2 (AACS 3, p. 355)

The criminal escape; Christ was condemned.. the one guilty of many crimes received a pardon; He who had remitted the crimes of all who confess was condemned. And yet the Cross itself also, if you reflect upon it, was a courtroom. In the middle of it stood the final judge.

St. Augustine, *Tractates on John*, Tractate 31.11 (FC 88, p. 40; AACS, p. 225)

The Dream

This dream was no small event. It should have been enough to stop them in their tracks when viewed in relation to the other proofs set in other things that occurred. Why didn't the dream come to Pilate? Perhaps she was more worthy. Or perhaps because, even if he had seen it, he would not have equally believed or perhaps he would not have even mentioned it. So it was providentially arranged that the wife should see it, in order that it might become more commonly known. And note that she does not only behold the dream but also suffers from it. One might imagine that Pilate might have been made so reluctant to participate in this murder, even from a feeling of sympathy toward his wife. The time of the dream also is significant, for it happened on that very night.

St. John Chrysostom, *Commentary on Matthew*, Homily 86.2 (NPNF 2:10, p. 512)

[Pilate's wife] took it upon herself to prevent her husband from passing sentence against Jesus…Thus, you may say it is better for someone to receive bad things in a dream than to receive them in life. Who indeed would not choose to receive bad things "in a dream" [rather than receive them] in life [unless one deserved such things, and it were better to receive bitter things in life and to receive minor troubles in a dream]?

The Scholar Origen, *Commentary on Matthew*, 122 (AACS 1b, p. 280)

Pilate Washed His Hands

Why then did Pilate allow Him to be sacrificed? Why didn't he rescue Him, like the centurion had rescued Paul? (Acts 27:1-44). For that man was too aware that he could have pleased the Jews and that a sedition may have taken place and a riot; nevertheless he stood firm against all these. But Pilate did not do so. He was extremely cowardly and weak. He joined in their corruption. He did not stand firm against the bullying crowd or against the Jewish leadership. In every way he allowed them an excuse. For they "cried out exceedingly," that is, cried out the more, "Let Him be crucified." For they desired not only to put Him to death but also that it should be on a trumped-up charge of iniquity. And even though the judge was contradicting them, they continued to cry out against Him.

St. John Chrysostom, *Commentary on Matthew*, Homily 86.2 (NPNF 2:10, p. 512

Pilate accepted that water in line with that prophetic saying, "I will wash my hands in innocence" (Psa. 25:6) that he might cleanse the works of the Gentiles by the washing of his hands and in some way separate us from the wickedness of the Jews who cried out, "Crucify Him!" What he intimated was this: I truly wanted to release an innocent Man, but a riot is breaking out and the charge of treason against Caesar has been brought against me. So "I am innocent of the blood of this just Man."

The judge who was induced to pass judgment against the Lord does not condemn the defendant but puts the blame on the plaintiffs. He declares Him to be a just Man who was meant to be crucified. "See to it yourselves," he says. "I am the administrator of the laws. It is according to your word that His Blood is being shed."

St. Jerome, *Commentary on Matthew*, 4.27.24 (AACS 1b, p. 282)

Pilate washed his hands as if to be clean of defilement, but his thoughts were evil. For he called Jesus a righteous Man and yet handed Him over to murderers.

The Blessed Theophylact, *TGM*, 242

"Your blood be upon us and our children."

What do they do? When they saw the judge washing his hands saying, "I am innocent," they cried out, "His blood be on us and our children." They were rendering a sentence against themselves. He was yielding Himself up that all should be done. Note how great their madness is—for passion and evil desire work on us like this. They did not permit anyone to see anything of what was right. They not only curse themselves, they draw down the curse upon their own children as well. They acted with unutterable madness. They acted both against themselves and against their children! Yet the Love of Mankind did not hold their own sentence against them. He did not confirm it upon their children or even upon them. Rather, He received both from them and from their children who repented. He counted them worthy of the good things beyond number. Think of who might have been among them! Even Paul, perhaps. Even some among the thousands that believed in Jerusalem, for it is said, "You see, brother, how many myriads of Jews there are who have believed" (Acts 21:20). And if some continued in their sin, to themselves let them impute their punishment.

St. John Chrysostom, *Commentary on Matthew*, Homily 86.2 (NPNF 1:10, p. 513)

His Suffering

The daughter of Zion repaid Him with evil for the immensity of His Grace. The Father had washed her from her blood, but she defiled His Son with her spitting (Ezek. 16:9; Matt. 26:67; Mk. 14:65). The Father had clothed her with fine linen and purpose, but she clothed Him with garments of mockery (Ezek. 16:10; Matt. 27:28; Mk. 15:17). He had placed a crown of glory on her head, but she plaited a crown of thorns for Him (Ezek. 16:12; Matt. 27:29; Mk. 15:17; Jn. 19:2). He had nourished her with choicest food and honey, but she gave Him gall (Ezek. 16:13, Matt. 27:34). He had given her pure wine, but she offered Him vinegar in a sponge (Jn. 19:29). The One who had put shoes on her feet, she made hasten barefoot towards Golgotha (Ezek. 16:10; Matt. 27:33; Mk. 15:22, Jn. 19:17). The One Who had girded her loins with sapphire, she pierced in the side with a spear (Ezek. 16:10-11, Jn. 19:34). When she had outraged the servants [of God] and killed the prophets, she was led into captivity to Babylon, and when the time of her punishment was completed, her return [from captivity] took place.

St. Ephrem the Syrian, *CTD*, 20.11, pp. 292-296 (AACS 2, pp. 210-211)

Why did Pilate have Jesus whipped? Either as one presumably condemned or to please the crowd, or as if he were willing to give their judgment some sort of standard legal expression. And yet he thought to have resisted them. For indeed even before this he had said, "You take Him and judge Him according to your law" (Jn. 18:31).

There were many reasons that Pilate and the others might have held back: the signs and the miracles, the great patience of the One who was suffering these things, and above all His benign silence. For since both by His defense of Himself and by His prayers, He had shown His humanity, again He now shows His glory and the greatness of His nature, both by His silence and by His indifference to what they said. This might have led them to marvel. But neither Pilate nor the crowd takes sufficient note of these evidences.

St. John Chrysostom, *Commentary on Matthew*, Homily 86.2 (NPNF 2:10, p. 513)

Jesus was handed over to the soldiers for scourging, and their whips did the work on that most sacred Body and that Bosom which held God. This came about so that, in keeping with the words "many cords of sins" and with the whipping of Jesus we might be free from scourging. As holy Scripture says to the just man, "The whip did not draw near to your tabernacle" (Psa. 90:10).

St. Jerome, *Commentary on Matthew*, 4.27.24 (AACS 1b, p. 283)

He Who has given the food of heaven was fed with gall (Mt 27:34); He Who has offered us the cup of salvation was given vinegar to drink (Matt. 27:48; Mk. 15:36; Lk. 23:36) He the innocent, He the just—no rather, innocence itself and justice itself is counted among criminals (Matt. 27:38; Mk. 15:27; Lk. 23:33; Jn. 19:18); and truth is concealed by false testimonies. He Who is to judge is judged and the Word of God, silent, is led to the Cross. The elements are disturbed, the earth trembles, night blots out the day (Matt. 27:45,51; Mk. 15:33; Lk. 23:44).

"There was darkness over the land" (Matt. 27:45) and its eyes lest it be forced to gaze upon the crime of the people. Though the stars are confounded at the crucifixion of the Lord, He does not speak, nor is He moved, nor does He proclaim His majesty, even during the suffering itself. He endures all things even to the end with constant perseverance so that in Christ a full and perfect patience may find its realization...

He Himself suffered the lash, in Whose Name His servants now scourge the devil and his angels. He Who now crowns the martyrs with eternal garlands was Himself crowned with thorns...He Who now gives true palms to victors was beaten in the face with hostile palms; He Who clothes all other with the garment of immortality was stripped of His earthly garment.

St. Cyprian, *The Good of Patience*, 7 (FC 36, p. 270; AACS 2, p. 225)

They "clothed Him in purple" in mockery; yet ironically it was a fulfillment of prophesy, for He was indeed a king. Even their parody indirectly served divine revelation. Even though they did it in a spirit of derision, still they did it, and His regal dignity was by that symbolically heralded. So, likewise, though it was with thorns they crowned Him, it was still a crown.

St. Cyril of Jerusalem, *Sermon on the Paralytic*, 12 (FC 64, p. 217; AACS 2, p. 226)

Pilate had Him whipped, either to gratify the people or else to show that it was he himself who had condemned Christ, and to make it appear that they were not about ho crucify an innocent Man, but rather One who was dishonorable. This was fulfilled this prophesy of Isaiah as well, "I gave My back to scourges" (Isa. 50:6).

The Blessed Theophylact, *TGM*, 242

Hear therefore also what follows. For after "they had mocked Him, they led Him to crucify Him," it is said, and when they had stripped Him, they took His garments, and sat down and watched Him, when He should die. And they divide His garments amongst them, which sort of thing is done in the case of very vile and abject criminals, and such as have no one belonging to them, and are in utter desolation. They parted the garments, by which such great miracles were done. But they wrought none now, Christ restraining His unspeakable power. And this was no small addition of insult. For as to one base and abject, as I said, and the vilest of all men; so do they dare to do all things. To the thieves at any rate they did nothing of the kind, but to Christ they dare it all. And they crucified Him in the midst of them, that He might share in their reputation.

St. John Chrysostom, *Homilies on Matthew* (NPNF 1:10, pp. 1083-1084)

Jesus, therefore, went to the place where He was to be crucified, bearing His Cross. What a grand spectacle! To the profane a laughing-stock, to the pious a mystery. Profaneness sees a king bearing a cross instead of a scepter; piety sees a King bearing a Cross, on which He nails Himself, and afterwards to nail it on the foreheads of kings. To profane eyes this was contemptible, which the hearts of saints would afterwards glory in.

For to Paul, who was yet to say, "But God forbid that I should glory, except in the Cross of our Lord Jesus Christ" (Gal. 6:14), he was commending that same Cross of His by carrying it on His own shoulders, and bearing the candlestick of that light that was yet to burn, and not to be placed under a bushel (cf. Matt. 5:15).

St. Augustine, *Tractates on John*, Tractate 117 (Jn. 19:17-22)

SIXTH HOUR: "THE CRUCIFIXION"

Num. 21:1-9; Isa.53:7-12; Isa.12:2-13:10; Amos 8:9-12
Gal. 6:14-18; Psa. 37:21,22; 21:16,17,18,8
Matt. 27:27-45; Mk. 15:26-33; Lk. 23:26-44; Jn. 19:13-27

Overview

As [the women] were "looking on," so we too gaze at His wounds as He hangs. We see His blood as He dies. We see the price offered by the Redeemer, and touch the scars of His Resurrection. He bows His head, as if to kiss you. His heart is made bare open, as it were, in love to you. His arms are extended that He may embrace you. His whole body is displayed for your redemption. Ponder how great these things are. Let all this be richly weighed in your mind. As He was once fixed to the Cross in every part of His Body for you, so may He now be fixed in every part of your soul.

Saint Augustine, *On Virginity* (AACS 2, p. 235)

There is only one theme for this entire hour: the Cross.

In this hour, God extends His arms on the Cross—in one hand carrying the sins of mankind from all generations; in the other declaring the love of God for man, forgiveness, and eternal life. Thus, He reconciled man with God on the Cross for our salvation.

The first prophesy, from **Numbers**, introduces Moses' brazen serpent—a symbol of the powerful Cross crushing Satan and all death. The Church daily reminds us of this message in the prayers of the sixth hour of the Agpeya. So we read of the power of the Cross, which acts as our cure and victory against sin.

The second prophesy in **Isaiah 53** is a powerful sign of Christ as the Lamb, brought to the slaughter. In the Jewish times, the lambs that were used for the temple sacrifices were born in Nazareth, grazed throughout Jerusalem, and then slaughtered on Golgotha outside of the temple. This practice amazingly foreshadows Christ, the true and perfect Lamb of God. This is one of the most powerful selections read throughout the week, prophesying about the Crucifixion, the burial, and the inheritance of salvation. Here, the Cross is the sacrificial wood that holds the Lamb of God.

The third prophesy, from **Isaiah 12**, speaks of the day of salvation that comes with a great joy, yet the sun will be darkened. This eclipse which took place on the Cross symbolizes the Lord as the Sun of Righteousness. On the

Cross, God gives us joyful waters to drink—of His precious blood mixed with the waters of baptism. Here, the Cross is our joy and steadfastness.

St. Gregory of Nyssa relates the third prophesy with man's thirst for salvation with the final prophesy of Amos, where man's thirst is only satisfied through "the hearing of the words of the Lord." **Amos** also prophesied that the sun would be darkened during His crucifixion. This demonstrates for us the hidden glory of the Cross.

Church Tradition and Rites

After these great prophesies are read, candles are then lit before the Icon of the Crucifixion. The presbyters, wearing their liturgical robes, cense the icon. In the presence of the bishop, they also cense and bow before him, without kissing his hand or his cross. Meanwhile, the congregation chants the hymn for the incense, Ϫⲁⲓϣⲟⲩⲣⲏ ("The Golden Censer") followed by the hymn Ⲫⲁⲓ ⲉⲧⲁϥⲉⲛϥ ("This is He"). In this hymn, we declare "This is He Who offered Himself on the Cross as an acceptable sacrifice for the salvation of our race. His Good Father smelled Him in the evening on Golgotha." Here, we taste the sweetness of the Cross.

After its paschal introduction is chanted, the Epistle of St. Paul to the Galatians is read. Its simple and essential theme: Glory in the Cross. Afterwards, six litanies are said by the priest, along with responses from the congregation. These prayers are patterned after those that follow the gospel readings in the Agpeya prayers.

Following this, the hymn of Ⲟⲩⲟⲛⲟⲅⲉⲛⲏⲥ ("O Only Begotten") is chanted. The initial part of the hymn discus the Incarnation and Crucifixion, and is accompanied by a somber paschal tune. Yet, near the end, there is hope when discussing the promise of the resurrection. Once the congregation chants "tramped down death..." (*Thanato Thanaton...*) the hymn regains life in a lively tempo and lighter beat. Here we hear of the hope of the Cross.

The Trisagion is then chanted twice, in two separate tunes, followed by the psalm and gospel readings. The psalm speaks directly about the piercing of His hands and feet. When Christ breathed His last, darkness came over all the land from the sixth to the ninth hour. The Church recreates this eclipse by turning off all of the lights in the Church after this one verse is read. Thus we see the light of the Cross.

After the reading of the Exposition, which sufficiently memorializes the events of this hour, the Church chants the hymn Ⲁⲣⲓⲡⲁⲙⲉⲩⲓ ("Remember me"). This hymn is based on the words spoken by the Thief on the Right, and expresses the desire of every believer to enter into God's Kingdom, which is opened for us through Christ's death and Resurrection. This hymn has 11 verses said by the reader, followed by repetitions of the thief's petition.

THE HYMN, Ⲫⲁⲓ ⲉ̀ⲧⲁ ϥⲉ ⲛ ϥ [5]

This is He Who offered Himself an acceptable sacrifice upon the Cross, for the salvation of our race.

His Good Father smelled His sweet aroma in the evening, on Golgotha.

Origins

The date and author of this hymn are both unknown. In addition, the theme of it is generic enough that it cannot be said with certainty whether it predates any Ecumenical Councils or was written as a result of them. The piece alone has themes that refute the heresies combated at all Three Councils, but it is not so direct that we can assume that with certainty. The only evidence that lends to suggesting that it is predates the Ecumenical councils, is that it has only one known tune. It would not be irrational to suggest that the indirectness of the Theological themes supports Pre-Council authorship, since hymns following the Councils usually combated specific heresies very vocally and directly so that all believers would be affirmed in their Orthodoxy. These, however, are only speculations, as nothing can be said with surety about the hymn, other than that it is authentically ours based on the tune and the fact that it is written in Coptic.

Note on Style and General Theme

Like most hymns of Great Friday, the theme Ⲫⲁⲓ ⲉ̀ⲧⲁϥⲉ ⲛϥ is our Redemption, which was accomplished on that Holy Day. This hymn, however, is stylistically more meditational than other hymns. The pronoun "our" is used, reinforcing the personal contemplative nature of the hymn, as it is each individual member of the Church looking toward the Savior on the Cross, and then sharing with the world the same prayer and proclamation. The Church looks at Him, mournfully, and then shares with humanity the message that they see in Him hanging upon the Tree of Life – this is God Incarnate who is hanging on that Tree for our salvation.

---

[5] Commentary by Fr. Antony Paul

Specific Themes

This hymn, despite its brevity, has in it the story of the Gospel— the story of Redemption. As such, it follows a natural order:

1. He is God.

2. His death was foretold in the prophecies.

3. He is the single and only acceptable sacrifice offered.

4. His sacrifice means the Salvation of our race.

5. His sacrifice was accepted before God the Father.

This is He...

1.

The Holy Bride of Christ, in pure adoration, makes it clear that she recognizes Who is on the Cross, and she says without hesitation, "This is He." Who is He? He is God; He is God Incarnate. This is the very basis to the hymn, which is why she can make the claim that all this was done for our Salvation. It has been discussed why only God can complete our Salvation by the Fathers of the Church at length, so it should suffice to argue that a limited man cannot take on the propitiation of sins of an unlimited sin. That is, a mere man under the bounds of natural time cannot take upon himself the sins of all generations – this is absurd. If I am in debt, it is impossible for me to take on the debt of my father – and I cannot in advance take on the debt of my child; working backwards, my father could not have made the same claim for his generations either. We appear to find ourselves in an endless dilemma, which would have no solution if we did not already recognize God, or rather, if He had not revealed Himself to us. It is abundantly clear that only "one" who has dominion over all properties of time, space, and Creation, can bear the full weight of such a sacrifice and not need a Savior for Himself – this "one" is no other than the one: God. As author of life and creator of Time, He is held by no such boundaries. As Lord of all Creation, He can make Himself the created. This, indeed, is He.

2.

How does the Church recognize, though, that this one on the Cross is the one spoken of? That indeed this is the one whose death was foretold? That the one should have been crucified? Saint Athanasius reminds us of some of these prophecies.

Moses was the first to tell us, when he said inspired by the Spirit, "And your life shall be in suspense before your eyes; and you shall be afraid by day and by night, and you shalt have no assurance of your life" (Deut. 28:66). The "life" here, is none other than the Life Himself - Moses has proclaimed that the one suspended is none other than God – the source of Life Himself.

Following this, Jeremiah prophesied and said, "But I was like an innocent lamb led to the slaughter, and I did not know they had devised evil against me, saying, 'Come and let us put wood into his bread, and let us utterly destroy him from off the land of the living, and let his name not be remembered any more'" (Jer. 11:19). The only "innocent" person is God Himself, as all others are born with the stain of sin, and "all have sinned and fallen short of the Glory of God" (Romans 3:23) – except God only. This means that the Innocent person is none other than God incarnate. The wood of which Jeremiah speaks is none other than the wood of the Tree of Life. He goes further to prophecy how the Jews wanted Him destroyed and that the memory of Him be blotted eternally.

Abundantly clear are the words of David the Prophet, "For many dogs have compassed me; the assembly of the wicked doers has beset me round; they pierced my hands and my feet" (Psalm 22:16). David's hands and feet were never pierced. Here He is seeing before himself Someone to Whom this has been done. "Wicked doers" surround Someone who is not wicked – this Someone must then have been innocent as well.

Of these three prophecies Saint Athanasius says, "Now a death raised aloft and that takes place on a tree, could be none other than the Cross; and again, in no other death are the hands and feet pierced, except on the Cross only."[6]

These, along with all the other prophecies about the Messiah's birth, life, death, and resurrection all confirm that indeed, "This is He", God, our Redeemer, Who is on that Holy Wood. Even John the Baptist recognized Him and said, "Behold, the Lamb of God, who takes away the sin of the world" (Jn. 1:29).

---

[6] St. Athanasius, *On the Incarnation*, 35, pp. 66-67

Who offered Himself an acceptable sacrifice upon the Cross...

3.

Having established that indeed it is God on the Cross and that this was the death by which He must die, we may then understand the words, "Who offered Himself an acceptable sacrifice upon the Cross." Since He is God, no others could offer Him. We could not choose for God to empty Himself and take the form of a servant. It is not within the power, no – it is blasphemous for anyone to put God under subjection. In fact, it is an absurdity. If God is under order of man, it means that man is lord over God, far be it from us to make such a statement. It is by realizing this absurdity, however, that we can appreciate the Divine Dispensation that was granted us – that He chose to offer Himself because He meets all the requirements of an acceptable sacrifice. An acceptable sacrifice need only be offered once; a continual sacrifice indicates that the previous sacrifice must have been incomplete. The Sacrifice on the Cross, however, was an Eternal Sacrifice:

> Why then, are they continually cured with the "same sacrifices"? For if they were set free from all their sins, the sacrifices would not have gone on being offered every day. For they had been appointed to be continually offered in behalf of the whole people, both in the evening and in the day. So that there was an arraignment of sins, and not a release from sins; an arraignment of weakness, not an exhibition of strength. For because the first had no strength, another also was offered: and since this effected nothing, again another; so that it was an evidence of sins. The "offering" indeed then, was an evidence of sins, the "continually," an evidence of weakness. But with regard to Christ, it was the contrary: He was "once offered."[7]

The fact that only one sacrifice was needed because it was God is reemphasized in another homily, "So then He forgave their sins, when He gave the Covenant, and He gave the Covenant by sacrifice. If therefore He forgave the sins through the one sacrifice, there is no longer need of a second."[8]

Saint John teaches that the sacrifice in the Old Testament was incomplete; it was simply an "arraignment," a process in which the transgressor was brought forth and called as an accused to answer for his

---

[7] St. John Chrysostom, *Commentary on Hebrews*, Homily 17 (NPNF 1:14, p. 959).
[8] St. John Chrysostom, *Commentary on Hebrews*, Homily 18 (NPNF 1:14, p. 966).

faults. The sacrifice made by our Lord, however, was no arraignment situation. He came bearing no faults of His own, but came bearing on Himself the faults of all sinners of all generations. Since not only did He not sin continually but not at all, He showed what is opposite to weakness – complete might. As a result, His sacrifice was all that was acceptable, as no other being, neither in the heavens nor below the heavens, can with boldness claim to be able to do the same – as all are created beings and bound by the laws He created. The heavenly are not of our kind and not unlimited, and hence could not take the sin of man, and as discussed, no man can take on the sins of all generations. God's sacrifice, again, is the only sacrifice that could be sufficient. He renewed our nature, He forgave our debt by His blood:

> This blood was ever typified of old in the altars and sacrifices of righteous men, This is the price of the world, by This Christ purchased to Himself the Church, by This He has adorned Her all. For as a man buying servants gives gold for them, and again when he desires to deck them out does this also with gold; so Christ has purchased us with His blood, and adorned us with His Blood.[9]

...for the salvation of our race

4.

It happened "for the salvation of our race." It has been established that He upon the Cross is God. He is the One spoken of by the prophets, and He is the acceptable sacrifice. Through this sacrifice, we are redeemed, since it has been established that the death of the Incarnate Word meant the debt of man was paid in full, once and for all. What follows, then, is quite logical: Salvation. We lost our Salvation when we were enemies with God, however the paying of this debt, this true Sacrifice, meant reconciliation with the heavens:

> "To appear," he says, "in the presence of God for us." What is "for us"? He went up (he means) with a sacrifice which had power to propitiate the Father. Why [tell me]? Was He an enemy? The demons were enemies, He was not an enemy. For that the Angels were enemies, hear what he says, "He made peace as to things on

---

[9] St. John Chrysostom, *Commentary on John*, Homily 46 (NPNF 1:14, p. 381).

earth and things in Heaven" (Col. 1:20). So that He also "entered into Heaven, now to appear in the presence of God for us." He "now appeared," but "for us."[10]

Salvation, however, does not merely mean reconciliation – though reconciliation is a mandatory step. It cannot be that man and God be at enmity with each other and dwell in the same heaven! Here, again, then, is the natural consequence of His Godhead. Because He is God, He conquered death by His death and Resurrection. He, as Saint John Chrysostom teaches us, entered heaven to appear for us, and after this Reconciliation and mediation for us, He Himself led to Paradise the spirits of those who had departed before His crucifixion – but in the hope of the Resurrection. It is the Redemption, Reconciliation and the Resurrection that together result for us in Salvation – man was saved from the bondage of sin and the consequence of it (death), and at last could enter with joy into Paradise:

> In order that while He might become a sacrifice for us all, we, nourished up in the words of truth, and partaking of His living doctrine, might be able with the saints to receive also the joy of Heaven.[11]

His Good Father smelled His sweet aroma in the evening, on Golgotha.

5.

Finally, we can comprehend how "His Good Father smelled His sweet aroma in the evening, on Golgotha." The Church is declaring in ecstasy and awe the fact that God the Father has accepted our prayers, and has accepted the Sacrifice offered before Him.

We were standing and praying as David did, saying, "Let my prayer be set forth before You as incense" (Psa. 141: 2), and we were joining those of the Old Testament of whom it is said "The whole multitude of the people was praying outside at the time of incense" (Lk. 1:10). Christ was our prayer because He was our only hope at Reconciliation, Redemption and Salvation – only if He was found acceptable could we live again – as such all our hope was (and is) in Him. Since we could not atone for our sins ourselves and reconcile ourselves to the Father, we stood by, "outside", watching and praying as Christ went in for us – as both our incense - our prayer and

[10] St. John Chrysostom, *Commentary on Hebrews*, Homily 17 (NPNF 1:14, p. 956).
[11] St. Athanasius, *Paschal Epistle* 18 (NPNF 2:4, p. 1307).

sacrifice– and our High Priest – making the offering Himself (Heb. 2:13). Because His Father found the aroma "sweet" on the Holy Cross on Golgotha, we could sigh in relief, and say, "Wherefore in all things it behooved him to be made like unto his brethren, that he might be a merciful and faithful high priest in things pertaining to God, "to make reconciliation for the sins of the people" (Heb. 2:17).

Our relief is more full, however, if we comprehend that the coal used to burn the incense, a type of Christ, confirms the propitiation of our sins as was told Isaiah, "Behold, this has touched thy lips, and will take away your iniquities, and will purge away your sins" (Isa. 6:7).

Now, then, we come full circle and marvel at all that this hymn contains – truly it is the story of our Redemption put in very simple words. Christ our God, of whom the prophets foretold, came to earth, took on our humanity while remaining God, suffered and died, buried and rose, was found as an unblemished sacrifice before God the Father, and hence reconciled us with God, redeemed us, and granted us Salvation.

The Prayer

This hymn is prayed in a very dramatic tune because we feel the guilt of our sins that made necessary this event. We point at the Lord on the Wood and proclaim that, yes, "This is He" indeed, very God and very Man, who is suffering on our behalf willingly, who offered Himself on our behalf. The full realization of the consequence of sin falls upon us, and so we cry out tragically, ϫⲁ ⲡⲟⲩϫⲁⲓ ("for the salvation"), as though we simultaneously accuse ourselves before Him of our sins, and cry out in wonder to preach to the world exactly what is occurring despite our wickedness.

In spite of the fact that we are living each moment of the Pascha and have not reached the climax, which is in the Resurrection, we still look forward to the hope that is in Him – recognizing that in His body hanging upon the Tree is also the promise of Life. It is for that reason that in our prayer we acknowledge that it is for our Salvation – even though Salvation is not achieved until the Resurrection. Since this hymn is also a preaching, it would be an incomplete witness if it did not bear with it the promise of Life that is in Christ our Risen Lord.

This is a prayer of repentance, only when we too can look at our Lord dying on our behalf, and realize that this is for us and because of us, can we continue to cry with genuine tears and say, "This is He. Amen. This is He."

This is He Who in old time was sacrificed as a lamb, He being signified in the lamb; but Who afterwards was slain for us, for "Christ our Passover is sacrificed." This is He Who delivered us from the snare of the hunters, from the opponents of Christ...and again rescued us His Church. And because we were then victims of deceit, He has now delivered us by His own self.[12]

THE HYMN, Ο ̄ Ο ̄ Ο Ο Ο ̄ Γ Є Ν Η C [13]

O Only-Begotten Son and Logos of God, Eternal and Immortal,

Who for our salvation did will to be incarnate of the Holy Theotokos and Ever-Virgin Mary.

Who without change became Man and was crucified, O Christ, our God.

Who trampled down death by death. One of the Holy Trinity, with the Father and the Holy Spirit, save us.

Introduction

Of all the hymns sung during the great Pascha, very few so elaborately tie together the dogmas of the Church with her general feeling of mourning. In essence, this hymn is perhaps a proof of the intrinsic relationship between theology and spirituality: they are inseparable. Everything about O monogenyc, from its words to its authorship is relevant for the Christian who wishes to derive from it all possible spiritual value.

A Note on Style

The author of this piece is bold, a fact which shall be discussed later, but not bold such that he forgets the boundaries of his mind, thoughts, and words. For in this piece, only adjectives, verbs or adverbs, are used to describe our God, never direct nouns. This is noteworthy only insofar as one recognizes how articulate the Greek language is - one can define virtually anything in Greek. Our fathers, however, like the Jews before them, understood that God could not be defined in terms of nouns or substances. He could only be described on what He has done, what He is *like*, *how* He works—in terms of His graces to us, or our relationship with Him. To attempt to say more would be risking blasphemy, as to claim a perfect

---

[12] St. Athanasius, *Paschal Epistle* 10 (NPNF 2:4, p. 1265).
[13] Fr. Antony Paul, "*O Monogenis:* A Spiritual and Historical Study of this Paschal Hymn."

understanding of God would be to presume one's own divinity. Hence, like our fathers who wrote the Creed at Nicaea, the author of this piece speaks of God *Who* is "Immortal," God *Who* has accepted everything, God Who became man or the one of the Holy Trinity. This reverence toward the Second Hypostasis and indeed toward the Holy Trinity must be noted and reflected in the way that this is sung, for though the hymn is bold, it is also humble

General Theological Themes

Before analyzing the specific themes of this piece, it is worth noting the overall theme: an affirmation of Christ's perfect Divinity, as well as His perfect Humanity. It is the perfect exposition on the words of Saint Cyril of Alexandria,

> If anyone does not acknowledge the Word of God the Father to be united hypostatically with the flesh and to be one Christ together with His own flesh, that is, the same subject as at once both God and man, let him be anathema.[14]

It is a hymn pleading for the mercy of our God, even as we relive His hanging and death upon the life-giving Tree. His perfect Divinity is revered and implored in our plea for mercy—for we do not ask the mercy for humanity from any mere human, but only from God. We revere and acknowledge His perfect humanity, as the sixth hour of the blessed day is the hour in which our Lord gave up His Spirit into the hands of His Father, which happened according to His perfect Humanity. Because He was both Human and Divine, salvation could be accomplished, and this we testify in this hymn, bowing before the Incarnate Logos, not just before His Divinity, nor before only His humanity.

Specific Theological Themes

Having recognized that the spirituality cannot be severed from the Theological let us then examine aspects of this hymn more directly.

First, Christ is declared as the Only-Begotten Son, hence His Sonship to the Father is declared. Even in the hour of His death, we sing with solemnity and hope and call Him "the Immortal," we acknowledge His perfect Divinity on the Cross, even as Demas did, knowing that no mere

---

[14] St. Cyril of Alexandria, *An Explanation of the Twelve Chapters*, Anathema 2

mortal by definition can be Immortal. "Before all ages" is then another cry out to affirm our belief that He is Divine, as we do not sing to a mortal man, one born of a woman as being "before all ages." Ever-existing and Eternal can only be attributed to God, no man can claim such an honor to himself. From this we can see how the writer may be referring directly to the Nicene Creed: "We believe in one Lord, Jesus Christ, the Only-Begotten Son of God, begotten of the Father before all ages." As we know, this very section of the Creed was written in order for the Church, the living body of Christ, to proclaim the perfect Divinity of Christ. Perhaps, then, it is meet to realize that the Creed here is being sung—the Orthodox Creed is not a mere document, it is a prayer.

"Who has accepted everything for our salvation..."

Here, then, is the proclamation of His Manhood. This is an indirect reference to the kenosis, the "emptying" of God, in which He "emptied Himself and took the form of a servant." For as God, He is not forced to "accept" anything, as he has the Divine authority merely to command and it shall be done, nothing is forced upon the Lord of Hosts. Because He emptied Himself, however, He accepted upon Himself the penalty that was given to our humanity, suffering and death as the price for our iniquities. He "accepted everything" in full, He Was not selective, He bore every pain, every tribulation, every temptation that is common to man, and took it upon Himself all "for our salvation."

"...the Incarnate of the Holy Theotokos, the Ever-Virgin Mary"

It is not clear as to why a reference was added to magnify the Theotokos here, though it is entirely appropriate. There are a few possible reasons one can consider for this section, one of which will be analyzed when considering the authorship of this piece.

It is possible that the Church saw it appropriate to magnify His Holy Mother who at this hour stood at the feet of her son and beheld Him dying. Indeed, we also include her and honor her in the verses of Sixth Hour chanted prior to this hymn. Reasons for veneration of the Theotokos in general already have books dedicated to it, but another reason for this inclusion is possible. It is not unlikely that this was another affirmation of His perfect one Nature, a defense of the title Theotokos made to oppose Nestorius, the deposed Patriarch of Constantinople in their Christological war. It is quite likely that the Church was considering all these possibilities, though the explanation of the latter may shed strong light upon who actually authored this piece.

"Who without change became man; Who was crucified...Who has trampled death by His death; the one of the Holy Trinity, glorified with the Father and the Holy Spirit, save us."

If it was not clear, here it is said with perfect clarity so that none may doubt, Christ is God the Word Who took flesh, and because He was perfect in His humanity, He died; and because He is perfect in His divinity, He conquered death and can be asked to save us. He is none other than the second hypostasis of the Trinity, and He, the Word of God, did suffer on our behalf and accept death.

> If anyone does not acknowledge that the Word of God suffered in the flesh, and was crucified in the flesh, and experienced death in the flesh, and became the first-born from the dead, seeing that as God He is both Life and life-giving, let him be anathema.[15]

This is then followed by a modified version of the Trisagion, the first two words of each verse affirming His Divinity, and the rest referring to His perfect humanity and the Incarnation. It restates all said in the first two verses in perhaps a more poetic way and corresponds again to the words of Saint Cyril,

> We understand Him to be the Word of God the Father Who has become incarnate and been made man, and if you call Him 'man', we acknowledge Him to be no less God who has by divine dispensation accommodated Himself to the limitations of the human state. We say that the intangible has become tangible, the invisible visible. For the body that was united to Him, which we say was capable of being touched and seen, was not something alien to Him. Those who do not believe this but, as I have said, separate the hypostases after the union, and consider them united by a mere conjunction simply in terms of rank or supreme authority, are excluded by this anathema from those who hold orthodox opinions.[16]

---

[15] St. Cyril of Alexandria, *An Explanation of the Twelve Chapters*, Anathema 12.
[16] St. Cyril of Alexandria, *An Explanation of the Twelve Chapters*, Anathema 3.

The *Trisagion* in and of itself presents a controversy relevant to the authenticity of the authorship. This shall be discussed in context below. It should suffice that it is again verifying the spiritual/theological basis of the first two verses. It seems fitting also to add here, that **Oⲙⲟⲛⲟⲅⲉⲛⲏⲥ** is a hymn that falls into the category of *Trisagion* hymns, accompanied by the *Trisagion* itself, and Megalou. The hymn itself was quite likely based on the hymn of the *Trisagion*.

The Prayer

This, then, is the prayer of **Oⲙⲟⲛⲟⲅⲉⲛⲏⲥ**: it is the prayer of all who worship Christ in His one Nature of God the Incarnate Logos, and it is the prayer that rings forth the truth of our Salvation. It is a hymn of power sung to the Lord crucified, in the hope of the Lord triumphantly resurrected.

Upon these words hang the fate of all Christians, and hence one who sings this cannot sing passively. The Church cannot put enough emphasis on this, because if Christ is not God, if He is not resurrected—then our faith is in vain, "And if Christ is not risen, then our preaching is empty and your faith is also empty" (1 Cor. 15:14). This religion is no longer the religion of hope, but it is a religion of death—for beyond the tomb there would be no eternal life, there would be a sentencing to Hades, but far worse and, God forbid, we would have believed a lie.

It is perhaps appropriate, then, to note the change in tune in these proclamations. We sing only the first word of each verse pathetically, but in our proclamations of the faith, we sing with a sudden solemnity. The tune is not hesitant, the tune is not dramatically tragic as the **Ϧⲁ ⲛ̄ⲟⲩⲭⲁⲓ** ("for the salvation") of **Ⲫⲁⲓ ⲉⲧⲁϥⲉⲛϥ**—rather it is one of dignity, mourning and respect, but also a tune of those proclaiming their God's perfection. It is not dramatic - it is solemn; it is the cry of the army to their Commander, Who is both one of them and far superior to them.

Authorship of the Piece

It has not been determined exactly who wrote **Oⲙⲟⲛⲟⲅⲉⲛⲏⲥ**. The Copts hold two traditions: Saint Athanasius the Apostolic according to some, and Saint Severus of Antioch according to others. Another tradition of note is that of the Chalcedonians, who hold that it was written by Emperor Justinian in the sixth century.

Emperor Justinian

Of the three possible authors, it seems most appropriate to eliminate consideration of Emperor Justinian for reasons of politics and Christology.

Politically, it makes very little sense that he wrote it. This Emperor favored his own in so far that he had our Pope Theodosius banished *from* Egypt, to live in Constantinople until his death. Furthermore, it was him who exiled Saint Severus of Antioch from his patriarchal chair *to* Egypt, after the blessed saint confessed his Orthodox belief in the *mia physis*. This bit of politics is relevant in that the Copts rejected Justinian. It is very unlikely that the Copts would accept a hymn to be forced upon them by a heterodox emperor, considering they were out of communion with the majority of the Christian world for their obstinate belief in Orthodoxy. It is implausible that they would succumb to even one hymn. It is equally unlikely that Justinian would have requested them to sing the hymn, since he knew that he was not in their favor, and also understood well the nature of the schism and what it entailed. He was in favor of a reunion of the Churches eventually, but there has not of yet been any evidence to suggest that he did request the Copts to sing a piece that he wrote. Furthermore, the tune is consistent with the tunes of all our other Paschal hymns - it would seem peculiar that the Copts were not only open to accepting the hymn he wrote, but that they would take it further to compose the music to accompany it. This is far from the personality of the Copts.

The other reason is partially related to the first, and it is based on Christology. As discussed previously, the hymn is Christological in nature, but far more importantly, the *Trisagion* is sung Christologically here, not in the Trinitarian way as is tradition among the Chalcedonians. In fact, to sing the *Trisagion* Christologically was virtually anathema in their Church from at least after Chalcedon, until their 5th Ecumenical Council. Emperor Justinian presided over this council, and acknowledged that the *Trisagion* could be used; however, it was more of an allowance than an encouragement. It was not popularly accepted even after sanction, and this is evidenced by the fact that it was later re-condemned by their John of Damascus—just two centuries later. It does not make sense that something so unpopular among the Theologians of his Church would be accepted by his own people. Even more against his favor, is the fact that the Greeks today *do not* chant O monogenyc with a Christological *Trisagion*. So highly is Justinian esteemed among the Chalcedonians, that it would seem odd that they would make intentionally such an omission - it would suggest acknowledging him as a saint while not recognizing his theology. So this alongside the very important political argument should not be dismissed or undermined. It may also suggest that the *Trisagion* might not have been initially included if Justinian wrote it, which is a possibility that does not allow us (on this basis) to reject him entirely as a candidate, though the issue of politics cannot be undermined. The very fact that Copts sing it, is a strong evidence that it could not have been written by an outsider. The Copts were closed to Greek additions and influence from Chalcedon until the time of Pope Cyril IV, the Great Reformer, just two centuries ago. So the only possible evidence in favor of Justinian is the universality of the hymn; this, as shall be discussed, perhaps can be explained better by attributing it to another author.

Finally, this piece is bold. No unskilled Theologian can write on the mystery of the Incarnation so succinctly and without fear, this is a person writing with experience and great insight into the truths of our faith - Justinian was an emperor, not a Theologian.

Saint Athanasius the Apostolic or Saint Severus of Antioch

It is the universality of this piece along with the Creedal nature that lends evidence that indeed this piece may have been authored by the great Saint Athanasius. Anything written by Athanasius was made known to the Church universal, as he died many years before the tragic split of the Church. This would give explanation as to why the hymn is currently in use between the Churches that are not even in communion with one another. The strong correlation between the first verse and the Creed must not be overlooked. The author, as discussed previously, even follows the same order of the clauses of the Creed. Furthermore, we know that the "Thirteenth Apostle" is the pillar to every Christian's understanding of the Incarnation, the major theme of this piece. It was Athanasius, who wrote,

> For He was made man that we might be made God; and He manifested Himself by a body that we might receive the idea of the unseen Father; and He endured the insolence of men that we might inherit immortality... And, in a word, the achievements of the Savior, resulting from His becoming man, are of such kind and number, that if one should wish to enumerate them, he may be compared to men who gaze at the expanse of the sea and wish to count its waves....[17]

---

[17] Saint Athanasius, *On the Incarnation of the Logos*, 54.

None knew or know the Incarnation as Saint Athanasius, nor is this piece inconsistent with his works.

One would feel content accepting the author as none other than the 20th Pope of Alexandria, but for three elements of the piece: the reference to the Theotokos, the words "Christ God," and the Christological Trisagion.

The strong message of the Incarnation does indeed seem to be some form of a direct attack on the Arian heresy to be included in our prayers, but the reference to the Theotokos poses more questions. It is not altogether impossible or unlikely for Saint Athanasius to be mentioning the Holy Virgin, however, referring to her as the Theotokos so directly, and in the context of **Ouonoɤenhc**, is more typical of Post-Ephesus writing. This piece is affirming His perfect oneness, which is inherent in the title of Theotokos. The Fathers emphasized usage of the term Theotokos after rejecting Nestorius' heresy that she is only the Christokos (the bearer of Christ), and not the Theotokos (the bearer of God). This was a direct influence of Saint Cyril the Great, who wrote,

> If anyone does not acknowledge Emmanuel to be truly God and therefore the Holy Virgin to be Theotokos (for she gave birth according to the flesh to the Logos of God made flesh), let him be anathema.[18]

This, alongside the Christological *Trisagion* seems awkward. If Athanasius used a Christological *Trisagion*, it is not only unlikely, but virtually impossible for the Chalcedonians to have rejected it so much or to hold it anathema. Division from the great fathers, particularly of Saint Athanasius meant immediate separation, as Athanasius' words gained him the title of Apostolic; so great was his authority that he was seen almost as an Apostle! It seems, especially because of the remaining piece of questionable writing, that this piece is post-Athanasius. We must also take into consideration, that the later fathers do not forget what was said before them—their sayings, quotes, and writings are collected alongside their own writings, such that the treasure of the Church's spiritual writings grows, not diminishes. That is, the Fathers of the Church quote the Fathers of the Church. So the Athanasian style of the first two verses does not demerit the possibility of Saint Severus' authorship of the piece.

---

[18] St. Cyril of Alexandria, *An Explanation of the Twelve Chapters*, Anathema 1.

The words "Christ-God" are highly *a*typical of Alexandrine school writing. Christ-God, is distinctive of Antiochene school writing, and it is a terminology that started to be used following the great controversy between Saint Cyril of Alexandria, John of Antioch, and Nestorius of Constantinople. The words 'Christ-God' are not used carelessly, they represent the heights of a far greater controversy, and it is these two words that open the possibility of Saint Severus' authorship.

Not only do these words support him as the writer, but also the strong emphasis on the one Nature of God the Incarnate Logos. These Cyrillian words used by Saint Dioscorus again at the Council of Chalcedon were the reason for the separation of the Diophysites from the Orthodox. It was these words that became the treasure of the Orthodox Copts for centuries, because it was for them the sentence that they were willing to be isolated for and estranged from all others. This strong influence on writings and hymns from this controversy are of course all post-Chalcedon, but more importantly, they were the words that stirred Saint Severus' heart, as he returned to the Orthodox Church - it is this statement of Saint Cyril's that Saint Severus and all the Orthodox confessed:

> Considering, therefore, as I said, the manner of His incarnation we see that His two natures came together with each other in an indissoluble union, without blending and without change, for His flesh is flesh and not divinity, even though His flesh became the flesh of God, and likewise the Logos also is God and not flesh, even though He made the flesh His own according to the dispensation. Therefore, whenever we have these thoughts in no way do we harm the joining into a unity by saying that he was of two natures, but after the union we do not separate the natures from one another, nor do we cut the one and indivisible Son into two sons but we say that there is one Son, and as the holy Fathers have said, there is one nature of the Logos (of God) made flesh.[19]

This being a strong emphasis of his time, coupled with his Antiochene schooling, give reasonable explanation for the strong leaning toward the Alexandrine Christologies while writing with Antiochene style—it gives reason for the "Christ-God" terminology not commonly used (though not altogether unused) during the time of Saint Athanasius.

---

[19] Saint Cyril of Alexandria, *Letter to Succensus.*

The only issue is again, not understanding its universal use. It is, at least, equally likely that the hymn could have spread from Alexandria if it had been spread from Constantinople. Perhaps we could also consider the possibility that he wrote it pre-exile, and that it was modified either by the non-Chalcedonians or by the Chalcedonians locally.

Though no author can be concluded beyond any doubt, it is not unreasonable to discount Justinian—as discussed previously. There is evidence that supports Saint Athanasius' authorship, though the evidence and themes favor most strongly Saint Severus.

Significance of the Authorship

One may question the spiritual significance of knowing the author of this piece altogether. The relevance of course, is relative—it is different to those who are praying alone than to those who are praying with the Church universal. Whether Saint Athanasius or Saint Severus, it is clear that this hymn not only is a proclamation and prayer of our faith, but it is also a condemnation on those who defame our God - the heretics. In that sense, it has also become a preaching; a preaching handed down by the fathers. By recognizing the author, we are sharing in the communion of the saints—the living and the dead. By singing with Athanasius or singing with Severus, we are joining them in their trials and tribulations that they endured for their God and faith; for the Truth of the one Nature. We are joining them in their triumph over the enemy; we are joining them in their love and passion for our Savior and Redeemer. More importantly, we find with them the same favor with God, for also preserving until now the same truths professed before the world centuries upon centuries ago. Through and with them, we learn to love Him more. The triumphant Church of God that sees no death stands in unity, proclaiming the mysteries of the faith, and uttering with boldness the Divine Mystery of our Salvation—it is first and last to the Glory of God.

Readings and Patristic Meditations

NUMBERS 21:1-9

Now The king of Arad, the Canaanite, who dwelt in the South, heard that Israel was coming on the road to Atharim, then he fought against Israel and took some of them prisoners. So Israel made a vow to the Lord, and said, "If You will indeed deliver this people into my hand, then I will utterly destroy their cities." And the Lord listened to the voice of Israel and delivered up the

Canaanites, and they utterly destroyed them and their cities. So the name of that place was called Hormah.

Then they journeyed from Mount Hor by the Way of the Red Sea, to go around the land of Edom; and the soul of the people became very discouraged on the way. And the people spoke against God and against Moses: "Why have you brought us up out of Egypt to die in the wilderness? For there is no food and no water, and our soul loathes this worthless bread." So the Lord sent fiery serpents among the people, and they bit the people; and many of the people of Israel died.

Therefore the people came to Moses, and said, "We have sinned, for we have spoken against the Lord and against you; pray to the Lord that He take away the serpents from us." So Moses prayed for the people. Then the Lord said to Moses, "Make a fiery serpent, and set it on a pole; and it shall be that everyone who is bitten, when he looks at it, shall live." So Moses made a bronze serpent, and put it on a pole; and so it was, if a serpent had bitten anyone, when he looked at the bronze serpent, he lived.

The brazen serpent was hung up as a remedy for the biting serpents, not as a type of Him that suffered for us, but as a contrast; and it saved those that looked upon it, not because they believed it to live, but because it was killed, and killed with it the powers that were subject to it, being destroyed as it deserved. And what is the fitting epitaph for it from us? "O death, where is your sting? O grave, where is your victory?" (Hos. 13:41; 1 Cor. 15:55). You are overthrown by the Cross; you are slain by Him who is the Giver of life; you are without breath, dead, without motion, even though you keep the form of a serpent lifted up on high on a pole.

St. Gregory Nazianzen, *Second Oration* (NPNF 2:8)

Moses, after the prohibition of [making an image of] any "likeness of anything," set forth a brazen serpent, placed on a "tree," in a hanging posture, for a spectacle of healing to Israel, at the time when, after their idolatry, they were suffering extermination by serpents, except that in this case he was exhibiting the Lord's Cross on which the "serpent" the devil was "made a show of," and, for every one hurt by such snakes—that is, his angels—on turning intently from the problem of sins to the sacraments of Christ's Cross, salvation was accomplished? For he who then gazed upon that [Cross] was freed from the bite of the serpents.

The Scholar Tertullian, *An Answer to the Jews*, 10 (ANF 3)

In a similar manner He points to the Cross of Christ...with Moses, when God commanded, "You shall not have any graven or image for your God," that he might reveal a type of Jesus. Moses then makes a brazen serpent, and places it upon a beam, and by proclamation assembles the people. When, therefore, they had come together, they beseeched Moses that he would offer sacrifice in their behalf, and pray for their recovery...[This is a symbol of] the glory of Jesus; for in Him and to Him are all things.

Epistle of Barnabas, 12 (ANF 1)

Didn't God, through Moses, forbid the making of an image or likeness of anything in the heavens or on earth? Yet, didn't He Himself have Moses construct the brazen serpent in the desert? Moses set it up as a sign by which those who had been bitten by the serpents were healed. In doing so, was Moses not free of any sin? By this, as I stated above, God through Moses announced a mystery by which he proclaimed that He would break the power of the serpent, who prompted the sin of Adam. He promises that He would deliver from the bites of the serpent (that is, evil actions, idolatries, and other sins) all those who believe in Him who was to be put to death by this sign, namely the Cross.

St. Justin Martyr, Dialogue with Trypho, 94 (FC 6, p. 297; AACS OT 3, p. 242)

The serpent struck Adam in paradise and killed him. [It also struck] Israel in the camp and annihilated them. "And as Moses lifted up the serpent in the wilderness, even so must the Son of Man will be lifted up" (Jn. 3:14). Just as those who looked with bodily eyes at the sign which Moses fastened on the Cross lived bodily, so too those who look with spiritual eyes at the Body of the Messiah nailed and suspended on the Cross and believe in Him will live [spiritually]. Thus it was revealed through this brazen [serpent], which by nature cannot suffer, that He who was to suffer on the Cross is one Who by nature cannot die.

St. Ephrem the Syrian, CTD, 16.15 (AACS OT 3, p. 242)

To be made whole of a serpent is a great mystery. What is it to be made whole of a serpent by looking upon a serpent? It is to be made whole of death by believing in one dead. And nevertheless Moses feared and fled (Exod. 4:3). Why did Moses flee from the serpent? What, brethren, except that which we know to have been done in the gospel? Christ died, and the disciples feared and withdrew from the hope wherein they had been.

St. Augustine, Explanation of the Psalms, 74.4 (NPNF 1:8, p. 344)

And since this great and wonderful dignity can only be attained by the remission of sins, He goes on to say, "And as Moses lifted up the serpent in the wilderness, even so must the Son of man be lifted up; that whoever believes on Him should not perish, but have eternal life." We know what at that time happened in the wilderness. Many were dying of the bite of serpents: the people then confessed their sins, and, through Moses, beseeched the Lord to take away from them this poison. Accordingly, Moses, at the Lord's command, lifted up a brazen serpent in the wilderness, and admonished the people that everyone who had been serpent-bitten should look upon the uplifted figure. When they did so they were immediately healed.

What does the uplifted serpent symbolize but the death of Christ, by that mode of expressing a sign, by which the thing which is effected is signified by that which effects it? Now death came by the serpent, which persuaded man to commit the sin, by which he deserved to die. The Lord, however, transferred to His own flesh not sin, as the poison of the serpent, **but He did transfer to it death, that the penalty without the fault might transpire in the likeness of sinful flesh, whence, in the sinful flesh, both the fault might be removed and the penalty.**

As, therefore, it then came to pass that whoever looked at the raised serpent was both healed of the poison and freed from death, so also now, whoever is conformed to the likeness of the death of Christ by faith in Him and His baptism, is freed both from sin by justification, and from death by resurrection. For this is what He says: "that whoever believes in Him should not perish, but have eternal life" (Jn. 3:15). What necessity then could there be for an infant's being conformed to the death of Christ by baptism, if he were not altogether poisoned by the bite of the serpent?

St. Augustine, *On the Merits and the Forgiveness of Sins and the Baptism of Infants*, 6 (NPNF 1:5)

He endured death, then; but death He hung on the Cross, and mortal men are delivered from death. The Lord calls to mind a great matter, which was done in a figure with them of old: "And as Moses," He said, "lifted up the serpent in the wilderness, so must the Son of man be lifted up; that everyone who believes on Him may not perish, but have everlasting life." A great mystery is here, as they who read know...the Lord Himself testifies in this passage, so that no man can give another interpretation than that which the Truth indicates concerning itself...

What are the biting serpents? Sins, from the mortality of the flesh. What is the serpent lifted up? The Lord's death on the Cross. For as death came by the serpent, it was figured by the image of a serpent. The serpent's

bite was deadly, the Lord's death is life-giving. A serpent is gazed on that the serpent may have no power. What is this? A death is gazed on, that death may have no power. But whose death? The death of life: if it may be said, the death of life.

Yes, for it may be said, but said wonderfully. But should it not be spoken, seeing it was a thing to be done? Shall I hesitate to utter that which the Lord has deigned to do for me? Is not Christ the life? And yet Christ hung on the Cross. Is not Christ life? **And yet Christ was dead. But in Christ's death, death died. Life slew death; the fullness of life swallowed up death; death was absorbed in the body of Christ.**

So also shall we say in the resurrection, when now triumphantly we shall sing, "O death, where is your victory? O death, where is your sting?" Meanwhile brethren, that we may be healed from sin, let us now gaze on Christ crucified; for "as Moses," He said, "lifted up the serpent in the wilderness, so must the Son of Man be lifted up; that whoever believes in Him will not perish, but have everlasting life." Just as they who looked on that serpent perished not by the serpent's bites, so they who look in faith on Christ's death are healed from the bites of sins. But those were healed from death to temporal life; whilst here He said, "that they may have everlasting life." Now there is this difference between the figurative image and the real thing: the figure procured temporal life; the reality, of which that was the figure, procures eternal life.

St. Augustine, *Tractates on John*, Tractate 12 (NPNF 1:7)

ISAIAH 53:7-12

He was oppressed and He was afflicted, yet He opened not His mouth; He was led as a lamb to the slaughter, and as a sheep before its shearers is silent, so He opened not His mouth.

He was taken from prison and from judgment, and who will declare His generation? For He was cut off from the land of the living; For the transgressions of My people He was stricken. And they made His grave with the wicked—but with the rich at His death, because He had done no violence, nor was any deceit in His mouth.

Yet it pleased the Lord to bruise Him; He has put Him to grief. When You make His soul an offering for sin, He shall see His seed, He shall prolong His days, and the pleasure of the Lord shall prosper in His hand. He shall see the labor of His soul, and be satisfied. By His knowledge My righteous Servant shall justify many, for He shall bear their iniquities.

Therefore I will divide Him a portion with the great, and He shall divide the spoil with the strong, Because He poured out His soul unto death, and He was numbered with the transgressors, and He bore the sin of many, and made intercession for the transgressors.

For when the Lord Himself had come, He came in order to suffer, He came hidden. And though He was strong in Himself, He appeared in the flesh, weak. For He must appear in this way so that He might not be perceived; but rather be despised, in order that He might be slain. There was semblance of glory in divinity, but it lay concealed in flesh. "For if they had known, they would never have crucified the Lord of glory" (1 Cor. 2:8).

So then He walked hidden among the Jews, among His enemies, doing marvels, suffering ills, until He was hung on the Tree, and the Jews seeing Him hanging both despised Him the more, and before the Cross wagging their heads they said, "If He is the Son of God, let Him come down from the Cross" (Matt. 27:39,40).

Hidden then was the God of gods, and He gave forth words more out of compassion for us than out of His own majesty. For whence, unless assumed from us, were those words, **"My God, My God, why have You forsaken Me?"** But when did the Father forsaken the Son, or the Son the Father? Are not Father and Son one God? How then, "My God, My God, why have You forsaken Me," except that in the flesh of infirmity there was acknowledged the voice of a sinner?

For as He took upon Him the likeness of the flesh of sin (Rom. 8:3) why should He not take upon Him the voice of sin? Hidden then was the God of gods, both when He walked among men, and when He hungered, and when He thirsted, and when fatigued He sat, and when with wearied body He slept, and when taken, and when scourged, and when standing before the judge, and when He made answer to him in his pride, "You could have no power against Me, except it had been given you from above" (John 19:11).

When He was led as a sacrifice, "as a sheep before His shearers," He was silent; and when He was crucified and buried, He was all the time the hidden God of gods.

St. Augustine, *Commentary on the Psalms*, 50.5 (NPNF 1:8)

When He was scourged He opened not His mouth! And when He was crucified He prayed for His crucifiers! How can I pay the Lord off for all what He had given me? The Chalice of salvation I take, and call the Name of the Lord!

St. Jerome, *Divine Love*, p. 246.

They crucified Him with robbers, involuntarily realizing the prophecy... What they did to insult Him has been meant to realize the strength of that great prophecy. The devil tried hard to conceal what took place, but in vain. Three have been crucified, among whom Jesus alone was glorified, to confirm His authority on all. Miracles happened, as the three of them were nailed on their crosses, yet no one referred those miracles to the other two, but to Jesus alone, putting the plan of the devil completely to no avail. One of the two robbers was saved, he who did not say wrong to the glory of the cross, but somehow contributed to it. What happened to him that led him to Paradise is not much less than an earthquake.

St. John Chrysostom, *Commentary on John*, Homily 85:1

He is sold, and very cheap, for it is only for 30 pieces of silver; but He redeems the world, and that at a great price, for the price of His own Blood.

As a sheep He is led to the slaughter, but He is the Shepherd of Israel, and now of the whole world also (cf. Isa. 53:7, Psa. 79:1).

As a Lamb He is silent, yet He is the Word, and is proclaimed by the voice of one crying in the wilderness.

He is bruised and wounded, but He heals every disease and every infirmity (Matt. 9:35).

He is lifted up and nailed to the Tree, but by the Tree of Life He restores us (Rev. 22:2, Gen. 2:9)

Yes, He saves even the Robber crucified with Him. Yes, He wrapped the visible world in darkness.

St. Gregory Nazianzen, *Third Theological Oration* (NPNF 2:7, p. 602)

Some of [the prophets said that] He Himself "shall take [upon Himself] our weaknesses and bear our sorrows"...some [predicted] a weak and inglorious man, and one who knew what it was to bear infirmity, and sitting upon the foal of a donkey (Zech. 9:9), He should come to Jerusalem, and that He should give His back to the smiters, and His cheeks to palms, and that He should be led as a sheep to the slaughter, and that He should have vinegar and gall given Him to drink (Psa. 68:21)...and that He should stretch forth His hands the whole day long (Isa. 65:2); and that He should be mocked and maligned by those who looked upon Him (Psa. 21:7)

St. Irenaeus of Lyons, *Against Heresies*, 4.32.11-12 (ANF 1, p. 510)

If it was for the sake of you and your sins that He numbered with transgressors, you should keep the law for His sake. Worship Him, Who was nailed on the Cross for your sake, even though you are yourself nailed... Purchase your salvation by your death, and enter together with Jesus into paradise, to remember, "from where you have fallen" (Rev. 2: 5).

St. Gregory Nazianzen, *Oration on Easter*, 34 (NPNF 2:7)

He intercedes for us every day, washing our feet. We likewise are in need of washing our own feet every day, through spiritually doing what is right; realizing and saying with the Lord's prayer: "And forgive us our debts, as we forgive our debtors" (Matt. 6:12).

St. Augustine, *Tractates on John*, Tractate 56:4 (NPNF 1:7, p. 426)

ISAIAH 12:2-13:10

Behold, God is my salvation, I will trust and not be afraid; "For God, the Lord, is my strength and song; He also has become my salvation."

Therefore with joy you will draw water from the wells of salvation

*And in that day you will say: "Praise the Lord, call upon His Name; declare His deeds among the peoples, make mention that His name is exalted. Sing to the Lord, for He has done excellent things; this is known in all the earth. **Cry out and shout, O inhabitant of Zion, for great is the Holy One of Israel in your midst!**"*

The burden against Babylon which Isaiah the son of Amoz saw.

"Lift up a banner on the high mountain, raise your voice to them; Wave your hand, that they may enter the gates of the nobles. I have commanded My sanctified ones; I have also called My mighty ones for My anger— Those who rejoice in My exaltation."

The noise of a multitude in the mountains, like that of many people! A tumultuous noise of the kingdoms of nations gathered together! The Lord of hosts musters the army for battle. They come from a far country, from the end of heaven— The Lord and His weapons of indignation, to destroy the whole land.

Wail, for the day of the Lord is at hand! *It will come as destruction from the Almighty. Therefore all hands will be limp, every man's heart will melt, and they will be afraid. Pangs and sorrows will take hold of them; they will be in pain as a woman in childbirth; they will be amazed at one another; Their faces will be like flames.*

Behold, the day of the Lord comes, cruel, with both wrath and fierce anger *to lay the land desolate; and He will destroy its sinners from it. For the stars of* *heaven and their constellations will not give their light; the sun will be darkened in its going forth, and the moon will not cause its light to shine.*

"Eat of My bread" (Prov. 9:5) is the bidding of Wisdom to the hungry; and the Lord declares those blessed who hunger for such Food as this, and says, "If any man thirst, let him come unto Me, and drink": and **"draw you therefore water with joy,"** is the great Isaiah's charge to those who are able to hear his sublimity. There is a prophetic threatening also against those worthy of vengeance, that they shall be punished with famine. But the "famine" is not a lack of bread and water, but a failure of the word—"not a famine of bread, nor a thirst for water, but a famine of hearing the word of the Lord" (Amos 8:11).

St. Gregory of Nyssa, *On the Making of Man*, 19.1 (NPNF 2:5, p. 408)

AMOS 8:9-12

"And it shall come to pass in that day," says the Lord God, "That I will make the sun go down at noon, and I will darken the earth in broad daylight; I will turn your feasts into mourning, and all your songs into lamentation; I will bring sackcloth on every waist, and baldness on every head; I will make it like mourning for an only son, and its end like a bitter day.

"Behold, the days are coming," says the Lord God, "That I will send a famine on the land, not a famine of bread, nor a thirst for water, but of hearing the words of the Lord. They shall wander from sea to sea, and from north to east; they shall run to and fro, seeking the word of the Lord, but shall not find it.

Suspended, then, and fastened to His Cross, Christ cried out to God the Father in a loud voice and willingly laid down His life. In that same hour, there was an earthquake, the veil of the temple that separated the two tabernacles was cut in two, and the sun was suddenly withdrawn, and from the sixth hour until the ninth hour there as darkness. The prophet Amos bears witness to this.

Lactantius, *Epitome on the Divine Institutes*, 4.1 (FC 49, p. 296; AACS OT 14, p. 112)

GALATIANS 6:14-18

But God forbid that I should boast except in the cross of our Lord Jesus Christ, by whom the world has been crucified to me, and I to the world. For in Christ Jesus neither circumcision nor uncircumcision avails anything, but a new creation. And as many as walk according to this rule, peace and mercy be upon them, and upon the Israel of God. From now on let no one trouble me, for I

*bear in my body the marks of the Lord Jesus. Brethren, the grace of our Lord
Jesus Christ be with your spirit. Amen.*

Now indeed [the Cross] appears to be a reprehensible thing, but only to
the world and to unbelievers. In heaven and for believers It is the highest
glory. For poverty also is reprehensible, yet it is a cause of boasting to us...
many mock simplicity, but we are disciplined by it. In this way the Cross
ironically is also a cause of boasting for us. Paul did not say, "I do not boast"
or "I do not wish to boast" but "God forbid," as though he was insulting
something absurd and calling on the aid of God to see this right. But what is
this boasting in the Cross? That on my behalf Christ took the form of a slave
and suffered what He suffered on account of me, the slave, the enemy, the
ingrate...

By "the world" he does not mean heaven nor earth, but the affairs of
life, human praise, distinguished positions, reputation, wealth and all things
that have a show of splendor, all such things are dead to me. Such should be
the case for all Christians. Nor is he satisfied only with the former ordinary
mode of dying, but he also introduces another kind of death: dying to the
world itself.

St. John Chrysostom, *Commentary on Galatians*, Homily 6.14 (AACS 8, p.
102)

Anyone who after Christ's coming is circumcised in the flesh does not
carry the marks of the Lord Jesus. Rather he glories in his own confusion.
But the One who was flogged beyond what the law required, frequently was
in prison, was beaten three times with rods, was once stoned and suffered all
the other things that are written in his catalogue of boasting (2 Cor. 11:23-
29)—this is the one who carries on his body the marks of the Lord Jesus.
Perhaps also the ascetic today who keeps his body under control and subjects
it to servitude so that he will not appear degenerate as he preaches to others
may in some way carry the marks of the Lord Jesus on his own body.

St. Jerome, *Epistle to the Galatians*, 3.16.17 (AACS 8, p. 104)

For [Saint Paul], who was able to make himself known by so many and
great miracles, says, "God forbid that I should glory in anything else than in
the Cross of Christ." And to the Corinthians he says that the word of the
Cross "to us who are being saved it is the power of God" (1 Cor. 1:18). To
the Ephesians, moreover, he describes by the figure of the Cross the power
that...holds together the universe...Rejoicing in these lacerations, Paul says
"I bear in my body the marks of Christ." He readily yields to his weakness in

all these misfortunes, through which the power of Christ is being perfected in virtue.

St. Gregory of Nyssa, *Commentary on Song of Songs*, 12.5.7 (AACS 8, p. 104)

What is the boast of the Cross? That Christ for my sake took on Him the form of a slave, the enemy, the unfeeling one. Yes, He so loved me as to give Himself up to a curse for me. What can be comparable to this!...Let us then not be ashamed of His unspeakable tenderness; He was not ashamed of being crucified for your sake, and shall you be ashamed to confess His infinite solicitude? It is as if a prisoner who had not been ashamed of his king, should after that king had come to the prison and himself loosed of the chains, become ashamed of him on that account. Yet this would be the height of madness, for this very fact would be an especial ground for boasting...

More clearly by those wounds than by any argument, than by any language, do I vindicate myself. For these wounds utter a voice louder than a trumpet against my opponents, and against those who say that I play the hypocrite in my teaching, and speak what may please men. For no one who saw a soldier retiring from the battle bathed in blood and with a thousand wounds, would dare to accuse him of cowardice and treachery, seeing that he bears on his body the proofs of his valor, and so should you, he says to judge of me.

St. John Chrysostom, *Commentary on Galatians* (NPNF 1:13)

PSALM 37:21,22

I am the Beloved, rejected as a despised Man; for they nailed My flesh. Do not abandon me, O my Master and my God.

It was fitting for Him to be silent during His passion; but He would not be so in His judgment, when He Who, in great humility, was sentenced, comes to judge all.

St. Augustine, *Commentary on the Psalms* (38) (NPNF 1:8)

"Do not forsake me, O Lord; O my God, do not depart from me" Let us speak in Him, let us speak through Him [for He Himself intercedes for us], and let us say, "Do not forsake me, O Lord my God." And yet He had said, "My God! My God! why have You forsaken Me?" and He now says, "O My God, do not depart from Me." If He does not forsake the body, did He forsake the Head? Whose words then are these but the first man's? To show then that He carried about Him a true body of flesh derived from him, He says, "My God, My God why have You forsaken Me?" God had not forsaken Him. If He does not forsake You, who believe in Him, could the Father, the Son, and the Holy Spirit, One God, forsake Christ? But He had transferred to Himself the person of the First Man.

We know by the words of an Apostle, that "our old man is crucified with Him." We should not, however, be divested of our old nature, had He not been crucified "in weakness." For it was to this end that He came that we may be renewed in Him, because it is by aspiration after Him, and by following the example of His suffering, that we are renewed. Therefore, that was the cry of infirmity; that cry, I mean, in which it was said, "Why have You forsaken Me?" Then was it said in that passage above, "the words of my offenses." As if He were saying, these words are transferred to My Person from that of the sinner.

"Depart not from me. Make haste to help me, O Lord of my salvation" (v. 22). This is that very "salvation," Brethren, concerning which, as the Apostle Peter said, "Prophets have inquired diligently," and though they have inquired diligently, yet have not found it. But they searched into it, and foretold of it; while we have come and have found what they sought for. And see, we ourselves too have not as yet received it; and after us shall others also be born, and shall find, what they also shall not receive, and shall pass away, that we may, all of us together, receive the "denarius of salvation in the end of the day" (Matt. 20:1-20) with the Prophets, the Patriarchs, and the Apostles. For you know that the hired servants, or laborers, were taken into the vineyard at different times; yet did they all receive their wages on an equal footing. Apostles, then, and Prophets, and Martyrs, and ourselves also, and those who will follow us to the end of the world, it is in the End itself that we are to receive everlasting salvation; that beholding the face of God, and contemplating His Glory, we may praise Him forever, free from imperfection, free from any punishment of iniquity, free from every perversion of sin: praising Him; and no longer longing after Him, but now clinging to Him for whom we used to long to the very end, and in whom we did rejoice, in hope. For we shall be in that City, where God is our Bliss, God is our Light, God is our Bread, God is our Life; whatever good thing of ours there is, at being absent from which we now grieve, we shall find in Him. In Him will be that "rest," which when we "call to remembrance" now, we cannot choose but grieve. For that is the "Sabbath" which we "call to remembrance;" in the recollection of which, so great things have been said already; and so great things should to be said by us also, and should never to cease being said by us, not with our lips indeed, but in our heart: for therefore do our lips cease to speak, that we may cry out with our hearts.

St. Augustine, *Commentary on the Psalms* (38:26-27) (NPNF 1:8)

PSALM 21:16-18,8

They pierced My hands and My feet; they counted all My bones. They look and stare at Me. They parted My garments among themselves, and for My clothing they cast lots. "He trusted in the Lord, let Him rescue Him; Let Him deliver Him, since He delights in Him!"

No words can better describe the stretching of His body upon the tree than these: "And all My bones are numbered."

St. Augustine

The Scholar Origen sees that these bones figuratively refer to the disciples of Christ and all His believers, who were scattered during His crucifixion in weakness, and through His resurrection they were gathered together as one body, and not one of these bones were broken:

"All My bones are scattered," although the bones of His body were not scattered, and not even one of them was broken. But when the resurrection itself takes place of the true and more perfect body of Christ, then those who are now the members of Christ, for they will then be dry bones, will be brought together, bone to bone, and fitting to fitting (for none of those who are destitute of fitting will come to the perfect man), to the measure of the stature of the fullness of the body of Christ. And then the many members will be the one body, all of them, though many, becoming members of one body.

The Scholar Origen, *Commentary on John*, 10.20 (ANF 10)

Many Fathers of the Church state that the true pious believers, "the bones of Christ," even if they become weak because of sufferings and martyrdom, the grace of God will support them, and one of these bones will never be broken. The bones of Christ are our inner faith, for through the temptation we may cry within our hearts, "How long, O Lord, will You forget me forever? How long will You turn Your face away from me?" How long must I bear pain in my soul, and have sorrow in my heart all the day? (Psa. 13:1,2) as if our God has left us alone, or our faith became feeble... But God works within us by His grace so that we may add the same words of the

Psalmist, "my heart rejoices in Your salvation" (Psa. 13:5), declaring that none of Christ's bones within us has been broken, even if they were temporary scattered.

Fr. Tadros Malaty, *Patristic Commentary on Psalms*

MATTHEW 27:27-45

Then the soldiers of the governor took Jesus into the Praetorium and gathered the whole garrison around Him. And they stripped Him and put a scarlet robe on Him. When they had twisted a crown of thorns, they put it on His head, and a reed in His right hand. And they bowed the knee before Him and mocked Him, saying, "Hail, King of the Jews!" Then they spat on Him, and took the reed and struck Him on the head. And when they had mocked Him, they took the robe off Him, put His own clothes on Him, and led Him away to be crucified.

Now as they came out, they found a man of Cyrene, Simon by name. Him they compelled to bear His cross. And when they had come to a place called Golgotha, that is to say, Place of a Skull, they gave Him sour wine mingled with gall to drink. But when He had tasted it, He would not drink. Then they crucified Him, and divided His garments, casting lots, that it might be fulfilled which was spoken by the prophet:" **They divided My garments among them, and for My clothing they cast lots."**

Sitting down, they kept watch over Him there. And they put up over His head the accusation written against Him: THIS IS JESUS THE KING OF THE JEWS.

Then two robbers were crucified with Him, one on the right and another on the left. And those who passed by blasphemed Him, wagging their heads and saying, "You who destroy the temple and build it in three days, save Yourself! If You are the Son of God, come down from the cross." Likewise the chief priests also, mocking with the scribes and elders, said, "He saved others; Himself He cannot save. If He is the King of Israel, let Him now come down from the cross, and we will believe Him. He trusted in God; let Him deliver Him now if He will have Him; for He said, 'I am the Son of God.'" Even the robbers who were crucified with Him reviled Him with the same thing.

Now from the sixth hour until the ninth hour there was darkness over all the land.

MARK 15:26-33

And the inscription of His accusation was written above: THE KING OF THE JEWS.

With Him they also crucified two robbers, one on His right and the other on His left. So the Scripture was fulfilled which says, "And He was numbered with the transgressors." And those who passed by blasphemed Him, wagging their heads and saying, "Aha! You who destroy the temple and build it in three days, save Yourself, and come down from the cross!" Likewise the chief priests also, mocking among themselves with the scribes, said, "He saved others; Himself He cannot save. Let the Christ, the King of Israel, descend now from the cross, that we may see and believe." Even those who were crucified with Him reviled Him.

Now when the sixth hour had come, there was darkness over the whole land until the ninth hour.

LUKE 23:26-44

Now as they led Him away, they laid hold of a certain man, Simon a Cyrenian, who was coming from the country, and on him they laid the cross that he might bear it after Jesus. And a great multitude of the people followed Him, and women who also mourned and lamented Him. But Jesus, turning to them, said, "Daughters of Jerusalem, do not weep for Me, but weep for yourselves and for your children. For indeed the days are coming in which they will say, 'Blessed are the barren, wombs that never bore, and breasts which never nursed!' Then they will begin to say to the mountains, 'Fall on us!' and to the hills, 'Cover us!' For if they do these things in the green wood, what will be done in the dry?" There were also two others, criminals, led with Him to be put to death. And when they had come to the place called Calvary, there they crucified Him, and the criminals, one on the right hand and the other on the left. Then Jesus said, "Father, forgive them, for they do not know what they do." And they divided His garments and cast lots. And the people stood looking on. But even the rulers with them sneered, saying, "He saved others; let Him save Himself if He is the Christ, the chosen of God." The soldiers also mocked Him, coming and offering Him sour wine, and saying, "If You are the King of the Jews, save Yourself." And an inscription also was written over Him in letters of Greek, Latin, and Hebrew: THIS IS THE KING OF THE JEWS.

Then one of the criminals who were hanged blasphemed Him, saying, "If You are the Christ, save Yourself and us." But the other, answering, rebuked him, saying, "Do you not even fear God, seeing you are under the same condemnation? And we indeed justly, for we receive the due reward of our deeds; but this Man has done nothing wrong." Then he said to Jesus, "Lord, remember me when You come into Your kingdom." And Jesus said to him, "Assuredly, I say to you, today you will be with Me in Paradise."

Now it was about the sixth hour, and there was darkness over all the earth until the ninth hour.

JOHN 19:13-27

When Pilate therefore heard that saying, he brought Jesus out and sat down in the judgment seat in a place that is called The Pavement, but in Hebrew, Gabbatha. Now it was the Preparation Day of the Passover, and about the sixth hour. And he said to the Jews, "Behold your King!" But they cried out, "Away with Him, away with Him! Crucify Him!" Pilate said to them, "Shall I crucify your King?" The chief priests answered, "We have no king but Caesar!" Then he delivered Him to them to be crucified. So they took Jesus and led Him away.

And He, bearing His cross, went out to a place called the Place of a Skull, which is called in Hebrew, Golgotha, where they crucified Him, and two others with Him, one on either side, and Jesus in the center. Now Pilate wrote a title and put it on the cross. And the writing was: JESUS OF NAZARETH, THE KING OF THE JEWS.

*Then many of the Jews read this title, for the place where Jesus was crucified was near the city; and it was written in Hebrew, Greek, and Latin. Therefore the chief priests of the Jews said to Pilate, "Do not write, 'The King of the Jews,' but, 'He said, "I am the King of the Jews."'" Pilate answered, "What I have written, I have written." Then the soldiers, when they had crucified Jesus, took His garments and made four parts, to each soldier a part, and also the tunic. Now the tunic was without seam, woven from the top in one piece. They said therefore among themselves, "Let us not tear it, but cast lots for it, whose it shall be," that the Scripture might be fulfilled which says: "**They divided My garments among them, and for My clothing they cast lots.**"*

*Therefore the soldiers did these things. Now there stood by the cross of Jesus His mother, and His mother's sister, Mary the wife of Clopas, and Mary Magdalene. When Jesus therefore saw His mother, and the disciple whom He loved standing by, He said to His mother, "**Woman, behold your son!**" Then He said to the disciple, "**Behold your mother!**" And from that hour that disciple took her to his own home.*

His Suffering: The Robe, Reed, and the Thorns

The **scarlet robe** was prefigured by the scarlet sign mentioned in Joshua the son of Nun, which Rahab used for her safety (Josh. 2:18), and mentioned in Genesis (38:28), which was placed on the hand of one of Tamar's newborn sons in token of the future Passion of Christ. So now, in taking up the "scarlet robe," He took upon Himself the blood of the world, and in that thorny "crown" plaited on His head He took upon Himself the thorns of our sins. As to the purple robe, it is written that "they took the purple off Him" (Mk. 15:20).

But as to the **crown of thorns,** the Evangelists mention nothing further. Apparently they wanted us to determine what happened to the crown of thorns placed on His head and never removed. My belief is that the crown of thorns disappeared from the head of Jesus, so that our former thorns no longer exist now that Jesus has removed them from us once and for all on His own distinguished head...

What can be said about the **reed** they placed "in His right hand"?...The reed embodied the hallow and fragile scepter that we all were leaning on before we saw it was a bad scepter, for we were trusting in the reed-shaped rod of Egypt or Babylon or some other kingdom opposed to God's kingdom (Isa. 36:6). Then he took that reed and rod of the fragile kingdom from our hands, to subdue it and break it into pieces on the Cross. In place of that reed we once were leaning on, He gave us the **scepter** of the heavenly kingdom and the **rod** mentioned in Scripture, "The rod of justice, the rod of Your kingdom" (Psa. 45:6). In other words, the rod that chastens those who need to be chastened, as the Apostle notes: "What do you want? Shall I come to you with a rod?" (1 Cor. 4:21). He also gave us a **staff** that we might celebrate the Paschal Feast (as scripture says, "And your staff in your hand" [Exod. 12:11]), laying down that reed-shaped rod we once had before we celebrated the Lord's Paschal Feast.

Then they took this fragile, hallow reed and struck the honorable head of Jesus with it, for that ever-adverse kingdom reviles and scourges God the Father, the head of the Lord and Savior. And amid all this, the Only-begotten Goodness itself was unharmed, nor did He suffer anything, "having become a curse for us" (Gal. 3:13), since by nature He is a blessing. But since He is a blessing, He destroyed, took away and dispelled all human malediction.

The Scholar Origen, *Commentary on Matthew*, 125 (AACS 1b, p. 285)

The beaten Lord is dressed in a scarlet robe, a purple cloak and a crown of thorns, and a reed is placed on His right hand. Bending their knees before Him, they mock Him. Having taken upon Himself all the infirmities of our bodies, He is covered with the **scarlet** blood of all the martyrs destined to reign with Him. He is cloaked with the high honor of the prophets and patriarchs in purple cloth. He is also **crowned** with thorns, that is, with the former sins of the remorseful Gentiles, so that glory might derive from the destructive and useless things, plaited on His divine head, which they contrive. The sharp points of **thorns** aptly pertain to the sins from which a crown of victory is woven for Christ. The **reed** symbolizes the emptiness and weakness of all those Gentiles, which is held firm in His grasp. His head, moreover, is struck. As I believe, not much harm was done to His head from being struck with the reed. However, the typical explanation for this is that the bodily weakness of the Gentiles that was previously held in Christ's hand finds comfort now in God the Father, for He is the head (1 Cor. 11:13). **But amid all this, while Christ is mocked, He is being adored.**

St. Hilary of Poitiers, *On Matthew*, 33.3 (AACS 1b, pp. 284-285)

He is stoned, but is not taken. He prays, but He hears prayer. He weeps, but He causes tears to cease. He asks where Lazarus was laid, for He was Man; but He raises Lazarus, for He was God. He is sold, and very cheap, for it is only for thirty pieces of silver; but He redeems the world, and that at a great price, for the Price was His own blood. As a sheep He is led to the slaughter, but He is the Shepherd of Israel, and now of the whole world also. As a Lamb He is silent, yet He is the Word, and is proclaimed by the Voice of one crying in the wilderness. **He is bruised and wounded, but He heals every disease and every infirmity. He is lifted up and nailed to the Tree, but by the Tree of Life He restores us.** Yes, He saves even the Robber crucified with Him. Yes, He wrapped the visible world in darkness. He is given vinegar to drink mingled with gall. Who? He who turned the water into wine, he who is the destroyer of the bitter taste, who is Sweetness and altogether desire. He lays down His life, but He has power to take it again and the veil is rent, for the mysterious doors of Heaven are opened; the rocks are cleft, the dead arise. He dies, but He gives life, and by His death destroys death. He is buried, but He rises again; He goes down into Hell, but He brings up the souls; He ascends to Heaven, and shall come again to judge the leaving and the dead, and to put to the test such words as yours. If the one gives you a starting point for your error, let the others put an end to it.

St. Gregory Nazianzen, *The Third Theological Oration* (NPNF 2:7, p. 602)

Today He who hung the earth upon the waters is hung upon the Cross. He who is King of the angels is arrayed in a crown of thorns. He who wraps the heaven in clouds is wrapped in the purple of mockery. He who in Jordan set Adam free receives blows upon His face. The Bridegroom of the Church is transfixed with nails. The Son of the Virgin is pierced with a spear. We venerate Your Passion, O Christ. Show us also Your glorious Resurrection.

Eastern Orthodox Church, *Antiphon 15* of Great Friday

Answer to those who are in doubt because He bears up with Him His body and the tokens of His Passion, which He had not when He came down, and who therefore inquire, **"Who is this King of Glory?"** that it is the **Lord strong and mighty,** as in all things that He has done from time to time and does, so now in His battle and triumph for the sake of humanity. And give to the doubting of the question the twofold answer. And if they marvel and say as in Isaiah's drama Who is this who comes from Edom and from the things of earth? Or how are the **garments red** of Him Who is without blood or body, as of one that treads in the full wine-press? Set forth the beauty of the array of the Body that suffered, adorned by the Passion, and made splendid by the Godhead, than which nothing can be more lovely or more beautiful....

St. Gregory Nazianzen, *Second Oration* (NPNF 2:8)

Simon of Cyrene

The Savior is led to the suffering that brings salvation. They laid His Cross on Simon of Cyrene. Another of the holy Evangelists said that Jesus Himself carried the Cross (Jn. 19:17). Now surely both are correct. For the Savior carried the Cross, and, having met the Cyrene **about half way,** they transferred the Cross to him. It is said about him through the voice of Isaiah, that "For unto us a Child is born, unto us a Son is given; and the government will be upon His shoulder" (Isaiah 9:6). Now the Cross has become the means by which He governs, through which He continues to rule over all heaven, since it is true that even as "far as death" He has become "...obedient to the point of death, even the death of the Cross. Therefore, God also has highly exalted Him..." (Philip. 2:8-9).

St. Cyril of Alexandria, Fragment 306 (AACS 1b, p. 287)

It is fitting not only for the Savior to take up His Cross but also for us to carry it, doing compulsory service for our salvation. Furthermore, we did not benefit by taking up His Cross then as much as we benefit by it now, since He takes it upon Himself and carries it.

The Scholar Origen, *Commentary on Matthew*, 126 (AACS 1b, p. 287)

After He took up the wood of His Cross and set out, they found and stopped a man of Cyrene, that is from among the Gentiles, and placed the wood of the Cross on Him. It was only right that they should have given the wood of the Cross voluntarily to the Gentiles, since in their rebellion, the Jews rejected the coming of Him Who was bringing all blessings. In rejecting it themselves, in their jealousy, they threw it away to the Gentiles. The Lord approved the welcoming Gentiles and thus provoked jealousy among their contemporaries through the Gentile's acceptance. By carrying the wood of His Cross Himself, Christ revealed the sign of His victory. Christ said that another person would not pressure Him to death, "I have power to lay it down, to lay it down or take it up again" (Jn. 10:18). Why should another person have carried the Cross? This showed that He, in Whom no sin could be found, went up on the Cross for those who rejected Him.

St. Ephrem the Syrian, *CTD*, 20.20 (AACS 3, pp. 357-357)

How blessed was Simon who deserved to be the first to bare so great a sign of victory! He was compelled to carry the Cross before the Lord because the Lord wanted to demonstrate His cross to be a singular grace of that heavenly mystery which is Himself: God and man, Logos and flesh, Son of God, and Son of Man. He was crucified as Man, but triumphed as God in the mystery of the Cross. His suffering was of the flesh, but His glorious victory was divine. Through His Cross, Christ defeated both death and the devil. Through the Cross, Christ mounted His chariot of victory and chose the four Evangelists, as through horses for His chariot, to announce so great a victory to all the world. Simon of Cyrene therefore was carrying the instrument of this great triumph in his arms. **He was a partaker of the Passion of Christ so that he might be a partaker of His resurrection, as the Apostle teaches, "For if we die with Him, we must also live with Him. If we endure, we shall also reign with Him" (2 Tim. 2:11-12). Similarly, the Lord Himself says in the Gospel, "And whoever does not bear his cross and come after Me cannot be My disciple" (Lk. 14:27).**

Cromatius, *Tractate on Matthew*, 19.5 (AACS, 1b, p. 287)

Golgotha, Wine and Gall

Just as it sufficed for the Lord only to taste "vinegar mixed with gall" so also was it sufficient for our benefit that He only taste death, which lasted no longer than three days. The other wine, however, which was not "mixed with gall" or with anything else, He took and drank, and when He "gave thanks," (Matt. 26:27) He gave it to His disciples, promising that He would drink it "anew in the Kingdom of God" (Matt. 26:29).

The Scholar Origen, *Commentary on Matthew*, 127 (AACS 1b, p. 288)

If it was for the sake of you and your sins that He was numbered with transgressors so that you should keep the law for His sake. Worship Him, who was nailed on the Cross for your sake, even though you are yourself nailed...Purchase your salvation by your death, and enter together with Jesus into paradise, to remember "from where you have fallen" (Rev. 2:5).

St. Gregory Nazianzen, *Oration on Easter*, 34 (NPNF 2:12)

Dividing His Garments

They distributed His clothes by casting lots for them rather than by cutting them up because this signifies the eternal incorruptibility of Christ's Body. The life and salvation of all things was hung from the Tree of Life with a thief on His left and a thief on His right. This demonstrates that the entire human race is called to the mystery of the Lord's suffering.

St. Hilary of Poitiers, *Commentary on Matthew*, 23.5 (AACS 1b, p. 288)

There are those who to this day do not have the Lord with them but do have His garments—namely the words of the Scripture. They do not have them in full but only in part. Nonetheless, the prophet had spoken that prediction which was now fulfilled (Psa. 22:18). Now as to whether any of His clothes were torn apart when they divided His garments or whether any of them remained intact and just what those items were, nothing is said by the first three Evangelists. But in John we read [of this division of the garments]. Therefore, not all but only one of the soldiers who had cast lots received it. Now anyone debating the differences between those who have the Lord's "Garments" will doubtless find some people who, although they do not have the Lord in their teachings, do have the "tunic" that was "woven from top to bottom."

The Scholar Origen, *Commentary on Matthew*, 127 (AACS 1b, p. 288)

It is important to consider what type of Man ascends. I see Him naked (Jn. 19:23). Let him who prepares to conquer this age ascend in this way so that he does not seek the help of the age. Adam, who desired clothing, was conquered (Gen. 3:7). He who laid down His clothes conquered. He ascended in the same way that nature formed us with God as Creator. In the same way as the first Adam lived in paradise, the Second Adam entered paradise (1 Cor. 15:47). In order not to conquer only for Himself but for all, He held out His hands (Isa. 65:2; Rom. 10:21) to draw all things to Himself. Having wrenched them from the bonds of death and hung them on the yoke of faith, He joined those of heaven to those who before were of earth (1 Cor. 15:48-49).

St. Ambrose of Milan, *Exposition of the Gospel of Luke*, 10.112-113 (AACS 3, p. 363)

The Cross depicts two complete pictures: the rage of God on sin which cost the Lord His life; and that of God's overwhelming Love which ruptured fountains of abundant grace."

Fr. Tadros Malaty, Patristic *Commentary on Jonah*, p. 35

The Dream

What then does Pilate say? "Did you not hear how many things they testify against You?" [Pilate wished Christ would] defend Himself and be acquitted. Therefore, he said these things. But since He answered nothing, [Pilate] devises something else. Of what nature was this? It was a custom for them to release one of the condemned, and by this means he attempted to deliver Him. For if you are not willing to release Him as innocent, yet as guilty pardon Him for the feast's sake.

See the order is reversed? For the petition in behalf of the condemned it was customary to be with the people, and the granting it with the rulers; but now the contrary has come to pass, and the ruler petitions the people; and not even so do they become gentle, but grow more savage and bloodthirsty, driven to frenzy by the passion of envy. For neither had they what they should accuse Him, and this though He was silent, but they were refuted even then by reason of the abundance of His righteous deeds, and being silent He overcame them that say ten thousand things, and are maddened...

[Her] dream too was no small thing. So why doesn't he see it himself? Either because she was more worthy, or because he, if he had seen it, would not have been equally believed; or would not so much as have told it. Therefore, it was ordered that the wife should see it so that it might be manifest to all. She does not merely see it, but also suffers many things, that from his feeling towards his wife, the man may be made more reluctant to the murder. And the time too contributed not a little, for on the very night she saw it.

But it was not safe, it may be said, for him to let Him go, because they said He made Himself a king. Then, he should have searched for proofs, and a conviction, and for all the things that are infallible signs of a usurpation— e.g., whether He levied forces, whether He collected money, whether he forged arms, whether He attempted any other such thing. But He is led away at random, therefore neither does Christ acquit him of the blame, in saying, "He the one who delivered me to you has the greater sin." So then it was from weakness that he yielded and scourged Him, and delivered Him up.

He then was humanly and weak; but the chief priests wicked and criminal. For since he had found out a device, namely, the law of the feast requiring him to release a condemned person, what do they contrive in opposition to that? "They persuaded the multitude," it is said, "that they should ask Barabbas."

St. John Chrysostom, *Commentary on Matthew*, Homily 86.1 (NPNF 2:10, p. 511)

The Two Thieves

There came to my ear from the Scripture which had been read a word that caused me joy on the subject of the thief; it gave comfort to my soul amidst the multitude of its vices, telling how He had compassion on the thief. O may He bring me too into that garden at the sound of Whose name I am overwhelmed with joy; my mind bursts its reins as it goes forth to contemplate Him.

St. Ephrem the Syrian, *Hymn on Paradise*, 12.10 (HOP, 131)

When He hung on the precious Cross, two thieves were hung with Him. What comes from this? It was truly a mockery as far as the plan of the Jews, but it was also the commemoration of prophesy. It is written, "He was also numbered with the transgressors" (Isa. 53:12). For our sakes, He became a curse. That is, He became accursed. It is written again, "for he who is hangs on a tree is accursed of God" (Deut. 21:23). His act did away with the curse that was on us. We are blessed with Him and because of Him. Knowing this, blessed David says, "Blessed are we of the Lord, who made heaven and earth" (Psa. 113:23). Blessings descend to us by His sufferings. He paid our debts in our place. He bore our sins. He was stricken in our place (Isa. 53:6), as it is written. He took our sins in His own Body on the Tree (1 Pet. 2:24), because it is true that His bruises heal us (Isa. 53:5). He also was sick because of our sins, and we were delivered from the sickness of the soul...

"This Man" he says, "has done nothing hateful." O how beautiful is this confession! How wise the reasoning and how excellent the thoughts! He became the confessor of the Savior's glory and the accuser of the pride of those who crucified Him...

Let us look at his most beautiful confession of faith. He says, "Lord, remember me when You come into Your kingdom." You see Him crucified and call Him a King. You expect the One who bears scorn and suffering to come in godlike glory. You see Him surrounded by a Jewish crowd, the wicked gang of the Pharisees, and Pilate's band of soldiers. All of these were mocking Him, and no one confessed Him.

St. Cyril of Alexandria, *Commentary on Luke*, Homily 153 (CLC p. 610)

They crucified Him with robbers, involuntarily realizing the prophecy...What they did to insult Him has been meant to realize the strength of that great prophecy...The devil tried hard to conceal what took place, but in vain. Three have been crucified, among whom Jesus alone was glorified, to confirm His authority on all. Miracles happened, as the three of them were nailed on their crosses, yet no one referred those miracles to the other two, but to Jesus alone, putting the plan of the devil completely to no avail. One of the two robbers was saved, he who did not say wrong to the glory of the Cross, but somehow contributed to it. What happened to him that led him to Paradise is not much less than an earthquake...

St. John Chrysostom, *Homilies on John*, 85:1 (NPNF 2:14)

In the beginning, God shaped man, and man was the image of the Father and the Son. God said, "Let Us make man in Our image, according to Our likeness" (Gen. 3:24). Again when he wished to bring the thief into Paradise, he immediately spoke the word and brought him in. Christ did not need to pray to do this, although He had kept all people after Adam from entering there. God put there the flaming sword to guard Paradise. By His authority, Christ opened Paradise and brought in the thief.

St. John Chrysostom, *Against the Anomoeans*, 9.15 (FC 72, p. 239)

Referring to the two robbers who were crucified with Him, it was written, "He was numbered with transgressors" (Isa. 53). They were both transgressors, but one of them is no more; the other, who rejected salvation until the end, though his hands were tied, yet his tongue kept blaspheming ... For one, it was the end of his life, but the beginning of his repentance and salvation. After rebuking his partner, he said to Jesus: "Lord, remember me when You come into Your kingdom" (Lk. 23:42).

Remember Me, O Lord, to you I cry out; the eyes of my mind are closed, but remember me! I do not say remember my deeds, for which I am frightened...Everyone is kind to his fellow traveler...I do not say remember me now, but when you come into your kingdom. What power has illuminated your soul? Who taught you to worship the despised who was crucified with you?

St. Cyril of Jerusalem, *Catechetical Lectures*, 13.30 (FC 64, p. 24; AACS 2, p. 231)

One robber said, "Are you not the Messiah? Save yourselves and us with You!" The Lord however did not take him down from the cross as he asked, in order to exalt the other robber on the right of the cross and who was believing in the crucified Savior. It would have been easy for Him to use a miracle to gain anyone as a disciple. He produced a more powerful miracle when He forced the scoffer of truth to adore Him. That is why the apostle said, "the weakness of God is stronger than men" (1 Cor. 1:25).

Stretch out Your arms toward the Cross, so that the crucified Lord may stretch out His arms toward you. The one who does not stretch out his hand toward the Cross cannot approach His Table either. He will deprive the guests of His table who should have come to Him hungry but instead came full. Do not fill yourself before going to the table of the Son. He might then make you leave the table while you are still hungry...

The hands that Adam stretched out toward the tree of knowledge, breaking the commandment, were unworthy of stretching out toward the Tree of Life to revive the gifts of the God Who they had despised. Our Lord took these hands and attached them to the Cross, so that He might kill their killer and arrive at His marvelous life. "You will be with Me in the garden of delights." "Remember me in Your Kingdom." Since he had seen with the eyes of faith the dignity of our Lord instead of His shame, and His glory instead of His humiliation, he said, "Remember me." What is apparent now, the nails and the Cross, will not make me forget what will be at the consummation and what is not yet visible: Your kingdom and Your glory.

St. Ephrem the Syrian, *CTD* 20.11, pp. 292-296 (AACS 2, pp. 210-211)

Two robbers were crucified with Him. [When the Jews] started by mocking Him; one followed the evil Jews in his behavior; the other, admirably took a different trend. He believed in Him; and amid his bitter suffering, condemned the vicious attitude of the Jews, and the blaspheming words of his partner crucified with him. Confessing his sins, and admitting that he is justly receiving the due reward of his deeds, he condemned his evil ways, to be forgiven by God, saying with the Psalmist, "I will confess my transgressions to the Lord. And You forgive the iniquity of my sin" (Psa. 32:5).

He presented Christ with a blameless testimony, rebuked the Jews for their lack of God's love, and condemned the verdict of Pilate, saying, "this Man has done nothing wrong" (Lk. 23:41) What a beautiful confession!...He gained the inheritance of saints, and his name is now written in heaven; after having been condemned to death, he was numbered among the dwellers of the exalted city.

St. Cyril of Alexandria, *Commentary on Luke*, Homily 153, pp. 720-721

Amid the courtroom of the Cross, one robber who believed was freed, the other who insulted Him was condemned (Lk. 23:39-43). He was then signifying in advance what He would do concerning the living and the dead, putting some on His right and some on His left (Matt. 25:31-33). The one robber was liken to those who would be on the left; the other, to those who would be on the right. He who was being judged was anticipating final judgment.

St. Augustine, *Tractates on John*, 31.11 (FC 88, p. 40)

Some scholars believe the two robbers refer to the nations of the Jews and the Gentiles; one of them was condemned to death through the Mosaic law, while the other, through the natural law. The Lord Christ was crucified between them, to bind them together in Him, being a corner stone for the Church, offering His blood a price for unity in Him!

Fr. Tadros Malaty, *Patristic Commentary on Mark*

That flaming, flashing sword (Gen. 3:24) was keeping Paradise safe. No one could open the gates that Christ closed. The thief was the first to enter with Christ. His great faith received the greatest of rewards. His faith in the kingdom did not depend on seeing Christ. He did not see Him in His radiant glory or behold Him looking down from heaven. He did not see the angels serving Him. To put it plainly, he certainly did not see Christ walking about in freedom, but on a scaffold, drinking vinegar and crowned with thorns. He saw Him fastened to the Cross and heard Him begging for help, "My God, My God, why have You forsaken me?" ...the Cross of Christ is the key to paradise. The Cross of Christ opened it. Has He not said to you, "the Kingdom of Heaven suffers violence, and the violent take it by force" (Matt. 11:12). Does not the one on the Cross cause the violence? There is nothing between the Cross and Paradise. The greatest of pains produces the greatest of rewards.

St. Jerome, *On Lazarus* (FC 57, pp. 209-210)

Darkness over the Earth

When they fasted to the Cross the Lord of all, the sun over their heads withdrew and the light at midday was wrapped in darkness, as the divine Amos had foretold, "There was darkness from the sixth to the ninth hour" (Amos 5:18). This was a plain sign to the Jews that the minds of those who crucified Him were wrapped in spiritual darkness, for blindness in part has happened to Israel (Rom. 11:25). In his love for God, David even curses them saying, "let their eyes be darkened, that they may not see" (Psa. 69:23).

St. Cyril of Alexandria, *Commentary on Luke*, Homily 153 (CLC pp. 610-611)

When Jesus was nailed to the tree between two thieves, it was the end of the sixth hour. It was between the sixth and ninth hour that the sun was obscured and the darkness prevailed, as we have it jointly attested on the authority of the three Evangelists, Matthew, Mark and Luke.

St. Augustine, *Tractates on John*, 117.1 (NPNF 2:7, p. 428)

Note how clearly was fulfilled the prophesy of our Savior's Passion. It was to be day in which "there shall be no light"…This was also fulfilled figuratively by His priestly accusers, for among them came darkness, cold and ice, following upon their indignities to the Anointed One. Their understanding also was darkened, so that the light of the gospel did not shine in their hearts, and their love to God grew cold. Then in the evening the light of the knowledge of the Christ arose, so that they who sat in darkness and the shadow of death saw a great light (Isa. 9:2; Matt. 4:16).

Eusebius of Caesarea, *Proof of the Gospel*, 10.7 (AACS 2, p. 233)

They worked on delivering the Author of life to death; so they crucified the Lord of glory. But, as they nailed the Lord of all to the Cross, the sun withdrew from over their heads, and the light was clothed with darkness, as previously indicated by the prophet Amos through Divine inspiration (Amos 5:18)… That should have been a clear sign for the Jews, that the minds of His crucifiers became darkened, as "blindness in part has happened to Israel" (Rom. 11:25). The prophet David, in his love for God, cursed them, saying, "Let their eyes be darkened, so that they do not see" (Psa. 69:23). Yes! Creation itself mourned its Lord; the sun was darkened, the rocks were split, and the temple itself, seemed to be saddened, as its veil was torn in two from top to bottom. That was What God meant, saying through the prophet Isaiah: "I clothe the heavens with blackness, and I make sackcloth their covering" (Isa. 50: 3).

St. Cyril of Alexandria, *Commentary on Luke*, Fragment 155, p. 722

At midday, that all that dwell on the earth may know it, when it was day all over the world; which was enough to convert them, not by the greatness of the miracle only, but also by its taking place in due season. For after all their insulting, and their lawless derision, this is done, when they had let go their anger, when they had ceased mocking, when they were satiated with their insults, and had spoken all that they were minded; then He shows the darkness, in order that at least so (having vented their anger) they may profit by the miracle. For this was more marvelous than to come down from the Cross, that being on the Cross He should work these things. For whether they thought He Himself had done it, they should have believed and feared...They should have been moved to compassion, for that darkness was a token of His anger at their crime. For that it was not an eclipse, but both wrath and indignation, is not hence alone manifest, but also by the time, for it continued three hours. Then, an eclipse immediately takes place.

St. John Chrysostom, *Commentary on Matthew*, Homily 83.1 (NPNF 2:10, p. 521)

"Father, forgive them for they do not know what they do."

He prayed as man, and as God with the Father, He heard the prayer. Even now He prays in us, for us, and is prayed to by us. He prays in us as our High Priest. He prays for us as our head. He is prayed to by us as our God. When He was praying as He hung on the Cross, He could see and foresee. He could see all His enemies. He could foresee that many of them would become His friends. That is why He was interceding for them all. They were raging, but He was praying. They were saying to Pilate, "Crucify," but He was crying out, "Father, forgive." He was hanging from the cruel nails, but He did not lose His gentleness. He was asking for pardon from those whom He was receiving such hideous treatment.

St. Augustine, Sermon 382.2 (AACS 3, p. 361)

The Glory of the Cross

Adam had been naked and fair, but his diligent wife labored and made for him a garment covered with stains. The garden, seeing him thus vile, drove him out. Through Mary, Adam had another robe which adorned the thief; and when he had become resplended at Christ's promise, the garden looking on embraced him in Adam's place.

St. Ephrem the Syrian, *Hymns on Paradise*, 12.10 (HOP, 164)

The crucified Jesus Christ, and His royal glory were radiating from the Cross.

St. Ambrose of Milan, *Commentary on Luke*, 23:33-49

Our Lord was crucified, carried on Himself the trespasses of the universe, and nailed the sin with nails, so as not to reign. He crucified it with Him on Golgotha to prevent it from killing further generations.

St. Jacob of Sarug

The Cross is glory. Look at what the evangelist says, "for the Holy Spirit was not yet given, because Jesus was not yet glorified" (Jn. 7:39).

The Cross has abolished the enmity between God and men, presenting reconciliation; turning earth into heaven; gathering angels together with humans; destroying the fortress of death; weakening the power of the devil; quenching the authority of sin; rescuing the world from transgression and reclaiming truth; chasing away the demons; devastating the temples of idols and canceling their sacrifices; sowing the virtue and establishing the Church!

The Cross is the will of the Father, the glory of the Son, and the joy of the Holy Spirit. It is the boast of the apostle Paul who says, "But God forbid that I should boast except in the cross of our Lord Jesus Christ, by whom the world has been crucified to me, and I to the world" (Gal. 6:14).

The Cross is brighter than the sun, of more splendor than its rays. When the sun darkened the cross shone; the sun darkened, not because it was put out, but because the light of the Cross surpassed it. The Cross breaks our chains, and shakes the foundation of the prison of death. It is the sign of God's love (Jn. 3: 16)...

The Cross is a fortified stronghold, protector for the rich; fountain for the poor; defender for the fallen in the nets; a shield for those in battle; a way to overcome lusts and gain virtues; an amazing and wonderful sign.

Fr. Tadros Malaty, *Divine Love*, pp. 378-380

Again, [St. Paul] reminds them of the Cross, thereby effecting two things; both showing His care [for them] and persuading them to bear all things nobly, looking to the Master. For (as He would say) if He who is worshiped by Angels endured to have a little less than the Angels for your sake, you who are inferior to the Angels should bear all things for His sake.

Then [St. Paul] shows that the Cross is "glory and honor," as He Himself also always calls it, saying, "that the Son of Man might be glorified" (Jn. 11:4); and, "the Son of Man should be glorified" (Jn. 12:23). If then He calls the [sufferings] for His servants' sake "glory," you should do the same and more.

See the fruit of the Cross, how great it is? Do not fear the matter: for it seems to you indeed to be depressing, but it brings forth countless good things.

St. John Chrysostom, *Commentary on Hebrews*, Homily 4.3 (NPNF 1:14)

Because Adam touched the tree he had to run to the fig; he became like the fig tree, being clothed in its vesture. Adam, like some tree, blossomed with leaves. Then he came to that glorious tree of the Cross, put on the glory from it, acquired radiance from it, and heard from it the truth that he would return to Eden once more.

St. Ephrem the Syrian, *Hymns on Paradise*, 12.10 (HOP, 164)

He has subjected all powers, He has subjugated kings, not with the pride of soldiery, but by the shame of the Cross; not by the fury of the sword, but by hanging on the Wood, by suffering in the body, by working in the Spirit. His body was lifted up on the Cross, and so He subdued souls to the Cross; and now what jewel in their diadem is more precious than the Cross of Christ on the foreheads of kings? In loving Him you will never be ashamed. ...[Therefore those who are] turning their thoughts to Christ, have run to the Church, have overcome, not any one, but the devil himself, him who hunts after the souls of the whole world. But they who in that hesitation have chosen rather to run to the [world], have assuredly been overcome by him whom the others overcame—overcame in Him who said, "Be of good cheer, I have overcome the world." For the Captain suffered Himself to be tried, only that He might teach His soldier to fight.

St. Augustine, Sermon 1.2 (NPNF 2:6)

He promised Paradise from the Cross, because He is God the King. He rejoiced upon the Cross, that all was finished when He drank the vinegar, because He had fulfilled all prophecy before He died. He was born for us, suffered for us, died for us, rose again for us. This alone is necessary for our salvation, to confess the Son of God risen from the dead: why then should we die in this state of godless unbelief? If Christ, ever secure of His divinity, made clear to us His death, Himself indifferent to death, yet dying to assure that it was true humanity that He had assumed: why should we use this very confession of the Son of God Who for us became Son of Man and died as the chief weapon to deny His divinity?"

St. Hilary of Poitiers, *On the Holy Trinity* (NPNF 2:9, p. 534)

For Christ is of those who are humble-minded, and not of those who exalt themselves over His flock. Our Lord Jesus Christ, the Scepter of the majesty of God, did not come in the pomp of pride or arrogance...but in a lowly condition, as the Holy Spirit had declared regarding Him. For He says, "Lord, who has believed our report, and to whom is the arm of the Lord revealed?" We have declared [our message] in His presence:

He is, as it were, a child, and like a root in thirsty ground; He has no form nor glory. Yes, we saw Him, and He had no form nor comeliness. But His form was without eminence, yes, deficient in comparison with the [ordinary] form of men. He is a man exposed to stripes and suffering, not acquainted with the endurance of grief: for His countenance was turned away; He was despised, and not esteemed. He bears our iniquities, and is in sorrow for our sakes; yet we supposed that [on His own account] He was exposed to labor, and stripes, and affliction.

But He was wounded for our transgressions, and bruised for our iniquities. The chastisement of our peace was upon Him, and by His stripes we were healed. All we, like sheep, have gone astray; [every] man has wandered in his own way; and the Lord has delivered Him up for our sins, while He in the midst of His sufferings opened not His mouth. He was brought as a sheep to the slaughter, and as a lamb before her shearer is dumb, so He opened not His mouth. In His humiliation His judgment was taken away; who shall declare His generation? For His life is taken from the earth.

For the transgressions of my people was He brought down to death. And I will give the wicked for His sepulcher, and the rich for His death, because He did no iniquity, neither was guile found in His mouth. And the Lord is pleased to purify Him by stripes. If you make an offering for sin, your soul shall see a long-lived seed. And the Lord is pleased to relieve Him of the affliction of His soul, to show Him light, and to form Him with understanding, to justify the Just One who ministered well to many; and the Himself shall carry their sins. On this account He shall inherit many, and shall divide the spoil of the strong; because His soul was delivered to death, and He was reckoned among the transgressors, and He bare the sins of many, and for their sins was He delivered."

And again He says, "I am a worm, and no man; a reproach of men, and despised of the people. All who see Me have derided Me; they have spoken with their lips; they have wagged their head, [saying] 'He hoped in God, let Him deliver Him, let Him save Him, since He delighted in Him.'" Do you see, beloved, what is the example which has been given us; for if the Lord thus humbled Himself, what shall we do who have through Him come under the yoke of His grace?

St. Clement of Alexandria, *Commentary on First Corinthians*, 16 (ANF 1, pp. 25-26)

"King of the Jews"

The superscription ["King of the Jews"] is fittingly above the Cross because Christ's kingdom does not belong to His human Body but to His divine authority. The superscription is fittingly above the Cross, He shines above the Cross with the majesty of a king.

St. Ambrose of Milan, *Exposition of the Gospel of Luke*, 10.112-113 (AACS 3, p. 363)

He was not hailed as the King of Glory by the angels until He had been censured on the Cross as "King of the Jews..." (Matt. 27:37; Mk. 15:26; Lk. 23:38; Jn. 19:19). You owe your life to Him as a debt for these favors. So try as best as you can to be accountable to Him in the same way that He became accountable for you. Or, do not be crowned with flowers at all if you cannot bear the thorns, because you cannot be crowned with flowers.

The Scholar Tertullian, *The Chaplet*, 14 (FC 64, p. 24; AACS 2, p. 231)

A Stumbling Block to the Jews

The Cross of Christ is indeed a stumbling-block to those that do not believe, but to the believing it is salvation and life eternal. "Where is the wise man? where the disputer?" Where is the boasting of those who are called mighty? For the Son of God, Who was begotten before time began, and established all things according to the will of the Father, He was conceived in the womb of Mary, according to the appointment of God, of the seed of David, and by the Holy Spirit.

For [the Scripture] says, "Behold, a Virgin shall be with Child, and shall bring forth a Son, and He shall be called Immanuel." He was born and was baptized by John, that He might ratify the institution committed to that prophet.

St. Ignatius of Antioch, *Epistle to the Ephesians*, 18 (ANF 1, p. 114)

The Cross is a crown of victory. It has brought light to those blinded by ignorance. It has released those enslaved by sin. Indeed, it has redeemed the whole of mankind. Do not, then be ashamed of the Cross of Christ; rather, glory in it. Although it is a stumbling block to the Jews and folly to the Gentiles, the message of the Cross is our salvation. Of course it is folly to those who are perishing, but to us who are being saved, it is the power of God. For it was not a mere man who died for us, but the son of God, God made man.

St. Cyril of Jerusalem

Our God, Jesus Christ, was, according to the appointment of God, conceived in the womb by Mary, of the seed of David, but by the Holy Spirit. He was born and baptized, that by His passion He might purify the water...The Cross of Christ is indeed a stumbling-block to those that do not believe, but to the believing it is salvation and eternal life.

St. Ignatius of Antioch, *Epistle To the Ephesians*, 18 (ANF 1, p. 120)

Because of us, we who have been uncovered because of sin; the God of Glory Jesus was stripped of His clothes, was tied to the post, and was whipped with ropes and rods in which there was a chain of bones...Until this innocent body is scattered and its flesh dispersed in compensation; and His blood is shed to protect our wounds and to cure them. May we praise Him, for it is He Who has killed death by death with His crown of thorns!

St. Ephrem the Syrian

Adam received the punishment, "Cursed is the ground in your labors; thorns and thistles shall it bring forth to you." For this reason Jesus assumes the thorns, that He may cancel the sentence; for this reason also was He buried in the earth, that the earth which had been cursed might receive the blessing instead of a curse.

St. Cyril of Jerusalem, *Catechetical Lecture 13* (NPNF 2:7, p. 123)

For the Lord died in those days, that we should no longer do the deeds of death. He gave His life, that we might preserve our own from the snares of the devil.

St. Athanasius, *Paschal Epistle 6* (NPNF 2:4, p. 1242)

You may ask, why didn't they all marvel [at this] and consider Him to be God? Because the race of man was then held in a state of great carelessness and corruption. This miracle was only one, and when it had taken place, immediately passed away; and no one was concerned to inquire into the cause of it, and great was the prejudice and the habit of ungodliness. They did not know what was the cause of that which took place, and they thought perhaps this happened so, in the way of an eclipse or some natural effect. And why do you marvel about them that are without, that knew nothing, neither inquired by reason of great indifference, when even those that were in Judea itself, after so many miracles, yet continued using Him despitefully, although He plainly showed them that He Himself performed this thing.

St. John Chrysostom, *Commentary on Matthew*, Homily 83.1 (NPNF 2:10, p. 521)

Do you turn this benefit into a reproach to God? Will you deem Him little on this account, that He humbled Himself for your sake, and because to seek for that which had wandered the Good Shepherd,[20] He who lays down His life for the sheep, came upon the mountains and hills upon which you used to sacrifice, and found the wandering one; and having found it, took it upon His shoulders, on which He also bore the wood; and having borne it, brought it back to the life above; and having brought it back, numbered it among those who have never strayed. That He lit a candle, His own flesh, and swept the house, by cleansing away the sin of the world, and sought for the coin, the Royal Image that was all covered up with passions, and calls together His friends, the Angelic Powers, at the finding of the coin, and makes them sharers of His joy, as He had before made them sharers of the secret of His Incarnation? That the Light that is exceeding bright should follow the Candle—Forerunner, and the Word, the Voice, and the Bridegroom, the Bridegroom's friend, that prepared for the Lord a peculiar people and cleansed them by the water in preparation for the Spirit? Do you Reproach God with this?

Do you conceive of Him as less because He girds Himself with a towel and washes His disciples, and shows that humiliation is the best road to exaltation; because He humbles Himself for the sake of the soul that is bent down to the ground, that He may even exalt with Himself that which is bent double under a weight of sin? How comes it that you do not also charge it upon Him as a crime that He eats with Publicans and at Publicans' tables, and makes disciples of Publicans that He too may make some gain. And what gain? The salvation of sinners. If so, one must blame the physician for stooping over suffering and putting up with evil smells in order to give health to the sick; and him also who leans over the ditch, that he may, according to the Law, save the beast that has fallen into it.

He was sent, but sent according to His humanity, since He was hungry and thirsty and weary, and was distressed and wept, according to the laws of human nature... For He is said on the one hand to have been betrayed, and on the other it is written that He gave Himself up; and so also that He was raised and taken up by the Father, and also that of His own power He rose and ascended. The former belongs to the Good Pleasure, the latter to His own authority... Do you stumble at His Flesh? So did the Jews.

St. Gregory Nazianzen, *Second Oration* (NPNF 2:8)

---

[20] Nicetas says that this refers to St. Gregory's father, who had ordained him Priest, to assist him in the Cure of Souls, and whose one desire was that his son might succeed him in the Bishopric. (footnote in NPNF).

Who were the first people to use crucifixion for punishment?[21]

The earliest known use of Crucifixion dates to the Persian period. Assyrians and the Persians practiced impalement (mounting a living body on a pointed stake). But the Persians also crucified as punishment, as the fifth century b.c. Historian Herodotus tells us. The earliest example we are aware of occurred in 522 BC, when a Persian official killed an opponent and then crucified him. A few years later Darius the Great crucified one of the royal judges but then relented and restored the man to a position of leadership. In neither case do we know what the cross looked like. Presumably the offenders were only tied to a cross.

Alexander the Great in 332 BC, after the fall of Tyre, crucified 2,000 men of military age and sold 30,000 others into slavery. The Hasmonean (Maccabean) Alexander Jannaeus (103-76 BC) near the end of His reign crucified 800 Pharisees after he put down a revolt in the rebellious town of Bemeselis, north of the city of Samaria. A few years later, in 71 BC, at the end of the Roman slave revolt led by Spartacus, 6,000 recaptured slaves were crucified on crosses set up along the Appian Way. Then, as is often observed, many Christians were crucified in Rome during the persecution of Nero, following the great fire of Rome.

We know that at the least Persians, Greeks, Phoenicians, Carthaginians, Jews, and Romans practiced crucifixion. They used crucifixion as a punishment or deterrent for crime and rebellion. It was especially a punishment for runaway slaves and robbers; slaves often became brigands. Our Lord, Himself, was crucified between two robbers (Mk. 15:27). Crucifixion was employed especially in the provinces and it was usually reserved for those who did not possess Roman citizenship. In time, however, some lower-class Romans suffered Crucifixion. Constantine finally abolished the practice.

---

[21] The following is the summary of an article written by Vos in *Nelson's New Illustrated Bible*.

Prayer

Today, He who hung the earth upon the waters is hung upon the Cross. He who is King of the angels is arrayed in a crown of thorns. He who wraps the heavens in clouds is wrapped in the purple of mockery. He who in the Jordan set Adam free, receives blows upon His face. The Bridegroom of the Church is affixed to the cross with nails. The son of the Virgin is pierced by a spear. We worship Your passions, O Christ. Show us also Your Holy Resurrection...

You have redeemed us from the curse of the law by Your precious Blood: nailed to the Cross and pierced by the spear, You have poured forth immortality upon mankind. O our Savior, glory be to You.

My Lord and Savior, Your body is torn by whips and I wear nice clothes, living lavishly and carelessly. You are given the myrrh to drink, and I enjoy the desires of life. You comfort my pains and sufferings and I refuse to repent. I ask You to have mercy upon me, for I know how tender is Your overflowing mercy.[22]

---

[22] *The Road to the Cross*, pp. 586-588. The picture above is a model of first-century Jerusalem—The upper city with some public buildings, but especially houses of the wealthy with their open courtyards. Photo of ancient Jerusalem model in Holyland Hotel in West Jerusalem.

NINTH HOUR: "THE CRUCIFIXION"

Jer. 11:18-12:13, Zech. 14:5-11

Philip. 2:4-11; Psa. 69:1,2, 21

Matt. 27:46-50; Mk. 15:34-37; Lk. 23:45-46; Jn. 19:28-30

Overview

"My spirit bows in adoration to the Cross, which is a stumbling-block to those who do not believe, but is to you for salvation and eternal life."

St. Ignatius of Antioch[23]

"O You Who gave up the Spirit into the hands of the Father when You were hung on the Cross in the Ninth Hour and guided the thief into entering Paradise; do not neglect me, O Good One..."

Litany of the Ninth Hour of the Agpeya

In this hour, the Church stands at the Cross, looking at His great act of love flowing from It. Our Savior has conquered death by death! Blessed is this moment in which our Lord bowed His head and gave up His Spirit. The moment terrified Satan and tied him down while those who had fallen asleep in Christ rejoiced.

"For this reason the gospel was preached also to those who are dead, that they might be judged according to men in the flesh, but live according to God in the spirit" (1 Pet. 4:6). It is the same moment during which the thief to the right entered Paradise, opening its door to the rest of the human race. The darkness of this frightening death was dissipated by the passing of our Savior through it. Death no longer has any dominion over those who die in Jesus Christ.

Jeremiah the prophet tells us in this hour, "But I was like a docile lamb brought to the slaughter; and I did not know that they had devised schemes against me, saying, "Let us destroy the tree with its fruit, and let us cut him off from the land of the living" (Jer. 11:19).

My Lord and Master, they were wrong to assume that they could eradicate You from life, when You are its origin, its provider, and its

---

[23] St. Ignatius of Antioch, *The Second Epistle to the Ephesians*, 18 (ANF 1, p. 202)

sustainer. By going through death You changed our human understanding of it. For now death in Christ became not only life, but also eternity.

Zechariah the prophet announces to us, "And in that day it shall be that living waters shall flow from Jerusalem, half of them toward the eastern sea and a half of them toward the western sea; and the Lord shall be King over all the earth" (Zech. 14:8-9). He is the living Water even though He did die from the Cross. However, we chant with the angels, saying, "Holy God, Holy Mighty, Holy Immortal." It seems that the Spirit in this prophesy wanted to reveal to us the totality of the kingdom of Christ, as living water to whoever wishes to come and drink—the Jews (the first eastern sea) and the Gentiles (the western sea). And the Lord shall be King over all the earth.[24]

Also the reading of **Philippians** explains the cry of the Lord in the **Gospels**. As Origen states, when the Lord "emptied Himself and took the form of a servant, He accepted the shame and death on the Cross, where virtually all of humanity abandons the Lord." During this time, the Lord did not abandon Him, as some commentators believe. Instead, the Lord glorified Him, accepted His sacrifice as a sweet aroma that was pleasing to Him (as we declare in the famous hymn, **Ⲫⲁⲓ ⲉⲧⲁϥⲉⲛϥ.**)

The spear supposedly entered from the right side, diagonally, ending in the heart. This was a prophesy mentioned in the **Psalms**: "My heart is wounded" (literally, pierced) (Psa. 109:21,22). The soldier who thrust this spear was named Longinus. After witnessing this majestic event, he confessed Christianity and became a martyr.

Church Tradition and Rites

During the 9th hour, candles are lit before the Icon of the Crucifixion. The presbyters, with their heads uncovered and wearing their liturgical robes, cense the icon. In the presence of the bishop, they cense and bow before him without kissing his hand or the cross.

The hymn "The Golden Censor" (**Ϯϣⲟⲩⲣⲏ**) is chanted while the priests begin to raise incense. Also chanted during this hour is the hymn "For the Resurrection" (**Ⲉⲑⲃⲉ ϯⲁⲛⲁⲥⲧⲁⲥⲓⲥ**), which points to the future resurrection, the hope in the Cross and the fruit of His death.

---

[24] Fr. Pishoy Kamel, *JTG*, 70.

Readings and Patristic Meditations

JEREMIAH 11:18-12:13

*Now the Lord gave me knowledge of it, and I know it; for You showed me their doings. But I was like a docile lamb brought to the slaughter; and I did not know that they had devised schemes against me, saying, "**Come, let us cast wood in His bread and let us cut Him off from the land of the living, that His name may be remembered no more.***"[25]

But, O Lord of hosts, You who judge righteously, testing the mind and the heart, let me see Your vengeance on them, for to You I have revealed my cause.

"Therefore thus says the Lord concerning the men of Anathoth who seek your life, saying, 'Do not prophesy in the name of the Lord, lest you die by our hand'— therefore thus says the Lord of hosts: 'Behold, I will punish them. The young men shall die by the sword, their sons and their daughters shall die by famine; and there shall be no remnant of them, for I will bring catastrophe on the men of Anathoth, even the year of their punishment.'"

Righteous are You, O Lord, when I plead with You; Yet let me talk with You about Your judgments. Why does the way of the wicked prosper? Why are those happy who deal so treacherously? You have planted them, yes, they have taken root; They grow, yes, they bear fruit. You are near in their mouth but far from their mind.

*But You, O Lord, know me; You have seen me, and You have tested my heart toward You. **Pull them out like sheep for the slaughter, and prepare them for the day of slaughter.** How long will the land mourn, and the herbs of every field wither? The beasts and birds are consumed, for the wickedness of those who dwell there, because they said, "He will not see our final end."*

"If you have run with the footmen, and they have wearied you, then how can you contend with horses? And if in the land of peace, in which you trusted, they wearied you, then how will you do in the floodplain of the Jordan? For even your brothers, the house of your father, even they have dealt treacherously with you; Yes, they have called a multitude after you. Do not believe them, even though they speak smooth words to you.

"I have forsaken My house, I have left My heritage; I have given the dearly beloved of My soul into the hand of her enemies. My heritage is to Me like a lion in the forest; It cries out against Me; therefore I have hated it. My heritage is to

---

[25] As Justin Martyr mentions, the Jews have cut out this one verse in Jeremiah, as well as many others, hundreds of years ago. Although the KJV and NKJV do contain this verse, however, the translation is slightly different than the original Septuagint. See the comments below.

Me like a speckled vulture; The vultures all around are against her. Come, assemble all the beasts of the field, bring them to devour!

"Many rulers have destroyed My vineyard, they have trodden My portion underfoot; they have made My pleasant portion a desolate wilderness. They have made it desolate; desolate, it mourns to Me; the whole land is made desolate, because no one takes it to heart. The plunderers have come on all the desolate heights in the wilderness, for the sword of the Lord shall devour from one end of the land to the other end of the land; no flesh shall have peace.

They have sown wheat but reaped thorns; They have put themselves to pain but do not profit. But be ashamed of your harvest because of the fierce anger of the Lord."

"Let us cast wood in His bread"

The Lord Christ speaks for Himself: "I was like a docile lamb brought to the slaughter; and I did not know...They thought about Me, saying: 'Let us cast wood in His bread.'" If the Jews have crucified Him, which we know for sure, how could we connect between this issue, and the last phrase? It is something difficult to understand!

The bread of the Lord Christ is the Word, the teaching on which we feed. When the Jews saw Him teaching the multitude, they intended to corrupt His teaching by crucifying Him, and said, "Let us cast wood in His bread." Adding the Crucifixion of the Lord Christ to His teachings, is like casting wood in His bread. When those people gathered together to plot against Him, they said, "Let us cast wood in His bread"

I have another view of this, which is: **The wood cast in His bread,** made it stronger and more effective. As the wood that was cast by Moses into the bitter water made it sweet (Exod. 15:25), likewise, when the "Tree" of love of the Lord Christ, was added to His teachings, it made His bread more sweet and delicate. Actually, before the "Tree" was added to His "bread"; namely during the time of His teaching that preceded the Cross, His words "have not gone out to the end of the world" (Psa. 19:4). But, once the "bread" gained power through the "Tree" that was cast in it, His words did go out to the end of the world.

The "tree" in the Old Testament had been a symbol of the love of the Lord Christ, by which the bitter water became sweet. For I believe that, if the law is not understood by the spiritual meaning, it would be "bitter water"; but by the coming of the "Tree" of the crucifixion of the Lord Christ, and the coming of His teachings, the law of Moses became sweet...

The One against whom they said: "Let us cut Him off from the land of the living; that His name may be remembered no more," says: "Unless a grain of wheat falls into the ground and dies, it remains alone; but if it dies it produces much grain" (Jn. 12:24). If the Lord Christ was not crucified and did not die, the grain of wheat would have stayed alone, and the multitudes would not have got fruit by Him and followed Him. But His death gave fruits, represented by all the Christians. So, if death has produced all these fruits, how much more would resurrection produce?!

The Scholar Origen, *On Jeremiah*, Homily 10.1-3

For of this tree [which symbolizes the Cross] likewise it is that God hints, through Jeremiah, that you would say, "Come, let us put wood into his bread, and let us wear him away out of the land of the living; and his name shall no more be remembered." Of course on His body that "wood" was put; for so Christ has revealed, calling His body "bread," whose body the prophet in bygone days announced under the term "bread." If you shall still seek for predictions of the Lord's cross, the twenty-first Psalm will at length be able to satisfy you, containing as it does the whole passion of Christ; singing, as He does, even at so early a date, His own glory.

The Scholar Tertullian, *An Answer to the Jews*, 6 (ANF 3)

ZECHARIAH 14:5-11

Then you shall flee through My mountain valley, for the mountain valley shall reach to Azal. Yes, you shall flee as you fled from the earthquake in the days of Uzziah king of Judah. Thus the Lord my God will come, and all the saints with You.

It shall come to pass in that day that there will be no light; the lights will diminish. It shall be one day which is known to the Lord—neither day nor night. But at evening time it shall happen that it will be light.

And in that day it shall be that living waters shall flow from Jerusalem, half of them toward the eastern sea and half of them toward the western sea; in both summer and winter it shall occur. And the Lord shall be King over all the earth. In that day it shall be— "The Lord is One," and His Name one.

All the land shall be turned into a plain from Geba to Rimmon south of Jerusalem. Jerusalem shall be raised up and inhabited in her place from Benjamin's Gate to the place of the First Gate and the Corner Gate, and from the Tower of Hananeel to the king's winepresses.

The people shall dwell in it; And no longer shall there be utter destruction, But Jerusalem shall be safely inhabited.

"Neither day nor night"

Christ was judged in the night, when it was cold, therefore a fire of coal was laid. He suffered in the third hour, and "from the sixth hour until the ninth hour there was darkness over all the land" (Matt. 27:45). But from the ninth hour there was light again. Are these details written down [in the prophets]? Let us see. Zechariah says, "And it shall come to pass in that day, and there shall be no light but cold and fronts through one day (the cold on account of which Peter warmed himself), and that day shall be known to the Lord." What did He not know other days? There are many days, but "this is the day which the Lord has made." (Psa. 118:24)

"And that day shall be known to the Lord—and that day shall be neither day nor night." What dark saying does the prophet utter? That day is neither day nor night. What then shall we call it? The gospel interprets it, telling of the event. It was not day, for the sun did not shine without interruption from rising to setting, but from the sixth hour to the ninth hour there was darkness. The darkness was interposed, but God called the darkness night. Therefore it was neither all light, so as to be called day, nor all darkness, so as to be called night; but after the ninth hour the sun shone forth. This also the prophet foretells; for after saying, "not day nor night" he adds, "and in the time of the evening there shall be light." Do you see the truth of the events foretold?

St. Cyril of Jerusalem, *Catechetical Lectures*, 13 (NPNF 2:2, p. 251)

PHILIPPIANS 2:4-11

Let each of you look out not only for his own interests, but also for the interests of others. Let this mind be in you which was also in Christ Jesus, who, being in the form of God, did not consider it robbery to be equal with God, but made Himself of no reputation, taking the form of a bondservant, and coming in the likeness of men. And being found in appearance as a man, He humbled Himself and became obedient to the point of death, even the death of the Cross. Therefore God also has highly exalted Him and given Him the name which is above every name, that at the name of Jesus every knee should bow, of those in heaven, and of those on earth, and of those under the earth, and that every tongue should confess that Jesus Christ is Lord, to the glory of God the Father.

He emptied Himself and took the form of a servant.

In emptying Himself He became a man and was incarnate while remaining truly God. Having become a man, He remained the God that He was. He assumed a body like our own, differing only in that it was born from the Virgin by the Holy Spirit....The Son, emptying Himself of His equality with the Father and showing us a way of knowing Him, was made an express image of His substance (Heb. 1:3) so that we who were unable to see the glory of pure light that is inherent in the greatness of His divinity might, through that which was made splendor for us, find a way of contemplating the divine light through the sight of that splendor.

The Scholar Origen, *On First Principles*, Preface, 1.2.8 (AACS 8, pp. 242-243)

He let Himself be emptied. It was not through any compulsion by the Father. He complied of His own accord with the Father's good pleasure.

St. Cyril of Alexandria, *Dialogues on the Trinity*, 1 (AACS NT 8, p. 243)

What sort of emptying is this? To assume the flesh, even in the form of a slave, a likeness to ourselves while not being like us in His own nature, but superior to the whole creation. Thus He emptied Himself, descending by His economy into mortal bounds.

St. Cyril of Alexandria, *That Christ is One* (AACS NT 8, p. 243)

God did all things through [Christ]. Therefore He is also said to have taken the form of a slave. It is not only the flesh of the slave that He assumed but the very nature of a slave that He assumed. He became a slave so that He could share human suffering in the flesh.

St. Clement of Alexandria, *Excerpts from Theodotus*, 19.4-5 (AACS NT 8, p. 245)

And even the word emptied clearly affirms that He was not always as He appeared to using history...He emptied Himself, as the Apostle says, by contracting the ineffable glory of His Godhead within our small compass. In this way what He was remained great and perfect and incomprehensible, but what He assumed was commensurate with the measure of our own nature...He emptied Himself, so that as much as nature could hold it might receive....The one who says that He took the form of a slave—and this form is flesh—is saying that, being Himself something else according to His divine form, something else in His Nature, He assumed the servile form.

St. Gregory of Nyssa, *Antirrheticus Against Apollinarius* (AACS, 8, pp. 242, 244, 245)

Since He is emptied on our account when He came down (and by emptying I mean as it were the reduction and lessening of His glory), He is for this reason able to be received.

St. Gregory of Nyssa, *Oration 37.2* (AACS, 8, p. 244)

He honored the Father all the more, not that you may honor Him less but that you may marvel all the more. Here we learn that He is truly a Son who honors His Father more than all else. No one could have honored God the Father more than God the Son. The measure of His humility corresponds with the depth of His humanity...It was a great thing, ineffably great, that He became a slave. But to undergo death was much greater. Where can anything be found more paradoxical than this? This death was the most shameful of all, the most accursed. And He in death appeared to be a criminal. This was not an ordinary death (Deut. 21:23; Gal. 3:13).

St. John Chrysostom, *Commentary on Philippians*, Homily 8.2.5-11 (AACS NT 8, pp. 249-250)

He is said to have emptied Himself in no other way than by taking the form of a servant, not by losing the form of God. For that nature by which he is equal to the Father in the form of God remained immutable while He took our mutable nature through which He was born of the Virgin.

St. Augustine, *Contra Faustum*, 3.6 (AACS 8, p. 242)

He emptied Himself not because as eternal Wisdom He underwent change. For as eternal Wisdom He is absolutely changeless. Rather without changing He chose to become known to humanity in such a humble form.

St. Augustine, *On Faith and the Creed*, 18 (AACS 8, p. 242)

The Son humbled Himself, taking the form of a slave. But meanwhile He remained above any slavery because He had no stain of sin.

St. Augustine, *On the Grace of Christ and On Original Sin*, 2 (28).33.18 (AACS 8, p. 244)

To assume the form of a slave, He emptied Himself out of obedience. He emptied Himself that is from the form of God, which means equality with God...**Humility is hard, since the One Who humbles Himself has something magnificent in His nature that works against His lowering.** The One Who becomes obedient, however, undertakes the act of obedience voluntarily. It is precisely through the act of humbling that He becomes obedient...

He tempered Himself to the form of the human state as far as was necessary to ensure that the weakness of the assumed humility would not fail to beat His immeasurable power. He went even so far as to tolerate conjunction with a human body. Just this far did His goodness moderate itself with an appropriate degree of obedience. But in making Himself empty and restraining Himself within Himself, He did nothing detrimental to His own power, since even within this lowliness of His self-emptying He nonetheless used the resources of the evacuated power within Him.

St. Hilary of Poitiers, *On the Holy Trinity*, 8.45, 11.30, 12.48 (AACS 8, pp. 242, 244, 250)

Read the record of His compassion. It please Him, being the Word of God, to take the form of a servant. So He willed to be joined to our common human condition. He took to Himself the toils of the members who suffer. He made out human maladies His own. He suffered and toiled on our behalf. This is in accord with His great love of humankind.

Eusebius of Caesarea, *Demonstration of the Gospel*, 10.1.22 (AACS 8, p. 245)

MATTHEW 27:46-50

And about the ninth hour Jesus cried out with a loud voice, saying, **"Eli, Eli, lama sabachthani!"** *that is,* **"My God, My God, why have You forsaken Me?"** *Some of those who stood there, when they heard that, said,* "This Man is calling for Elijah!" *Immediately one of them ran and took a sponge, filled it with sour wine and put it on a reed, and offered it to Him to drink. The rest said,* "Let Him alone; let us see if Elijah will come to save Him." *And Jesus cried out again with a loud voice, and yielded up His spirit.*

MARK 15:34-37

And at the ninth hour Jesus cried out with a loud voice, saying, **"Eloi, Eloi, lama sabachthani?"** *which is translated,* **"My God, My God, why have You forsaken Me?"** *Some of those who stood by, when they heard that, said,* "Look, He is calling for Elijah!" *Then someone ran and filled a sponge full of sour wine, put it on a reed, and offered it to Him to drink, saying,* **"Let Him alone; let us see if Elijah will come to take Him down."** *And Jesus cried out with a loud voice, and breathed His last.*

LUKE 23:45-46

Then the sun was darkened, and the veil of the temple was torn in two. And when Jesus had cried out with a loud voice, He said, "Father, into Your hands I commit My spirit." *Having said this, He breathed His last.*

JOHN 19:28-30

After this, Jesus, knowing that all things were now accomplished, that the Scripture might be fulfilled, said, "I thirst!" Now a vessel full of sour wine was sitting there; and they filled a sponge with sour wine, put it on hyssop, and put it to His mouth. So when Jesus had received the sour wine, He said, "It is finished!" And bowing His head, He gave up His spirit.

"My God, My God why have You forsaken Me."

Certain people, in an outward of piety for Jesus, because they are unable to explain how Christ could be forsaken by God, believe that this saying from the Cross is truly only an expression of His humility. We, however, who know that He who was "in the form of God" (Philip. 2:6) descended from the greatness of His stature and emptied Himself, "taking the form of a servant" (Philip. 2:7) according to the will of the One who sent Him understand that He was indeed forsaken by the Father inasmuch as He who was the form of the invisible God and the Image of the Father "took the form of a servant."

He was forsaken for people so that He might shoulder so great a work and come "even to death" and "the death of the Cross" (Philip. 2:8), a work which seems thoroughly shameful to most people. For it was the height of His abandonment when they crucified Him with thieves and when "those who passed by blasphemed Him, wagging their heads" (Matt. 27:39). The chief priests and scribes said, "'He saved others; Himself he cannot save'" (Matt. 27:42). At that time, "even the robbers who were crucified with Him reviled Him" (Matt. 27:44).

Clearly then you will be able to understand the saying "Why have You forsaken Me." When you compare the glory Christ had in the presence of the Father with the contempt He sustained on the Cross, for His throne was "like the sun in the presence of God and like the moon established forever; and He as His faithful witness in heaven" (Psa. 88:36-37).

The Scholar Origen, *Commentary on Matthew*, 135 (AACS, 1b, p. 294)

[After the eclipse of the sun] He speaks, so that they might learn that He was still alive. He did this so they might become by this also more gentle. He said, "*Eli, Eli, lama sabachthani?*" **that unto His last breath they might see that He honors His Father, and is no adversary of God.** Therefore He also uttered a certain cry from the prophet, even to His last hour bearing witness to the Old Testament, and not simply a cry from the prophet, but also **in**

Hebrew, so as to be plain and intelligible to them, and by all things He shows how He is of one mind with Him Who begat Him.

What shamelessness, and greed, and folly! They thought (it is said) that it was Elijah whom He called, and straightway they gave Him vinegar to drink. But another came to Him, and "pierced His side with a spear." What could be more lawless, what more brutal, than these men; who carried their madness to so great a length, offering insult at last even to a dead body?

St. John Chrysostom, *Commentary on Matthew*, Homily 83.1 (NPNF 2:10, p. 521)

Others again are said in the manner of association and relation, as, "My God, My God, why have You forsaken Me?" and He has made Him to be sin for us, Who knew no sin, and being made a curse for us. Also, "Then shall the Son also Himself be subject unto Him Who puts all things under Him." **For neither as God nor as man was He ever forsaken by the Father, nor did He become sin or a curse, nor did He require to be made subject to the Father. For as God He is equal to the Father and not opposed to Him nor subjected to Him;** and as God, He was never at any time disobedient to His Begetter to make it necessary for Him to make Him subject. Appropriating, then, our person and ranking Himself with us, He used these words. For we are bound in the fetters of sin and the curse as faithless and disobedient, and therefore forsaken.

John of Damascus, *Concerning our Lord's Praying* (NPNF 2:9, p. 850)

In His most compassionate humanity and through His servant form we may now learn what is to be despised in this life and what is to be hoped for in eternity. In that very passion in which is proud enemies seemed most triumphant, **He took on the speech of our infirmity,** in which "our old man was crucified with Him" (Rom. 6:6) that body of sin might be destroyed, and said, "My God, My God why have You forsaken Me."…Thus the Psalm begins, which was sung so long ago, in the prophesy of His Passion and the revelation of the Grace in which He brought to raise up His faithful and set them free….

Out of the voice of the Psalmist, which our Lord then transferred to Himself, in the voice of this infirmity of ours, He spoke these words, "My God, My God why have You forsaken Me" (Psa. 22:1; Matt. 27:46; Mk. 15:34; Lk. 23:44). He is doubtless forsaken in the sense that His plea was not directly granted. **Jesus appropriated the Psalmist's voice to Himself, the voice of human weakness.** The benefits of the Old Covenant had to be refused in order that we might learn to pray and hope for the benefits of the New Covenant. Among those goods of the Old Covenant which belonged to the old Adam there is a special appetite for the prolonging of this temporal life. But this appetite itself is not eternal, for we all know that the day of death will come. Yet all of us, or nearly all, strive to postpone it, even those who believe that their life after death will be a happier one. Such force has the sweet partnership of flesh and soul (Eph. 5:29).

St. Augustine, *Letter 140 to Honoratus*, 5-6 (FC 20, pp. 16-69; AACS 2, p. 234)

"MY GOD, MY GOD..."
St. Cyril of Alexandria[26]

A. So if He said "My God, My God, why have you forsaken Me" (Matt. 27:26), how do these people understand it?"

B. They would regard these words, I suppose, as coming from the man that was assumed.

A. From a broken man, doubtless, who found the assaults of this trial so hard that it seemed unsupportable? Or how else?

B. They would regard them as the sayings of one who was distraught because of human faintheartedness, or so it would seem. For He also said to His disciples, "My soul is exceedingly sorrowful even to death" (Matt. 26:38), and He fell down before the Father Himself, saying "'O My Father, if it is possible, let this cup pass from Me; nevertheless, not as I will, but as You will'" (Matt. 26:39).

A. But isn't this exactly the same as what we have spoken of earlier? That is, "Who in the days of His flesh, when He had offered up prayers and supplications, with vehement cries and tears to Him Who was able to save Him from death" (Heb. 5:7). Yet if anyone thinks that Christ had fallen so low into such faintheartedness as to be so "sorrowful and cast down" (Matt. 26:37) that He could no longer bear His sufferings but was overcome by fear and mastered by weakness, then he assuredly convicts Him of not being God, and also shows that He apparently had no right to rebuke Peter.

B. What do you mean?

---

[26] The following is written by St. Cyril in his great work *That Christ is One* which is written as a dialogue between Cyril (A) and one of his disciples (B). (McGuckin, pp. 103-106).

A. Well, Christ said, "Behold we are going up to Jerusalem and the Son of Man shall be betrayed into the hands of sinful men, and they shall mock Him and shall crucify Him, and on the third day He shall rise again." But then this lover of God said, "May He be merciful to You Lord, that this shall not happen to You" (Mk. 10:34, Matt. 16:22). Then what did Christ say to him? "Get behind Me, Satan! For you are an offense to Me; for you are not mindful of the things of God, but the things of men" (Matt. 16:23). How did the disciple make an improper suggestion in wanting this trial to be removed from his Master if it was going to prove insufferable for Him, and so completely unbearable that it would undoubtedly cast Him down to cowardice and break His spirit? After all, He Himself had commanded His disciples to stand fast against their fears of death and reckon suffering as nothing in the course of fulfilling the will of God. I am amazed how such people are able to say that such a man has been conjoined to the Only Begotten or go on to maintain that He has shared in the divine dignities, when they then subject Him to the fears of death and expose Him as naked just like any one of us. He presumably gained no benefit at all from His divine dignities?

B. How can we understand the form of the economy in these matters?

A. It is mystical, profound and truly wonderful, for those who know the mystery of Christ correctly. Look at the sayings which refer to the emptying out, and are accommodated to the limitations of the manhood; look how they come at just the right time, when they are needed, so that He who is above all creation might be revealed as having become like us in all respects. Another conclusion follows from this.

B. Tell me what it is.

A. We had become accursed through Adam's transgression and had fallen into the trap of death, abandoned by God. Yet all things were made new in Christ (2 Cor. 5:17) and our condition was restored to what it was in the beginning. It was entirely necessary that the Second Adam, who is from heaven (1 Cor. 15:45) and superior to all sin, that is Christ, the pure and immaculate first-fruits of our race, should free that nature of man from judgment, and once again call down upon it heavenly graciousness of the Father.

He would undo our abandonment by His obedience and complete submission: "Who committed no sin" (1 Pet. 2:22), but the nature of man was made rich in all blamelessness and innocence in Him, so that it could now cry out with boldness, "'My God, My God, why have You forsaken Me'" (Matt. 27:46). Understand that in becoming man the Only Begotten spoke these words as one of us and on behalf of all nature. It was as if He were saying this:

"The first man has transgressed. He slipped into disobedience, and neglected the commandment he received, and he was brought to this state of willfulness by the wiles of the devil; and then it was entirely right that he became subject to corruption and fell under judgment.

"But You Lord have made Me a second beginning for all on the earth, and I am called the Second Adam. In Me You see the nature of man made clean, its faults corrected, made holy and pure. Now give Me the good things of Your kindness, undo the abandonment, rebuke the corruption and set a limit on Your anger. I have conquered Satan himself who ruled of old, for he found in Me absolutely nothing of what was his."

In my opinion this is the sense of the Savior's words. He did not invoke the Father's graciousness upon Himself, but rather upon us. The effects of God's anger passed into the whole of human nature as from the original rootstock, that is Adam: "Nevertheless death reigned from Adam up to Moses, even over those who had not sinned according to the likeness of the transgression of Adam" (Rom. 5:14). In the same way, however, the effects of our new first-fruits, that is Christ, shall again pass into the entire human race. The all-wise Paul confirms this for us when he says: "For if by one man's offense many died, much more" (Rom. 5:15) shall come to life because of the righteousness of One. And again: "As in Adam all die, even so in Christ all shall be made alive" (1 Cor. 15:22).

The Sponge and Vinegar

One can use the spiritual sense of this text profitably against those who write malicious things against Christ. Concerning them, Isaiah says "Woe to those who write wickedness" (Isa. 10:1). If those who publish such things are speaking "iniquity in the highest" (Psa. 72:8), some will use this text with a view toward those who, constructing a narrative gathered from pagan tongues, fill the sponge not with the word that is drinkable or with the wine which "gladdens the heart" (Psa. 103:15) or with the water of restoration (Psa. 22:2). But, on the contrary, with poisonous, undrinkable, unwise vinegar. They place this sponge on the reed of their writing and (as far as they are able) seem to offer a swallow of these diatribes for Jesus to drink. Others give Jesus to "drink wine mixed with gall" which Jesus the Son of God does not want. Others offer Him vinegar instead of wine. Others offer Him "wine mixed with gall" when they, having understood the doctrine of the Church, live unworthily of it. **Those who attribute to the lips of Christ** doctrines that are alien to the truth turn the metaphor around, and fill the sponge with vinegar, place it on a reed and drink it themselves.

The Scholar Origen, *Commentary on Matthew*, 137 (AACS 1b, p. 295)

Among the other things prophesied about Him, it was also written, "They gave Me poison for drink and for My thirst they gave Me vinegar to drink" (Psa. 69:21). We know in the gospel how these things happened. First, they gave Him gall. He took it, tasted it, and spit it out. Later, while hanging on the Cross, that all prophesies might be fulfilled, He said, "I thirst!" (Jn. 19:28). They took a sponge full of vinegar, fasted it on a reed, and offered it to Him as He hung there. He took it and said, "It is finished" (Jn. 19:30). What does "It is finished" mean? All that had been prophesied before My Passion has been fulfilled. What then is there still for Me to do?

St. Augustine, *Tractates on John*, Tractate 37.9 (FC 88, pp. 102-103)

He gives up His Spirit

Those robbers crucified next to Him, did they breathe their last when they wanted to? They were held fast by the chains of the flesh because they were not the creators of the flesh. Fastened by nails, they were tormented for a long time because they were not masters of their infirmity (Jn. 19:32-33). But the Lord took on flesh in the Virgin's womb when He wished it. He came forth to humanity when He wished it. He departed from the flesh when He wished it. This is a sign of power, not of necessity.

St. Augustine, *Tractates on John*, Tractate 37.9 (FC 88, p. 103)

He departed by His own [power]; for He had not come by necessity. And so some marveled more at His power of dying than at His power of performing miracles.

St. Augustine, *Tractates on John*, Tractate 31.6 (FC 88, p. 35)

"When Jesus had cried out with a loud voice, He yielded up the spirit." This refers to what He had earlier said, "I have power to lay it down, and I have power to take it up again" and "I lay it down of Myself" (Jn. 10:18). So for this reason He cried with the voice, that it might be shown that the act is done by His own power.

St. John Chrysostom, *Commentary on Matthew*, Homily 88.1 (NPNF 2:10, p. 521)

He suitably "gave up" the Spirit because He willingly gave Him up. Matthew says "yielded up His Spirit" because what is yielded is spontaneous, but what is lost is unavoidable. Since this is true, he added, "with a loud voice." He did this with a glorious declaration that He descended to death for our sins. I do not blush to confess what Christ did not blush to proclaim in a loud voice. This was a clear revelation of God witnessing to the separation of the Godhead and the flesh.

St. Ambrose of Milan, *Exposition of the Gospel of Luke*, 10.127 (AACS 3, p. 369)

If giving up the spirit or (according to John) handing over the Spirit were simply tantamount to dying, it would be easy to understand this passage. However, since discerning minds define death to be nothing other than the separation of the soul from the body, we can see that yielding up one's spirit is something more than simply dying physically. It is quite something else to "cry out with a loud voice and give up the spirit" (as in Matthew) or to commit one's spirit to the hand of God (as in Lk. 23:46) or to bow one's head and hand over his spirit (as in John 19:30). It is for all people to die, including the evil, because the soul of every person, including the unrighteous, will be separated from the body.

But to cry out with a loud voice and give up the spirit, which is equivalent to committing the spirit to the hand of God, or to bow the head and hand over the spirit, is reserved only for the saints who, like Christ Himself, have prepared themselves for God through good works so that when they leave this world they might with confidence commit themselves to the hand of God, or hand over their spirits.

If therefore we now understand what it means to cry out with a loud voice and thus to give up the spirit, that is, to commit oneself to the hand of God (as we have explained above in accordance with Luke's Gospel) and if we understand what it means to bow the head and hand over the spirit, let us hasten to guard the conduct of our lives so that, upon our deaths, we also, like Jesus, might be able to cry out with a loud voice and thus to give up our spirit to the Father.

The Scholar Origen, *Commentary on Matthew* 138 (AACS, 1b, pp. 295-296)

The Testimony of All Creation in His Death

Creation itself mourned its Lord. The sun was darkened, the rocks were split, the temple put on mourner's clothes. Its veil was split from the top to the bottom. This is what God signified to us by the voice of Isaiah, saying, "I clothe the heavens with blackness, and make sackcloth their covering."

St. Cyril of Alexandria, *Commentary on Luke*, Homily 153 (CLC pp. 610-611)

If He had been the son of a foreign god, the sun would not have eclipsed when the Lord was raised on His Cross. The Creator would have spread out a more intense light, because His enemy would have been withdrawn from His sight. He would have cause His light to shine on the Jews, because they would have been doing His will. He would have clothed the temple with a curtain of glory, because its enemy's death would have purified its sad impurities, and the breaker of its law would have gone out from it.

St. Ephrem the Syrian, *CTD*, 21.3 (AACS 3, p. 368)

ELEVENTH HOUR: "THE FOUNTAIN OF LIVING WATER AND THE PASSOVER LAMB"

Exod. 12:1-14, 43; Lev. 23:5-15; Psa. 142:6,7; 30:5

Matt. 27:51-56; Mk. 15:38-41; Lk. 23:47-49; Jn. 19:31-37

Overview

This is the hour of the Passover Lamb. Included in this hour are three passages by Fr. Pishoy Kamel, Fr. Tadros Malaty, and St. Gregory Nazianzen regarding Christ as the Passover Lamb.

In the Ninth Hour, the Lord thirsted. He reminded us of the thirst which He mentioned to the Samaritan Woman. But truly, we were in need of the Living Water that flows from the Spring that the Logos spoke of to her. During this hour, we read of the Fountain of Living Water that sprang as the water of salvation, both in the Old and New Testaments.

First, we read of the story of Moses in **Exodus**, who struck the rock in the desert. Water sprang that quenched the thirst of the Israelites in the desert. Then, we read the institution of the covenant by God's people to remember the Passover each year.

The **Psalmist** echoes this desire to be given the spiritual drink, imploring the Lord, "My soul thirsts for You as a dry land." But who thirsts for whom? We thirst for the living Water, the waters of baptism, the blood that purges all of our sins, the salvation of our souls, bodies and spirits. But truly He thirsts for our tears, our repentance, our love for Him.

Another prophesy within this psalm concerns the other main event in this hour—the end of the struggle and sacrifice of our Lord. For in this hour, we meditate on the words spoken by our Lord, *"It is finished!"* (Jn. 19:30). This is the Lord's declaration that all of His promises have been completely fulfilled for all of humanity. After He declares this, Longinus the soldier pierces the side of our Savior with the spear, blood and water came out from His wound.

The **Gospels** speak to us of this sacrifice. As Fr. Pishoy Kamel said, "He is in our midst, now crucified. He opens His arms the whole day for our entire life. His blood pours out of His wounded side—a sign on our homes and our hearts as the new Covenant which takes us from death to life. The water cleanses us and grants us purity, meekness, peace and love. These are the fruits of the Spirit given to us through baptism (the water). Your pierced side, Jesus is the stain of blood for us to be partners in Your Cross. The water is for the beginning of the new life and the end of the authority of sin. In the ninth hour, You were thirsty. Actually, You wanted me to feel thirsty and drink from Your living water. Now in the Eleventh Hour, You offer me this water."[27]

This fountain is both of blood and water, as prophesied in the book of Joel, "the mountains shall drip with new wine, the hills shall flow with milk, and all the brooks of Judah shall be flooded with water; a fountain shall flow from the house of the Lord" (Joel 3:18).

Christ, the Passover Lamb

According to the instructions the Lord gave to Moses mentioned in Exodus 12, the Passover lamb was:

1) without blemish (Exod. 12:15);

2) a young male, (v. 15);

3) examined four days from the selection of the sacrifice (10th of Nissan);

4) slain in public;

5) roasted in the fire (v. 8, 9);

6) left without none of its bones broken (v. 46);

7) a saving lamb for the children of Israel, if they placed its blood on the doorposts of the Israelites (v.7).

These seven characteristics were fulfilled through the coming of our Lord Jesus Christ. Thus, St. John the Baptist declares Him to be "the Lamb of God Who takes away the sins of the world" (Jn. 1:29). In this manner, the Passover lamb is a type of our beloved Lord, for He:

1) was without blemish, in whom was found no guile or deceit (Jn. 1:47);

2) was a young male, estimated to be 30 years old at the start of His ministry and 33 at the time of His Crucifixion;

3) entered into Jerusalem on the 10th of Nissan to be heavily examined by the Jews;

4) was brutally slain on the most populated time of the year in Israel;

5) endured the fire of sufferings, accusations and ridicule;

---

[27] Fr. Pishoy Kamel, *FTG*, 72-73.

6) was crucified without any of His bones broken (Jn. 19:36);

7) whose blood shed on the Cross saves us all from our sin (Rom. 5:9) and redeems us from our condemnation (Col. 1:14; Heb. 9:12-13, 22; Rev. 1:5).

If we enquire further into the significance of Jesus being pointed out by John, when he says, "This is the Lamb of God who takes away the sin of the world," we may take our stand at the dispensation of the bodily advent of the Son of God in human life, and in that case we shall conceive the Lamb to be no other than the Man. For the Man "was led like a sheep to the slaughter, and as a lamb, dumb before his shearers," saying, "I was as like a gentle lamb led to the slaughter." Hence, too, in the Apocalypse a Lamb is seen, standing as if slain (Rev. 5:6). This slain lamb has been made, according to certain hidden reasons, a purification of the whole world, for which, according to the Father's love to man, He submitted to death, purchasing us back by His own blood from him who had got us into his power, sold under sin. And He who led this lamb to the slaughter was God in man, the great High-Priest, as He shows by the words: "No one takes it from Me, but I lay it down of Myself. I have power to lay it down, and I have power to take it again" (Jn. 10:18).

The Scholar Origen, *Commentary on John*, 6.35 (ANF 10)

Readings and Patristic Meditations

EXODUS 12:1-14, 43

Now the Lord spoke to Moses and Aaron in the land of Egypt, saying, "This month shall be your beginning of months; it shall be the first month of the year to you. Speak to all the congregation of Israel, saying: 'On the tenth day of this month every man shall take for himself a lamb, according to the house of his father, a lamb for a household. And if the household is too small for the lamb, let him and his neighbor next to his house take it according to the number of the persons; according to each man's need you shall make your count for the lamb. Your lamb shall be without blemish, a male of the first year. You may take it from the sheep or from the goats. Now you shall keep it until the fourteenth day of the same month. Then the whole assembly of the congregation of Israel shall kill it at twilight. And they shall take some of the blood and put it on the two doorposts and on the lintel of the houses where they eat it. Then they shall eat the flesh on that night; roasted in fire, with unleavened bread and with bitter herbs they shall eat it. Do not eat it raw, nor boiled at all with water, but roasted in fire—its head with its legs and its entrails. You shall let none of it remain until morning, and what remains of it until morning you shall burn with fire. And thus you shall eat it: with a belt on your waist, your sandals on your feet, and your staff in your hand. So you shall eat it in haste. It is the

Lord's Passover. For I will pass through the land of Egypt on that night, and will strike all the firstborn in the land of Egypt, both man and beast; and against all the gods of Egypt I will execute judgment: I am the Lord. Now the blood shall be a sign for you on the houses where you are. And when I see the blood, I will pass over you; and the plague shall not be on you to destroy you when I strike the land of Egypt. So this day shall be to you a memorial; and you shall keep it as a feast to the Lord throughout your generations. You shall keep it as a feast by an everlasting ordinance...

And the Lord said to Moses and Aaron, "This is the ordinance of the Passover: No foreigner shall eat it."

The First Passover: Overcoming Temptation and Sin

The Passover first began with the commandment of the Lord given to Moses, that the blood of the lamb be placed on the door posts of the houses of the Israelites in Egypt. That night, they were to eat bitter herbs, have their loins girded, their sandals on their feet, and their staff in their hand (Exod. 12).

It continued that through the shedding of blood of the lamb, there came forgiveness. "And according to the law almost all things are purified with blood, and without shedding of blood there is no remission" (Heb. 9:22).

On the night of their exodus from Egypt, the Lord commanded the Israelites to roast the lamb, and eat unleavened bread with bitter herbs (Exod. 12:8). The meat that the Jews would feast upon was not raw or unbaked, but cooked in fire. The lamb had to suffer through fire, it had to suffer. This meat had a sweet smell, but a bitter taste. Such is the great reminder of sin—however pleasing it may seem to our senses, however alluring it may be to us, we must never forget the bitter sadness of its consequences. This bitterness lies within the Cross: "He has filled me with bitterness, he has made me drink wormwood" (Lam. 3:15).

The Christian life is full of bitter herbs that bring forth a sweet, saintly aroma. One type of herb comes from loving of our enemies. Another comes from serving the Lord in difficult circumstances—either a family difficulty or a conflict in our schedules. There is a garden of bitter herbs awaiting you in prayer and vigil in times of weakness, sorrow, or confusion. When you fast, you taste of these bitter herbs...you have experienced the Cross. By choosing to take this narrow and difficult path, by submitting to travel along the *Via Dolorosa*, "We are to God the fragrance of Christ among those who are being saved and among those who are perishing" (2 Cor. 2:15).

Christ, Himself became the true and ultimate Passover Lamb, the fulfillment of this prophesy. "For indeed Christ, our Passover, was sacrificed for us" (1 Cor. 5:7). After the disciples had eaten the Passover meal, the Old Testament had been fulfilled. Our Lord and Savior perfected the Passover meal by offering His Body and Blood in the form of bread and wine. This was the "marriage supper of the Lamb" discussed in Revelation 19:9.

That is why Christ proclaimed that "Every time you shall eat of this bread and drink from this cup you proclaim My death and confess My resurrection." Thus, every liturgy brings forth an epiphany; every communion becomes a sermon. This however, was only the first Passover.

The Second Passover: Faith and Baptism

The Second Passover was the crossing of the Red Sea by Moses and the Israelites. Just as Moses had parted its waters and crushed Pharaoh's soldiers, Christ had destroyed the soldiers of Satan at the bottom of the sea. Moses used His staff; Christ used the cross. They both spread their arms as an eagle, one divided waters between two nations; the Other separated the gap between two worlds.

In our lives, this Passover is the grave importance of baptism. Just as the waters of the Jordan saved the Israelites from the evil army of Pharaoh, so does the baptismal waters save us from Satan's forces. Once the Jews had crossed the river, they began a new life and were in search of a new home. So too do we begin this Christian Journey through baptism, seeking for eternal rest in Heavenly Jerusalem.

To live this new life in Christ, we cannot seek after the sacramental waters of baptism without faith. An ancient Jewish legend has it that the parting of the Red Sea did not actually take place when Moses had spread His arms, but when the first person took the first step on the water. This legend demonstrates that this miracle was based on the faith that God would fight and work a miracle for His people. We are no longer slaves to doubt, captives of anxiety; we are princes of confidence, kings of faith. As Saint Paul so boldly declared, "We walk by faith, not by sight" (2 Cor. 5:7).

LEVITICUS 23:5-15

*On **the fourteenth day** of the first month at **twilight** is the Pascha to the Lord. Then on the fifteenth day of the same month is the Feast of Unleavened Bread to the Lord; **seven days** you shall eat unleavened bread. On the first day you shall have a holy convocation; you shall **do service work** on it. But you shall* *offer a whole burnt offering to the Lord for seven days. The seventh day shall be a holy convocation; you shall do no service work.*

And the Lord spoke to Moses, saying, Speak to the children of Israel, and say to them, 'When you come into the land which I give to you and reap its harvest you shall bring a sheaf of the firstfruits from your harvest to the priest. He shall wave the sheaf before the Lord, to be accepted on your behalf; on the morning after the first day the priest shall offer it. Then you shall offer on that day on which you offer the sheaf a **sheep of the first year, without blemish, as a whole burnt offering to the Lord.** *Its grain offering shall be two-tenths of an ephah of fine flour mixed with oil, a sacrifice to the Lord, for a sweet aroma to the Lord; and its drink offering shall be of wine, one-fourth of a hin. You shall eat neither bread nor roasted fresh ears until the same day that you have offered gifts to your God;* **it shall be an ordnance forever throughout your generations in all your dwellings.**

'Then you shall count for yourselves from the morning following the Sabbath day, from the day that you brought the sheaf of the deposit: seven full weeks.'"

The mystery of the lamb which God ordered you to sacrifice as the Passover was truly a type of Christ, with whose Blood the believers, in proportion to the strength of their faith, anoint their homes (Exod. 12:7), that is, themselves. You are all aware that Adam, the result of God's creative act, was the abode of His inspiration (1 Cor. 3:16). Similarly, God's precept concerning the paschal lamb was only temporary.

St. Justin Martyr, *Dialogue with Trypho*, 40:1-3

The door-posts of the Jews were sealed with the blood of the slaughtered animal: with the blood of Christ are our foreheads sealed. And that sealing — for it had a real significance — was said to keep away the destroyer from the houses that were sealed: Christ's seal drives away the destroyer from us, if we receive the Savior into our hearts. But why have I said this? Because many have their door-posts sealed while there is no inmate abiding within: they find it easy to have Christ's seal in the forehead, and yet at heart refuse admission to His word. Therefore, brethren, I have said, and I repeat it, Christ's seal drives from us the destroyer, if only we have Christ as an inmate of our hearts…The Lord therefore came as it were to the victim's place, that the true Passover might be ours, when we celebrated His passion as the real offering of the lamb.

St. Augustine, *Tractates on John* (11), Tractate 50 (NPNF 2:7, p. 560)

"THE PASSOVER LAMB AND THE RESURRECTION OF THE MESSIAH"
Fr. Tadros Malaty

The Passover is considered a turning point in the history of the old people, through which they crossed from the land of bondage to the wilderness, to set forth toward the land of promise. The Passover lamb, with all its rites, carried special concepts: "It shall be the first month of the year" (Exod. 12:2); "This day shall be to you a memorial; and you shall keep it as a feast to the Lord throughout your generations" (Exod. 12:14); and it is to be kept by the whole assembly of the congregation (Exod. 12:6). It also carried a spiritual concept that touches the life of the congregation of the Church in its relationship with God. The Passover lamb is not merely a memorial of a historical event that took place in the past, but it represents a present and continuous work of God in the life of His people. The Passover feast also means a personal relationship between every member of the congregation and God Himself, concerning the symbol of the Passover lamb. But as the Lord Christ offered Himself a true "Passover" for the whole world, His Passion, crucifixion, burial, and resurrection become a continuous and permanent Passover in the life of the Church that it celebrates, not only once every year, but in every Divine Liturgy, and experiences its strength throughout every day. That divine Passover work became the subject of meditation for every true believer, through which he passes over from glory to glory, to enter, by the Holy Spirit, into the Father's bosom.

That made the two chapters: 11 and 12 of the Book of Exodus, the center of the whole Book, if not, of the whole Old Testament, as the crucifixion and the resurrection of the Lord Christ are the center of the Bible as a whole. That is why I find it imperative, to present an accurate, yet concise study, as much as possible, of the Passover Lamb, in the light of the old Jewish traditions known at that time, and the passion, crucifixion, and resurrection, in order to know its significance in the life of the catholic (universal) or global Church, and in each of its members.

The Passover and the Old Traditions

In the days of the first Adam, his two sons offered two different offerings to the Lord. Abel, as a man of hunting, offered a blood sacrifice, as atonement for his sins – which he obtained after his parents, while Cain, as a worker in the land, brought an offering to the Lord of the fruit of the land. Anyhow, humanity received those two actions, and disfigured them, through deviation from the divine way. The nomadic Bedouins, used to splash the sign of blood over their tents, with the assumption that it chases away the evil spirits. Those laboring in agriculture adopted a different tradition, abstaining from eating leavened bread, for several days, at the beginning of the new agricultural season, lest the leaven of the old crop would get into the new one. By that, they start a new year with new food, and a new life.

Let us note that those two rites (splashing of blood and abstaining from leavened bread) had their origin in pure faith; yet humanity deviated from their way of faith. So, the rite of Passover came to return them back to another and better way of life.

The Passover carries the "sign of blood," with the concept of reconciliation between God and man, through the blood of the Redeemer. The believer feels himself like a Bedouin with no place here to settle down in a permanent Passover, in a continuous movement toward the higher Jerusalem. He puts blood on the two doorposts and on the lintel, namely on his heart and mind, not to drive away the evil spirits, but to pass over with all his thoughts and feelings to the Fatherly bosom, through his union with the Savior, defeating the hosts of evil under his feet.

As to the second rite, concerning eating only unleavened bread, and removing the leaven from his house, it concerns the life of the believer, who, although, in a permanent movement toward the heavenly, and in a state of sojourn on the earth, he feels from within that he is leaning on the bosom of the Lord, working in the vine of the new land. Hence, he eats unleavened bread for the seven days of the week - keeps on eating, all the days of his life, the new food that will never get old. He will continuously enjoy the new life, enjoy the food of the angels, and sing the new praise, saying with the apostle, "behold, all things have become new" (2 Cor. 5:17).

It is amazing how the Church, in her celebration of the feast of Passover (Resurrection), has practiced since the early days two integrated rites together: the Baptism of the catechumens (the new converters to Christianity), and the Eucharist. In the eve of the Passover, the Bishop baptizes the catechumens, to let them bear the sign of blood on their inner foreheads and in their hearts, to enjoy the reconciliation with God the Father, in His Son Jesus Christ, by His Holy Spirit, and to enjoy the spirit of sonship, that will help them cross over to the divine glories. Then they would approach, together with the rest of believers to partake of the other rite - the Eucharist - in which the Church, striving on earth, appears, as though she, amid her strife, has settled down around the eternal divine altar, feeding on the forever new unleavened Bread, and enjoying the holy Body and Blood, that would never get old. This is our new Passover, the shadow and symbol of which the old Passover bore.

A Personal Passover

God commanded the whole congregation to keep the Passover. It is the Passover of all the Church, united to her Groom. Later on, He commanded to hold it only in Jerusalem, the city that carries His name, as it is a Passover of the Lord.

That vivid collective image did not disregard the personal role of every member of the congregation, but rather it concentrated on it, through the union of every member with the congregation. Not only did God command that every house should be splashed with blood, but also committed every man and woman to eat the flesh of the Passover lamb, roasted on fire. The act of eating here is a sign of a personal relationship, and of personal partaking of that rite. Indeed, it was not possible for very little children to take part of it, yet they attended the rite and rejoiced in it, besides getting saved through the faith of their parents, who partook of eating the flesh of the Passover lamb.

It was not just a matter of the crossing over of the congregation as a whole, but for every individual person, whether it be a man, woman, or child. But, even after the crossover, while keeping the feast year after year, along the ages, every single partaker of that feast is considered as though he or she has personally enjoyed the fellowship of faith, together with those who have been saved, and as though they received a portion of the freedom gained by the early forefathers. In the Book of Exodus it is said, "You shall keep the feast of unleavened bread... for in it you came out of Egypt" (Exod. 23:15), addressing every single member of the congregation, as though he or she came out of Egypt. And in the Book of Deuteronomy, it is said, "Observe the month of new corn, and keep the Pascha to the Lord your God, for in the month of new corn He brought you out of Egypt by night" (Deut. 16:1). That command was addressed to every believer along the ages, as though he or she has come together with the early forefathers by night out of the land of Egypt.

That is also confirmed by the Jewish tradition, saying in the *Didache*: "Your forefathers were not saved alone; but, while saving them, He saved us as well." Therefore, celebrating the feast of Passover, even in the sound Jewish thought, carried an inner trend, that touches every believer's life and his personal relationship with God, through his union with the congregation. It is the same thing meant by the Church, as it celebrates the new feast of

Passover, in order, for every believer to enter into the enjoyment of the new resurrected life, through his crossing and settling in the bosom of God, as a member in the holy congregation.

From the Law to the Messiah

The feast of Passover had its special rites for the Jews, that is recorded in the twelfth chapter of the Book of Exodus, that carries certain other traditions that included prayers of blessing, praises, and psalms, mentioned in the 'Mishnah', (which I previously dealt with) as well. That feast was rich in its memories and promises that carried God's care for man, especially through the salvation presented by the Messiah. They used to recognize that night as an anniversary of the creation of the world, of the circumcision of Abraham, the sacrifice of Isaac, the release of Joseph from the prison, the anticipated release from captivity, the appearance of the Messiah, the coming of Moses and Elijah, the resurrection of the fathers, and the end of the world. That is why the Lord Christ offered Himself a Passover to the world in the feast of Passover, in order to proclaim that the Truth swallows up the symbol, and brings it on to the consummation of its goal.

Father Melito, Bishop of Sardis says, "The secret of Passover is realized in the body of the Lord... He was led like a lamb, and was slain like a she-goat; saving us from the bondage of the world (Egypt), and setting us free of the servitude of the devil (Pharaoh), putting His seal on our souls by His Spirit, and on our body members by His blood... He is the One who brought us from servitude to freedom, from darkness to light, from death to life, and from oppression to eternal Kingdom... He is our Passover to salvation... He is the silent Lamb that was taken out of the flock and slain in the evening, and buried by night... for that, that feast was bitter. As said in the Holy Book, 'with unleavened bread and bitter weeds they shall eat it' (Exod. 12: 8). Bitter for you were the nails that were used... bitter was the tongue that blasphemed... bitter was the false testimony uttered against Him...Contemplate, O dear brother, how the secret of Passover is new and old, eternal and mortal, non-corruptible and corruptible... It is old according to the Law, and is new according to the Logos. It is mortal through the symbol, and eternal in the words of grace... corruptible through the death of the lambs, and non-corruptible through the life of the Lord. So are the sacrifice of the lambs, the rite of Passover, and the letter of the Law, all of which have been realized in Jesus Christ. In place of the Law came the Logos, so that the old became new, the commandment became grace, and the symbol became fact."

From the Earthly Passover to the Heavenly Passover

The Jews celebrate the earthly Passover, yet deny the heavenly one. But we celebrate the heavenly Passover crossing over the earthly one. The Passover they celebrate is a symbol of the salvation of the firstborns of the Jews. The death of the firstborns of the Egyptians, while the Jewish firstborns were saved, occurred because they were protected by the symbol, by the blood of the Passover sacrifice. But the Passover we celebrate brings salvation to all people, starting with the firstborns who are saved...

St. Hippolytus

And now, as you celebrate the Pascha, the holy Passover, you should know, O brethren, what the Pascha is! Pascha means "Passover." So this feast is so called, as in it, the Son of God passed over from this world to His Father.

St. Ambrose of Milan

What would be your benefit from celebrating this Feast, if you do not follow the example of Him, Whom you are worshipping... and pass over from the darkness of wicked deeds to the light of virtue, and from the love of this world to the love of the heavenly home?! There are many people who celebrate and observe this holy Feast, yet they do that unworthily because of their evil, and because they do not pass over beyond this world to their Father, and because they do not pass over from the carnal lusts of this world to the love of heaven. How miserable Christians they are?! They are still under the authority of the devil, and comfortable with his evil...

That is why, I am warning you, my brethren, that you should celebrate this Feast as you should by passing over. If any of you is still in sin, let him sanctify this Feast, passing over from the wicked deeds to the life of virtue. As for him, who walks in a holy life, let him pass over from virtue to virtue, and hence, none of you would not be passing over.

St. Athanasius, in his Passover messages, spoke often of passing over from the worldly Passover to the heavenly Passover. "Now, my brethren, Satan (Pharaoh) is slain; that tyrant who antagonizes the whole world. Now, we are not dealing with a worldly feast, but a permanent heavenly one, proclaiming it, not through shadows (and letters), but in Truth. Those, after getting fulfilled through eating the flesh of the dumb lamb, and splattering the doorposts of their houses with its blood, they consummated the feast, and were saved from the destroyer. But now, as we eat the 'Word of the Father,' and splatter our hearts with the blood of the New Testament, we recognize the grace, granted to us by the Savior, Who says, "Behold, I give you the authority to trample on serpents and scorpions, and over all the power of the enemy" (Lk. 10: 19). As death has no more authority, but life reigns in place of death; The Lord says: 'I am... the Life' (Jn. 14: 6). Everything is filled with joy and happiness, as it is written: 'The Lord reigns, let the earth rejoice'" (Psa. 97:1).

We should come to the feast with zeal and joy; so by starting with joy here, our souls would yearn to the heavenly feast. If we actively celebrate here, we shall surely receive the complete joy that is in heaven. And as the Lord says: "With fervent desire I have desired to eat this Passover with you before I suffer; for I say to you, I will no longer eat of it, until it is fulfilled in the Kingdom of God" (Lk. 22:15, 16).

For those who keep this feast with purity, the Passover will be their heavenly food. I wish we do not celebrate the Feast in an earthly way, but rather like keeping a feast in heaven with the angels. Let us glorify God through life of virtue and righteousness! Let us rejoice, not in our souls, but in the Lord to be with the saints!

The Rites of the Passover

St. Melito, Bishop of Sardis, believes that the Law was an introduction to the covenant of grace, not only through commandments and words, but also through the symbol saying, "The words and acts of the rite, brethren, are meaningless, if they are severed from what they symbolize." This is actually the view of the Church that it received, with an evangelical Spirit, since its beginning.

And now, let us speak about the rite of the Passover, as it came in the Book of Exodus, and what it symbolizes, with the help of biblical texts and the writings of the fathers.

Why did it happen by night?

The Lord says to Moses: "About midnight I will go out into the midst of Egypt" (Exod. 11:4). And He confirms in the Book of Deuteronomy: "for in the month of new corn He brought you out of Egypt by night" (Deut. 16:1). St. Hippolytus interprets this by saying, "The strike took place by night in the darkness as in the veil of darkness, away from the bright light of the day, justice is realized in the devil and his dark crimes. "And I will show wonders in the heavens and in the earth: blood and fire and pillars of smoke. The sun shall be turned into darkness, and the moon into blood, before the coming of the great and terrible day of the Lord" (Joel 2:30, 31), and "Woe to you who desire the day of the Lord! For what good is the day of the Lord to you? It will be darkness, and not light. It will be as though a man fled from a lion, and a bear met him! Or as though he went into the house, leaned his hand on the wall, and a serpent bit him! Is not the day of the Lord darkness, and not light? Is it not very dark, with no brightness in it? (Amos 5:18-20)."

It is as though, while the devil dwells in darkness, the Lord is destroying him in his den. While he is sure that there is no one to oppose him, he will be destroyed together with all his works. The Lord (our new Passover) delivered His Spirit by the end of the day, and entered by night into Hades, to set those captivated in the darkness free, and to bring them forth to the light of paradise, without darkness!

In the Month of Abib, the beginning of months

The Lord spoke to Moses and Aaron saying, "This month shall be your beginning of months; it shall be the first month of the year to you" (Exod. 12:1). It is as though, with every Passover, they enter a new year, to live in a continuous state of renewal within the heart, through the slain Jesus Christ.

As the Lord Christ (our Passover) is the head of creation, and is its Firstborn, this month became the "firstborn" of ages, and the beginning of the new life. According to the words of the apostle, "Or do you not know that as many of us as were baptized into Christ Jesus were baptized into His death? Therefore we were buried with Him through baptism into death, that just as Christ was raised from the dead by the glory of the Father, even so we also should walk in newness of life" (Rom. 6:3,4).

St. Hippolytus says, "That means that the true sacrifice of Passover to us, is the beginning of eternal life." The symbolic Passover came at the beginning of the months; but the Lord (the true Passover) came at the end of ages (Heb. 9:26), to proclaim that He is the end and goal of the Law (Rom. 10:4). It is noteworthy that the word "Abib" means a head of grains, as though, through Passover, the soul becomes the "head of grain" of the Lord, namely, His harvest.

Taking the lamb on the tenth day of the month (Exod. 12:3)

That was a reference to the entrance of the Lord Christ into Jerusalem, to be kept there, until He offers Himself a Passover for our sake. Choosing the tenth day refers to His coming after the Law (the Ten Commandments) to consummate the commandment that was broken by man, granting us the possibility of its fulfillment.

Keeping it until the fourteenth day (Exod. 12:6)

In the fourteenth day, the moon becomes full; for the sun is a symbol of the Lord Christ, and the moon of the Church. It is as though, through Christ (our Passover) (1 Cor. 5:7), the enlightenment of the Church is consummated, and its splendor is proclaimed.

The days of keeping are five (10-15 of Abib), representing the five beginnings of the world, in the history of salvation. With it, Adam began the human race; Noah, began the new world after the great flood; Abraham began as a father to believers, (from whose seed came the people of God); Moses began the world in the written Law; and finally Christ came on the fifth day to begin the age of grace, in which He offered Himself a Passover, having its activity in all the five eras.

The five days also refers to the activity of the true Passover, for all those who work in any of the five hours of the day; those who began their work in the first hour, the third, the sixth, the ninth, or the eleventh hour.

Inviting the neighbor next to his house (Exod. 12:4)

This refers to the invitation of the Gentiles, being the (next neighbor), to share in the enjoyment of the true Passover.

The lamb should be without blemish (Exod. 12: 5)

It should be either a lamb, a symbol of meekness, according to the words of the prophet Isaiah, "He was oppressed and He was afflicted, yet He opened not His mouth; He was led as a lamb to the slaughter, and as a sheep before its sheerer is silent" (Isa. 53:7), or "one male kid from the goats for a sin offering" (Num. 7:16).

The Savior Lord Jesus Christ was called a Lamb, as in the Book of Jeremiah said, "I was like a docile lamb brought to the slaughter, and I did not know that they had devised schemes against Me, saying, 'Let us destroy the tree with its fruit, and let us cut Him off from the land of the living, that His name may be remembered no more'" (Jer. 11: 9). And as seen by St. John the Baptist, who said, "Behold, the Lamb of God who takes away the sin of the world" (Jn. 1:29). In heaven, St. John the evangelist saw Him, "in the midst of the elders, stood a Lamb as though it had been slain" (Rev. 5: 6).

Being perfect and without blemish, is because the Lord Christ, holy and without sin, is capable of atoning our sins by His own blood (Heb. 9:14). And according to the apostle, we have been redeemed by a perfect blood, as though of a lamb without spot, the blood of Christ.

Being a male, that refers to His status, as a Groom to all believers (2 Cor. 11:2); and "He who has the bride is the bridegroom" (Jn. 3:29).

Being "Of the first year", means that it should be young and strong; to stay new in our lives forever, though He is the Old of age, the Eternal.

Because the Lord Christ alone, without blemish or spot in every virtue, presents all righteousness, from the beginning to the end. Having said of Himself: "it is fitting for us to fulfill all righteousness" (Matt. 3:15).

St. Hippolytus

The whole assembly of the congregation of Israel shall kill it (Exod. 12:6)

On one side, this had been realized in the Person of the Lord Christ, of Whom it is said, "For truly against Your holy Servant Jesus, whom You anointed, both Herod and Pontius Pilate, with the Gentiles, and the people of Israel, were gathered together" (Acts 4:27). On another side, the Lord Himself was the One who came forward to offer Himself as a sacrifice of love for our sake. St. John Chrysostom says, "The Lord Christ was not commanded to do that, but came forward to offer Himself as a sacrifice to God."

Despite the great number of families that offer lambs, yet all of them share in one sacrifice. The Lord Christ had offered Himself as One Passover, for the atonement of all nations and peoples gathering all around Him, as though in one house. Concerning this, St. Hippolytus says, "As it was the case with the houses of the Hebrews, although numerous, yet counted as one house. Churches, though numerous in a city, they represent one Church. Christ, Who is whole, is undivided in various houses, as is said by the apostle Paul, that we are one in Christ."

It should be kept inside the house. St. Hippolytus says, "It is one assembly and one house. It is one Church where the Holy Body of Christ is eaten. It is not to be moved out of that one house or Church. Whoever eats it in any other place, will be condemned as a wicked thief."

To be killed at twilight (Exod. 12:6)

Is a reference to the fact that the Lord Christ has offered Himself for the world at the fulfillment of ages.

The blood to be put on the two doorposts and on the lintel of the houses (Exod. 12:7)

Speaking of the activity of the blood, He says, "When I see the blood, I will pass over you" (Exod. 12:13). "Without shedding of blood, there is no remission" (Heb. 9:22).

The Egyptians, no doubt have seen the slaying of the lambs and the sprinkling of the blood, and mocked the Israelites for it, but they perished. If any Hebrew had tied the lamb to the door, instead of slaying it, he would also perish, as there is no salvation for us, except through the death of the Lord Christ, and the shedding of His blood. That is why He says: "Most assuredly, I say to you, unless a grain of wheat falls into the ground and dies, it remains alone; but if it dies, it produces much grain" (Jn. 12:24).

The blood of the lamb was a symbol of the blood of the Lord Christ; without it, there is no salvation. And as St. Lactantius says, "The Hebrews were alone saved by the sign of blood. Not because the blood of the lamb had in itself the activity to save mankind, but because it was a symbol of the coming things."

St. Hippolytus says concerning the power of the sign of blood that "It is put on the houses as well as in the souls, where the Spirit of God finds its holy dwelling." And he also says, "The blood on the upper lintel, namely on the Church; and on the two doorposts, namely, on the two peoples (the Jews and the Gentiles)."

St. Gregory of Nyssa believes that putting the blood on the upper lintel and on the two doorposts, refers to the sanctification of the three sides of the soul: the mental, the emotional, and the spiritual. Man is sanctified with all his mental energies, desires, emotions, and inner feelings.

So, it was the belief of the fathers, as far as the sign of blood is concerned, that it implies the sanctification of the catholic, or global Church, as well as the human soul, as a member in that Church.

It is noteworthy that the blood is not to be put on the doorstep, lest it would be trampled over with the feet. The apostle says, "Of how much worse punishment, do you suppose, will he be thought worthy, who has trampled the Son of God underfoot, counted the blood of the covenant, by which he was sanctified a common thing, and insulted the Spirit of grace?" (Heb. 10: 29). As to our strife to enjoy the fruit of that Blood, St. Athanasius says, "It is fitting for us to prolong our prayers, fasts, and watching, so that we can anoint the doors of our houses with the precious blood, to let the destroyer pass over them."

God does not allow the paschal lamb to be sacrificed in any other place than where His Name is invoked (that is in the Temple at Jerusalem; Deut. 16:5-6), for He knew that there would come a time, after Christ's Passion, when the place in Jerusalem (where you sacrificed the paschal lamb) would be taken from you by your enemies, and then all sacrifices would be stopped.

St. Justin, *Dialogue with Trypho*, 40:1-3 (ANF 1)

Although, as a sheep He was led to the slaughter (Isa. 53:7; Acts 8:32), yet He was not a sheep; although as a lamb, speechless, yet neither was He a lamb for the model indeed existed, but then the reality appeared. For instead of the lamb there was a Son; and instead of the sheep, a Man; and in the Man, Christ, Who has comprised all things (Col. 1:17; Heb. 1:3).

Melito of Sardis, *On Pascha*, pp. 1-10, Introduction.

Use of a bunch of hyssop (Exod. 12:22)

"Then you shall take a bunch of hyssop, dip it in the blood in the basin, and strike the lintel and the two doorposts with the blood" (Exod. 12:22). Scholars cannot reach a definite view about that hyssop; however the traditional one is that it is the *Zaatar* plant. This plant was used, according to the holy Book, to purify from leprosy (Lev. 14:4,6) and from sin (Psa. 51:7), for ritual purification (Num. 19:6,8), and was also used to lift up a sponge filled with sour wine, and presented to the Lord Christ on the cross (Jn. 19:29). It is said that hyssop is an aromatic plant that grows on walls and rocks.

St. Augustine believes "that hyssop, although a weak and lowly weed, yet has deep and strong roots. It is as though it penetrates with its roots deep into love, "to comprehend with all the saints what is the width, length, depth, and height (of love)" (Eph. 3:17,18), and to recognize the Cross of our Lord." Through the blood, springing from the limitless love, we are sanctified, we destroy the leprosy of sin, receive healing from all of our sicknesses, our souls are purified, and we share with Christ His Passion on the Cross.

To eat it "roasted in fire" (Exod. 12:9)

The rite does not stop at the splattering of blood, but the believers should eat the flesh of the lamb, roasted in fire to unite with the Lord Christ, Who went through the divine justice, as through fire.

We should not stop at believing in the suffering Lord Christ, Who passed through fire for our sake, but we should also partake of the communion of His Body and Blood shed for us, so as to have the fellowship of His Passion, to recognize the power of His Resurrection, and to abide in Him and He in us.

St. Gregory, Bishop of Nyssa, believes that the food of Passover is "the hot and flaring faith." The Scholar Origen also says about it, "Let us have the hot Spirit, and get hold of the fiery words presented to us by God, as He did with the prophet Jeremiah, saying to him: 'Behold, I will make My words in your mouth fire' (Jer. 5:14). Let us make sure that the flesh of the lamb is well cooked, so that those who partake of it, would say with the two disciples of Emmaus, 'Did not our heart burn within us while He talked with us on the road, and while He opened the Scriptures to us?' (Lk. 24:32)."

It was the custom to roast the lamb on two crossing iron bars that symbolizes the cross. Thus, St. Justin Martyr says that the roasting was a symbol of the Cross by its shape.[28]

"Do not eat it raw, nor boiled at all with water" (Exod. 12:9)

He wants us to enjoy the divine Word, flaming with fire, and not to eat it raw nor boiled with water - not to receive it with a lukewarm attitude (like water), but with a hot spirit, serious in enjoying it. He wants us to receive faith through the cross and Passion, and not by a loosely spirit.

"Its head with its legs, and its entrails" (Exod. 12:9)

As we eat our new Passover, we enter into the head, the feet, and the entrails. We recognize the love of Christ, with the hope of comprehending its height (head), its depths (feet), and its width (entrails), and we shall find it surrounding us from all sides.

St. Hippolytus, the Roman, believes that the head is the Law that revealed the "secret of the Passover", the feet are the disciples, who preached peace on the mountains of Zion, while the entrails are the Passover itself that we came to know through the Law and the Bible.

"With unleavened bread" (Exod. 12:8)

The leaven refers to "malice and wickedness" (1 Cor. 5:7,8), and to hypocrisy. That is why St. Ambrose advises us, saying, "If people (the Jews)

---

[28] St. Justin, *Dialogue with Trypho*, 40:1-3 (ANF 1); reprinted in Cantalamessa, *Easter in the Early Church*, 40.

celebrated the feast of Passover by eating unleavened bread for seven days, every Christian is committed to eat of the body of the true lamb, Christ, and to lead a simple holy life all along the seven days, all the days of his life. Be careful to keep away of the old leaven, and do not remain in it, O brethren. According to the warning of the apostle, 'purge out the old leaven' (1 Cor. 5:7), that is to say, purify yourself of it. If you kept yourself away from all the evil, so called the old leaven, and fulfilled by faith all your resolutions when you were baptized, then you will be true Christians."

St. Athanasius, the apostolic, comments on the words of the apostle, "Let us keep the feast, not with old leaven, nor with the leaven of malice and wickedness, but with the unleavened bread of sincerity and truth" (1 Cor. 5:8)... 'that you put off, concerning your former conduct... that you put on the new man which was created according to God, in true righteousness and holiness' (Eph. 4:22, 24), with meditations from God's law day and night, with a humble mind and a pure conscience. Let us then, cast away from us every hypocrisy and deceit, get away from every pride and malice. Let us promise to love God and our neighbor to become a new creation... we would then be celebrating the feast as we should."

Some fathers like Origen believe that the old Passover was connected to the unleavened bread, so as to keep the believers from getting leavened by the leaven of the world anticipating the new leaven of the Kingdom of God (Matt. 13:33).

It is noteworthy that the Lord Christ, in the sacrament of the Eucharist, used leavened bread, as He carried our sins in His body.

"With bitter herb, they shall eat it" (Exod. 12:8)

St. Jerome believes that God forbid the use of honey in the offerings; yet, at the same time, commanded eating the lamb of Passover on bitter herb, as though He does not want us to lead a spoiled life, but bear the affliction in this world.

The bitter herb reminds the people of the bitterness of servitude, from which they are set free through the lamb of Passover.

The bitter herb refers to our commitment to approach the Sacrament of the new Passover, with bitterness of heart and spirit because of our sins. When our mouth is embittered, because of sin, our heart would get filled with the sweetness of the Lord's Body and Blood. In other words, we do not enjoy the sacrament of the Eucharist without repentance and confession.

"You shall let none of it remain until morning" (Exod. 12:9)

A reference to the sacrament of Passover was the secret of "the new life." Our Church is keen to let no divine Sacrament remain to the next day.

"Nor shall you break one of its bones" (Exod. 12:46)

This refers to the Lord Christ, who, "when they came to Jesus and saw that He was already dead, they did not break His legs" (Jn. 19:33). St. Hippolytus believes that, by this, we can recognize His Resurrection (Jn. 20: 27). He carried the marks of several wounds, but it was not fitting for Him to rise with broken legs.

As the bones of the Lord were not broken, it is fitting for us to receive the "Word of God," that we eat, enflamed with fire, yet without breaking its bones - to understand it, not in a killing human literal way, but through the constructive Spirit.

And as the bones of the Passover are not broken, so also, the righteous, united with the Lord Christ, their Passover, will have their bones unbroken, as King David the Psalmist said, "He guards all their bones; not one of them is broken" (Psa. 34:20). And as St. Augustine says, "The Psalmist does not mean the bones in the literal sense, but the unbreakable living faith, as we see from the incident of the right-hand robber, who although his feet bones were broken, yet the bones of his soul were kept by the Lord. In the moments of bitter affliction, he abided in the faith to be worthy to enter paradise, to be kept in the hands of God."

They will eat, ready to depart (Exod. 12:11)

"Thus you shall eat it: with a belt on your waist, your sandals on your feet, and your staff in your hand. So you shall eat it in haste; It is the Lord's Passover" (Exod. 12:11).

St. John Chrysostom says that this phrase has two interpretations:

1) A historical interpretation: to let the Jews take into consideration that they are going to depart; as though by so doing, they say, "We are ready to depart; we are going out of Egypt to the land of promise; we are departing." As those people were known for their forgetfulness, He gave them that commandment to remind them of the goal of the Passover.

2) A symbolic interpretation: saying, "For indeed, Christ, our Passover, was sacrificed for us" (1 Cor. 5:7)...We should eat it "with a belt on our waist, and sandals on our feet."

Why? So we also may be ready to depart and rest. I wish everyone eats this Passover without looking down to Egypt (the world), but up to heaven, to the higher Jerusalem. Bracing with a belt is an indication of the departure of the soul. Listen to what God says to a righteous man: "Brace yourself like a man; I will question you, and you shall answer Me" (Job 38:3). That is what He also said to all prophets, and to Moses. The Lord Himself appeared in a similar way to Ezekiel, and the angels, being soldiers, appear likewise (Rev. 15:6). Let us then brace ourselves and courageously stand. We should have no fear, because the Leader of our exodus is Jesus and not Moses!

They were therefore, eating it, ready to depart and to pass over from the land of bondage, heading to the land of promise; ready by their bodies (the belt), their hands (the staff), and their feet (the sandals). That is the same concept of getting ready to partake of the sacrament of the Eucharist; in having it, we yearn to pass over to where the Lord Christ is sitting.

The belted waist refers to controlling the body lusts, so man could walk, not according to the desires of his body, but to those of the heavenly Spirit. That is why John Cassian, speaking of, why a monk braces his waist with a belt, he says, "So that the soldier of Christ, will have his mind ready to carry out any work in the monastery; to have his movement unhindered by his clothes, and to comprehend that, using a belt made out of dead animal skin, implies his putting to death all his members, that contains the seeds of fornication and uncleanness, and in order to abide all the time in the commandments of the Bible, saying, 'Therefore put to death your members which are on the earth: fornication, uncleanness, passion, evil desire, and covetousness, which is idolatry'" (Col. 3:5).

The sandals on the feet refer to what happened with the prophet Moses, when he took off his sandals, made out of dead animal skin, in order to be able to enjoy the burning bush. But here, we put on sandals of a different kind, that of the Lord, of which St. John, the Baptist said that he is not worthy to bow and loosen its straps. Therefore, let us have the sandals of the Lord, so that, as He walked, we do likewise, not fearing the thorns of this life, nor the violence and authority of Pharaoh, but to trample over all the forces of evil under our feet. And as St. Ambrose says, "Whoever celebrates the Passover of the Lord, and the Lamb, should have his feet protected against the fierce spiritual beasts, and the stings of the serpent."

The staff in our hands is the rod of God, also called the rod of Moses, and the rod of Aaron. We lean on the power of God for salvation (the Cross), hold the rod of commandment (Moses), and practice the spiritual worship (Aaron). Some Church Fathers see in the staff, the hope on which the soul leans, on her way to heaven, to cast away the destructive threats of the devil, as a traveler does to chase away dogs with his staff.

Finally, St. Athanasius, the apostolic, speaks of the readiness to that trip, saying, "Our Lord Jesus Christ is the true light, who is our royal staff, and in place of the unleavened bread, is the Bread descending from heaven. And in short, the Lord leads us, by all that, to His Father."

As to eating it in haste (Exod. 12:11), St. Hippolytus says, "Whoever approaches that great and exalted Body, should be watching and fasting;" he should be ready to set forth.

"You shall keep it as a feast to the Lord throughout your generations" (Exod. 12:14)

As a confirmation of the eternal Passover and also, so that the old people would remain anticipating for the coming of the true Passover, Whose Blood will be forever sanctified.

"No outsider shall eat it" (Exod. 12:43,48)

No uncircumcised should partake of it, only the circumcised. Therefore, nobody can enjoy communion of the holy sacraments, except he who gained the spiritual circumcision, the Baptism by which he became a son to God, having the right to unite with Him in Christ Jesus.

In his fourth homily on the Resurrection, St. Athanasius, the apostolic, says, "The deceitful person, with impure heart, and defiled soul... is surely a foreigner to the saints, and counted unworthy of eating the Passover. For this reason, when Judas assumed that he could keep the Passover while plotting a deceit against the Savior, he turned as a foreigner to the city up high and a stranger to the apostolic company. The Law commanded that the Passover should be eaten with fitting caution, yet Judas, while eating it, the devil entered his soul (Jn. 13:27)."

"It is the Lord's Passover" (Exod. 12:11)

The Holy Book differentiates between the "Lord's Passover", and the "Jews' Passover." In the Law, He does not say "Your Passover" or "The Jews' Passover", but He says "The Lord's Passover" in reference to Himself. But when the people fell to evil, and lived without repentance, He refers it to them, saying: "The new moons, the Sabbaths, and the calling of assemblies - I cannot endure... your new moons and your appointed feasts My soul hates" (Isa. 1:13,14)

The Scholar Origen noticed that this thing happens with all sorts of worship, calling the Sabbath, "the Lord's Sabbath"; and in the Book of Numbers, He says: "My gifts, My presents, My burnt offerings, you shall take care to offer Me as a sweet aroma in My feasts" (Num. 28:1). He also calls the people "My people"; yet when they deviated from worshipping Him, He said to Moses: "'Go, quickly! Get down from here! For your people whom you brought out of the land of Egypt are transgressing the law'" (Exod. 32:7).

It is no longer the people of God, but that of Moses.

Killing the firstborn

The Scholar Tertullian believes that the Egyptians have paid the price of what they have done to the Hebrew children by throwing them in the rive; the Lord punished them by their own deeds.

God allowed all the firstborns to be killed, even those of the beasts with no exception. That is a symbol of God's work in devastating evil. Yet His children, even the hairs of their heads are counted and under His care.

St. Gregory, Bishop of Nyssa, sees in killing of the firstborns as a reference to the destruction of every cause of sin, saying, "It is fitting for whoever seizes evil through virtue, to destroy it since its onset. By this he destroys everything that would follow. That is what the Lord teaches us in the Bible, inviting us, very clearly, to kill the firstborns of evil... instructing us to destroy lust and anger, and not to be afraid before the sins of adultery and murder. Those two do not come all of a sudden, but the anger produces murder, and the lust gives birth to adultery... thus by destroying the firstborns (lust and anger), we kill all that would follow. If we take the serpent as an example, by crushing its head, all of its body would be killed at the same time."

"REQUIREMENTS OF THE PASSOVER FULFILLED"
St. Gregory Nazianzen[29]

Now we will partake of a Passover which is still typical; though it is plainer than the old one. For that is ever new which is now becoming known. It is ours to learn what is that drinking and that enjoyment, and His to teach and

---

[29] St. Gregory Nazianzen, *Second Oration* (NPNF 2:8).

communicate the Word to His disciples. For teaching is food, even to the Giver of food. Come here then, and let us partake of the Law, but in a Gospel manner, not a literal one; perfectly, not imperfectly; eternally, not temporarily. Let us make our Head, not the earthly Jerusalem, but the heavenly City; not that which is now trodden under foot by armies, but that which is glorified by Angels. Let us sacrifice not young calves, nor lambs that put forth horns and hoofs, in which many parts are destitute of life and feeling; but let us sacrifice to God the sacrifice of praise upon the heavenly Altar, with the heavenly dances; let us hold aside the first veil; let us approach the second, and look into the Holy of Holies. Shall I say that which is a greater thing yet? Let us sacrifice ourselves to God; or rather let us go on sacrificing throughout every day and at every moment. Let us accept anything for the Word's sake. By sufferings let us imitate His Passion, by our blood let us reverence His Blood; let us gladly mount upon the Cross. Sweet are the nails, though they be very painful. For to suffer with Christ and for Christ is better than a life of ease with others...

Thus then and for this cause the written Law came in, gathering us into Christ; and this is the account of the Sacrifices as I account for them. And that you may not be ignorant of the depth of His Wisdom and the riches of His unsearchable judgments, He did not leave even these unhallowed altogether, or useless, or with nothing in them but mere blood. But that great, and if I may say so, in its first nature **unsacrificeable Victim,** was intermingled with the Sacrifices of the Law, and was a purification, not for a part of the world, nor for a short time, but for the whole world and for all time. For this reason a Lamb was chosen for its innocence, and its clothing of the original nakedness. For such is the Victim, Who was offered for us, Who is both in Name and fact the Garment of incorruption. And He was a **perfect** Victim not only on account of His Godhead, than which nothing is more perfect; but also on account of that which He assumed having been anointed with Deity, and having become one with That which anointed It, and I am bold to say, made equal with God.

A **male,** because offered for Adam; or rather the Stronger for the strong, when the first Man had fallen under sin; and chiefly because there is in Him nothing feminine, nothing unmanly; but He burst from the bonds of the Virgin-Mother's womb with much power, and a Male was brought forth by the Prophetess, as Isaiah declares the good tidings.

And of **a year old,** because He is the Sun of Righteousness setting out from heaven, and circumscribed by His visible Nature, and returning unto Himself. And "The blessed crown of Goodness,"—being on every side equal to Himself and alike; and not only this, but also as giving life to all the circle of the virtues, gently commingled and intermixed with each other, according to the Law of Love and Order. And Immaculate and guileless, as being the Healer of faults, and of the defects and taints that come from sin. For though He both took on Him our sins and bare our diseases, yet He did not Himself suffer anything that needed healing. For He was tempted in all points like as we are yet without sin for he who persecuted the Light that shines in darkness could not overtake Him.

What more? The **First Month** is introduced, or rather the beginning of months, whether it was so among the Hebrews from the beginning, or was made so later on this account, and became the first in consequence of the Mystery; and the tenth of the Month, for this is the most complete number, of units the first perfect unit, and the parent of perfection. And it is kept until the fifth day, perhaps because the Victim, of Whom I am speaking, purifies the five senses, from which comes falling into sin, and around which the war rages, inasmuch as they are open to the incitements to sin. And it was chosen, not only out of the lambs, but also out of the inferior species, which are placed on the left hand —the kids; because He is sacrificed not only for the righteous, but also for sinners; and perhaps even more for these, inasmuch as we have greater need of His mercy. And we need not be surprised that a lamb for a house should be required as the best course, but if that could not be, then one might be obtained by contributions (owing to poverty) for the houses of a family; because it is clearly best that each individual should suffice for His own perfecting, and should offer His own living sacrifice holy unto God Who called him, being consecrated at all times and in every respect. But if that cannot be, then that those who are akin in virtue and of like disposition should be made use of as helpers. For I think this provision means that we should communicate of the Sacrifice to those who are nearest, if there be need.

Then comes the **Sacred Night**, the Anniversary of the confused darkness of the present life, into which the primeval darkness is dissolved, and all things come into life and rank and form, and that which was chaos is reduced to order. Then we flee from Egypt, that is from sullen persecuting sin; and from Pharaoh the unseen tyrant, and the bitter taskmasters, changing our quarters to the world above; and are delivered from the clay and the brick-making, and from the husks and dangers of this fleshly condition, which for most men is only not overpowered by mere pretentious calculations.

Then the Lamb is slain, and act and word are sealed with the Precious Blood; that is, habit and action, the side-posts of our doors; I mean, of course, of the movements of mind and opinion, which are rightly opened and closed by contemplation, since there is a limit even to thoughts. Then the last and gravest plague upon the persecutors, truly worthy of the night; and Egypt mourns the first-born of her own reasonings and actions which are also called in the Scripture the Seed of the Chaldeans removed, and the children of Babylon dashed against the rocks and destroyed; and the whole air is full of the cry and clamor of the Egyptians; and then the Destroyer of them shall withdraw from us in reverence of the Unction. Then the removal of leaven; that is, of the old and sour wickedness, not of that which is quickening and makes bread; for seven days, a number which is of all the most mystical, and is coordinate with this present world, that we may not lay in provision of any Egyptian dough, or relic of Pharisaic or ungodly teaching.

Well, let them lament; we will feed on the Lamb toward evening—for Christ's Passion was in the completion of the ages; because He too communed His Disciples in the evening with His Sacrament, destroying the darkness of sin; and not soaked, but **roast**—that our word may have in it nothing that is unconsidered or watery, or easily made away with; but may be entirely consistent and solid, and free from all that is impure and from all vanity.

And let us be aided by the good **coals**, kindling and purifying our minds from Him Who comes to send fire on the earth, Who shall destroy all evil habits, and to hasten its kindling. Whatever then there be, of solid and nourishing in the Word, shall be eaten with the inward parts and hidden things of the mind, and shall be consumed and given up to spiritual digestion; yes, from head to foot, that is, from the first contemplations of Godhead to the very last thoughts about the Incarnation. Neither let us carry none of it abroad, **nor leave it till the morning;** because most of our Mysteries may not be carried out to them that are outside, nor is there beyond this night any further purification; and procrastination is not creditable to those who have a share in the Word. For just as it is good and well-pleasing to God not to let anger last through the day, but to get rid of it before sunset, whether you take this of time or in a mystical sense, for it is not safe for us that the Sun of Righteousness should go down upon our wrath; so too we should not to let such Food remain all night, nor to put it off till to-morrow.

But whatever is of bony nature and not fit for food and hard for us even to understand, this must not be broken; that is, badly divined and misconceived (I need not say that in the History not a bone of Jesus was broken, even though **His death was hastened by His crucifiers** on account of the Sabbath); nor must it be **stripped off and thrown away**, lest that which is holy should be given to the dogs, that is, to the evil hearers of the Word; just as the glorious pearl of the Word is not to be cast before swine; but it shall be consumed with the fire with which the burnt offerings also are consumed, being refined and preserved by the Spirit Who searches and knows all things, not destroyed in the waters, nor scattered abroad as the calf's head which was hastily made by Israel was by Moses, for a reproach for their hardness of heart.

Nor would it be right for us to pass over the manner of this eating either, for the Law does not do so, but carries its mystical labor even to this point in the literal enactment. Let us consume the Victim in haste, eating It with unleavened bread, with **bitter herbs,** and with our loins girded, and our shoes on our feet, and leaning on staves like old men; with haste, that we fall not into that fault which was forbidden to Lot by the commandment, that we look not around, nor stay in all that neighborhood, but that we escape to the mountain, that we be not overtaken by the strange fire of Sodom, nor be congealed into a pillar of salt in consequence of our turning back to wickedness; for this is the result of delay.

With bitter herbs, for a life according to the Will of God is bitter and arduous, especially to beginners, and higher than pleasures. For although the new yoke is easy and the burden light, as you are told, yet this is on account of the hope and the reward, which is far more abundant than the hardships of this life. If it were not so, who would not say that the Gospel is more full of toil and trouble than the enactments of the Law? For, while the Law prohibits only the completed acts of sin, we are condemned for the causes also, almost as if they were acts. The Law says, "You will not commit adultery;" but you may not even desire, kindling passion by curious and earnest looks. "You shalt not kill," says the Law; but you are not even to return a blow, but on the contrary are to offer yourself to the smiter. How much more ascetic is the Gospel than the Law! "You shalt not forswear yourself" is the Law; but you are not to swear at all, either a greater or a lesser oath, for an oath is the parent of perjury. "You will not join house to house, nor field to field, oppressing the poor;" but you are to set aside willingly even your just possessions, and to be stripped for the poor, that without encumbrance you may take up the Cross and be enriched with the unseen riches.

And let the **loins** of the unreasoning animals be unbound and loose, for they have not the gift of reason which can overcome pleasure (it is not needful to say that even they know the limit of natural movement). But let that part of your being which is the seat of passion, and which cries, as Holy Scripture calls it, when sweeping away this shameful passion, be restrained by a girdle of continence, so that you may eat the Passover purely, **having mortified your members** which are upon the earth, and copying the girdle of John, the Hermit and Forerunner and great Herald of the Truth...

And it is in respect of this too that God says in an oracle to Job, "No, but gird up your loins like a man, and give a manly answer." With this also holy David boasts that he is girded with strength from God, and speaks of God Himself as clothed with strength and girded about with power—against the ungodly of course—though perhaps some may prefer to see in this a declaration of the abundance of His power, and, as it were, its restraint, just as also He clothes Himself with Light as with a garment. For who shall endure His unrestrained power and light? Do I enquire what there is common to the loins and to truth? What then is the meaning to St. Paul of the expression, "Stand, therefore, having your loins girt about with truth?" Is it perhaps that contemplation is to restrain evil desire, and not to allow it to be carried in another direction? For that which is disposed to love in a particular direction will not have the same power towards other pleasures.

And as to **shoes**, let him who is about to touch the Holy Land which the feet of God have trodden, put them off, as Moses did upon the Mount, that he may bring there nothing dead; nothing to come between Man and God. So too if any disciple is sent to preach the Gospel, let him go in a spirit of philosophy and without excess, inasmuch as he must, besides being without money and without staff and with but one coat, also be barefooted, that the feet of those who preach the Gospel of Peace and every other good may appear beautiful. But he who would flee from Egypt and the things of Egypt must put on shoes for safety's sake, especially in regard to the scorpions and snakes in which Egypt so abounds, so as not to be injured by those which watch the heel which also we are bidden to tread under foot....

And concerning the staff and the signification of it, my belief is as follows. There is one I know to lean upon, and another which belongs to Pastors and Teachers, and which corrects human sheep. Now the Law prescribes to you the staff to lean upon, that you may not break down in your mind when you hear of God's Blood, and His Passion, and His death; and that you may not be carried away to heresy in your defense of God; but without shame and without doubt may eat the Flesh and drink the Blood, if you are desirous of true life, neither disbelieving His words about His Flesh, nor offended at those about His Passion. Lean upon this, and stand firm and strong, in nothing shaken by the adversaries nor carried away by the plausibility of their arguments. Stand upon your High Place; in the Courts of Jerusalem place your feet; lean upon the Rock, that your steps in God be not shaken.

HOMILY OF ST. ATHANASIUS
THE APOSTOLIC[30]

It is so written in the Scriptures, "If our souls are following the law of God, the powers of darkness will not overpower us, but if we drift away from God they will prevail on us." It is said again, "You O man, who wants to be saved, teach yourself to swim in the depth of the richness and wisdom of God" (cf. Rom. 11:33).

Spread your arms in the likeness of the Cross to traverse a great sea, which is this age, that you may come to God.

The hindering doubts are for those who live away from the Catholic Church, questioning outside the faith, which are these: fornication, detraction (slander), and love of money that is the root of all evils (1 Tim. 6:10).

But the sign of the Cross is spread over all creation. If the sun could not emit its rays it would not be able to illuminate, neither the moon. Likewise, the birds in the sky, if they do not spread their wings they cannot fly, and if the ships could not spread their sails, they would not sail.

Behold, Moses the Archprophet spread his arms and defeated Amalek. Daniel was saved form the lion's den, Jonah from the fish's belly and Thekla when they threw her to the lions she was saved by the likeness of the Cross. Also Susanna from the hands of those two old men, Judith from Holofernes and the Three Holy Youth from the burning fiery furnace. All those were saved by the likeness of the Cross.

Again it is said, "May Your place of habitation be in one place," which is this, the Church, receiving nourishment from the words of Scripture and the Heavenly Bread and the Blood of Christ, strengthening yourself at all times with the words of Scripture.

PSALM 142:6,7; 30:5

I spread forth my hands to You; my soul thirsts for You, as a dry land. Hear me speedily, O Lord; my spirit has failed; do not turn away Your face from me, lest I shall be like them that go down to the pit.

---

[30] Homily 21, MS Copte 70 Bibl. nat. fol. 255r-256r.

Into Your hands, will I commit my spirit. You have redeemed me, O Lord, God of Truth.

Again here we see the cry of the thirsty for water. St. Augustine says that the Lord stretching out His hands to us is like the rain from heaven to plant fruit. "For the Lord shall give sweetness, that our land may give her fruit." "I have stretched forth my hands to You; my soul is as a land without water," not to me, but "to You." I can thirst for You, I cannot water myself." St. John Chrysostom also likens this psalm to the eclipse of the sun which we also read in this hour.[31]

"Hear me speedily, O Lord." For what need of delay to inflame my thirst, when I already thirst so eagerly? You did delay the rain, that I might drink and swallow, [and] not to reject Your entrance. If then You did for this cause delay, now give; for "my spirit has failed." Let Your Spirit fill me. This is the reason why You should speedily hear me. I am now become "poor in spirit," make me "blessed in the Kingdom of Heaven.''...

St. Augustine, *Commentary on Psalms* (143:7-9) (NPNF 2:8)

Psalm 30:5 is the last utterance of our dying Savior (Lk. 23:46) and is sacred to every believer. It is a great help and support for him in the hour of his death. This simple and proof of his trust, by virtue of which he entrusts his whole life into the hands of his God, sounds like the utterance of a man who breathes a sigh of relief as he reaches the protection of the walls of the fortress after a hard battle and is conscious of being now out of danger.

Fr. Tadros Malaty, *Patristic Commentary on the Psalms*

MATTHEW 27:51-56

Then, behold, the veil of the temple was torn in two from top to bottom; and the earth quaked, and the rocks were split, and the graves were opened; and many bodies of the saints who had fallen asleep were raised; and coming out of the graves after His resurrection, they went into the holy city and appeared to many. So when the centurion and those with him, who were guarding Jesus, saw the earthquake and the things that had happened, they feared greatly, saying, "Truly this was the Son of God!" And many women who followed Jesus from Galilee, ministering to Him, were there looking on from afar, among whom were Mary Magdalene, Mary the mother of James and Joses, and the mother of Zebedee's sons.

---

[31] St. John Chrysostom, *Commentary on the Psalms*, trans. Robert Charles Hill, ed. v. 2, p. 315.

MARK 15:38-41

Then the veil of the temple was torn in two from top to bottom. So when the centurion, who stood opposite Him, saw that He cried out like this and breathed His last, he said, "Truly this Man was the Son of God!" There were also women looking on from afar, among whom were Mary Magdalene, Mary the mother of James the Less and of Joses, and Salome, who also followed Him and ministered to Him when He was in Galilee, and many other women who came up with Him to Jerusalem.

LUKE 23:47-49

So when the centurion saw what had happened, he glorified God, saying, "Certainly this was a righteous Man!" And the whole crowd who came together to that sight, seeing what had been done, beat their breasts and returned. But all His acquaintances, and the women who followed Him from Galilee, stood at a distance, watching these things.

JOHN 19:31-37

Therefore, because it was the Preparation Day, that the bodies should not remain on the cross on the Sabbath (for that Sabbath was a high day), the Jews asked Pilate that their legs might be broken, and that they might be taken away. Then the soldiers came and broke the legs of the first and of the other who was crucified with Him. But when they came to Jesus and saw that He was already dead, they did not break His legs. But one of the soldiers pierced His side with a spear, and immediately blood and water came out. And he who has seen has testified, and his testimony is true; and he knows that he is telling the truth, so that you may believe. For these things were done that the Scripture should be fulfilled, "Not one of His bones shall be broken." And again another Scripture says, "They shall look on Him whom they pierced."

The Veil of the Temple

Anyone who searches the scriptures with some diligence will see that there were two curtains, an inner curtain which covered the Holy of Holies and another curtain exterior to either the tabernacle or the temple. These two curtains are figures of the holy tabernacle which the Father prepared from the beginning (Exod. 25:9,40). Of these two curtains, one was "torn in two parts from the top all the way to the bottom." This happened at the time when Jesus "cried out with a loud voice and gave up His Spirit." (Mat. 27:50)

By this the divine mystery was revealed that in the Passion of the Lord our Savior, the outer curtain was torn from the top, which represents the beginning of the world. Thus by tearing of the curtain the mysteries were disclosed, which with good reason had been hidden until the coming of Christ. Both the outer curtain and the inner curtain would have been torn if it had not been the case that we still know only "in part" (1 Cor. 13:9) and if it had not been the case that everything were already revealed to the beloved disciples of Christ who constitute His Body.

As it is, however, because we are being brought gradually to the knowledge of new things, only the outer curtain is "torn from top to bottom." But when the perfect comes (1 Cor. 13:10) and the other things which now remain hidden are revealed then the second curtain may also be removed. We will then see even the things which were hidden within the second curtain: the true ark of the covenant, the cherubim, the true mercy seat and the storehouse of manna in a golden bowl, and all of these clearly (Heb. 9:35)—and even things greater than these. All of this has been revealed through the law of Moses when God said to him, "Make them according to the pattern shown unto you on the mountain" (Exod. 25:40).

The Scholar Origen, *Commentary on Matthew*, 138 (AACS, 1b, p. 296)

The veil is torn. This declared the division of the two peoples or the profanation of the mysteries of the synagogue. The old veil is torn so that the Church may hang the new veils of its faith. The veil of the synagogue is taken away, so that we may see the inner mysteries of religion with unveiled eyes of the mind (2 Cor. 3:14). Even the centurion confesses the Son of God Whom he had crucified.

St. Ambrose of Milan, *Exposition of the Gospel of Luke*, 10.128 (AACS 3, p. 368)

He surrenders His life, yet He has power to take it again (Jn. 10:17-18). Yes, the veil is torn, for things of heaven are being revealed, rocks split, and dead men have an earlier awakening.

St. Gregory Nazianzen, *Oration 29*: On the Son, 20 (AACS 3, p. 235)

Perhaps the Spirit, when He saw the Son hanging naked, lifted Himself up [from its dwelling in the Holies of holies] and tore in two the clothing.

Perhaps the symbols when they saw the Lamb of symbols, tore the curtain apart and went out to meet Him.

Perhaps the spirit of prophesy, which was dwelling in the temple and had come down to herald His coming to humanity, flew away at that very instant to announce in the heights concerning our Lord's ascent into heaven.

"The rocks split apart" (Matt. 27:51) so that He might show that He could have torn the wood of the Cross apart. He did not tear apart the Cross through which the Kingdom would be torn from Israel. He did not shatter the Cross through which sin would be chased out from the middle of the Gentiles. Instead, the Spirit tore the curtain apart. To show that the Sprit had come out from the temple, it summoned the righteous that came out of the tombs (Matt. 27:52-53) as a witness to His going out from the temple. These two departures were proclaiming each other mutually. The Spirit anointed and sacrificed the kingship and the priesthood. The Spirit, wellspring of these two offices...

The curtain was torn. [This was] to show that [the Lord] had taken the kingdom away from them and had given it to others who would bear fruit (Matt. 21:43).

An alternative explanation is by the analogy of the torn curtain, the temple would be destroyed because His Spirit had gone away from it. Since the high priest had torn his robe, the Spirit tore the curtain to proclaim the audacity of the pride [of the Jews], by means of an action on the level of created beings. Because [the high priest] had torn his priesthood and had cast it from him, [the Spirit] also split the curtain apart (Matt. 27:51).

Or [alternatively], just as the temple in which Judas had thrown the gold (Matt. 27:5) was dissolved and rejected, so too [the Lord] pulled down and rent asunder the curtain of the door through which [Judas] had entered.

Or, [it was] because they had stripped Him of His garments that He rent the curtain in two. For the heart of the rock was burst asunder (Matt. 27:51) but their own hearts did not repent.

St. Ephrem the Syrian, *CTD* 21.6 (AACS 3, p. 369; AACS 1b, p. 235)

The earth shook, the rocks split, and the graves were opened

Many indeed are the miracles of that time: God crucified; the sun darkened and again rekindled; for it was fitting that the creatures should suffer with their Creator; the veil rent; the Blood and Water shed from His Side; the one as from a man, the other as above man; the rocks rent for the Rock's sake; the dead raised for a pledge of the final Resurrection of all men; the Signs at the Sepulcher and after the Sepulcher, which none can worthily celebrate; and yet none of these equal to the Miracle of my salvation. A few drops of Blood recreate the whole world, and become to all men what rennet is to milk, drawing us together and compressing us into unity.

St. Gregory Nazianzen, *On the Holy Pascha*, Oration 45.1 (NPNF 2:8)

And the earth shook, that is, all flesh trembled when the new word, the realities of the new covenant, the new song and all new heavenly things came upon them. This is what the prophet wrote concerning this very event, "All [namely, the disciples of Christ] who saw these things trembled and everyone was afraid" (Psa. 63:9).

The Scholar Origen, *Commentary on Matthew*, 139 (AACS 1b, p. 297)

The literal meaning of the great signs is undoubtedly that both heaven and earth and all things within them wished to acclaim their crucified Lord. It seems to me, however, that the trembling earth and other signs also represent a type of believers, namely, those who once were comparable to a graveyard but who, having abandoned the errors of their former ways and having softened their stony hearts, have come to acknowledge the Creator.

St. Jerome, *Commentary on Matthew*, 4.27.51 (AACS 1b, p. 297)

The earth shook. For the earth could not hold this dead Man. The rocks split for the Word of God and the power of His eternal goodness rushed in, penetrating every stronghold and principality. Graves were opened, for the gates of death had been unlocked. And a number of the bodies of the saints who had fallen asleep arose. Dispelling the shadows of death and illuminating the darkness of hell, Christ destroyed the spoils of death itself at the resurrection of the saints, who saw Him immediately. The centurion and the guards who witnessed this disturbance of the entire natural order confessed Him to be the Son of God.

St. Hilary of Poitiers, *Commentary on Matthew*, 23.7 (AACS 1b, 297)

The person who crucified the Author of his salvation and afterward did not beg for forgiveness is not free from sin. Granted, he did not know previously Whom he was persecuting. Nevertheless, he should have recognized that the One placed on the Cross was the Lord of all the elements. All the elements trembled beneath Him. The sky was darkened. The sun fled away. The earth split apart. The tombs of the dead lay open, and the dead regained the company of the living. For this reason also the centurion said, "truly this man was the Son of God." The centurion recognizes a stranger, but the Levite does not know his own. The Gentile worship Him, but the Hebrew denies Him. It was reasonable that the pillars of the world be moved when the chief priests did not believe.

St. Ambrose, *The Prayer of Job and David*, 1.5.13 (FC 65, p. 336; AACS 2, p. 369)

The Women Served Him

Certain women were notably present as these things occurred. They were most inclined to feel for Him, to grieve over His sufferings. See how great their dedication is! They had followed Him ministering to Him, wherever He went—even in time of great dangers. They had witnessed all these events—how He wept, how He yielded up His Spirit, how the rocks were split, and all the rest.

The women were first to see Jesus at His death and burial. The gender that is most likely to be ridiculed was first to enjoy the sight of His resurrected blessings. They most steadily showed their courage. Even when the disciples had fled in the darkness, these women were still present.

Among these women was His mother, for she is called Mary.... But another evangelist said, that many also lamented over the things that were done. They beat their breasts, which above all shows the cruelty of the Jews, for that they gloried in things for which others were lamenting, and were neither moved by pity, nor checked by fear. For indeed the things that were done were of great wrath, and were not merely signs, but signs of anger all of them—the darkness, the cloven rocks, the veil rent in the midst, the shaking of the earth, and great was the excess of the indignation....

Let us men imitate the women; let us not forsake Jesus in temptations. For they for Him even spent so much and exposed their lives, but we (for again I say the same things) neither feed Him when hungry, nor clothe Him when naked, but seeing Him begging, we pass Him by.

Yet, if you saw Himself, everyone would strip himself of all his goods. But even now it is the same. For He Himself has said, I am He. Why then do you not strip yourself of everything? For indeed even now you have heard Him say, "You have done it for Me;" and there is no difference whether you give to this [poor] man or to Him; you have nothing less than these women that then fed Him, but even much more...

St. John Chrysostom, *Commentary on Matthew*, Homily 88.2 (NPNF 2:10, p. 522)

Women attended to the food and clothing of their masters from their own possessions. This was according to Jewish custom. This practice did not proceed from Gentile law and even could have been a scandal among the Gentiles. Paul himself mentioned that he was unable to continue this custom, "Do we have no right to take along a believing wife, as do also the other apostles, the brothers of the Lord, and Cephas?" (1 Cor. 9:5). These women waited on the Lord out of their own resources. He reaped from their physical support as they benefited from His spiritual blessing. It was not because the Lord of all creatures was out of necessity looking for food, but rather that He might present a model of teaching and discipleship for them. Note carefully, though what sort of attendants He had: Mary Magdalene from whom He cast out seven demons. Mary the mother of James and Joseph, and her own aunt, the sister of Mary, the mother of the Lord. The mother of Zebedee's sons, a woman who had sought the kingdom for her children. And there were other women present.

> St. Jerome, *Commentary on Matthew*, 4.27.55 (AACS 1b, p. 298)

Isaiah is said to have prophesied concerning these women when he wrote, "Women are coming to the spectacle for this is not a wise people" (Is. 27:11). He calls women who had been distant and were looking upon Jesus from afar. He calls them to the Word, that they might abandon a foolish, forsaken people and come to the New Covenant. I consider these women blessed who were elevated to beatitude their vision by the Word and by the bodily death of Jesus; for everything in Christ, if seen truly, beautifies the beholder.

> The Scholar Origen, *Commentary on Matthew*, 141 (ACCS 1b, p. 298)

The Blood and Water

He caused the fountain of remission to spring forth for us out of His holy and immaculate side water for our regeneration, and the washing away of sin and corruption; and blood to drink as the hostage of life eternal.

> John of Damascus, *Exposition*, 4.9 (NPNF 2:9, p. 78)

Eve was created only when Adam slept; just as the Church was created when the Lord slept on the Cross.

> St. Augustine, *Commentary on Genesis*, FC

Would you like to know how the Church is built up from water and blood? First, through the baptism of water, sins are forgiven; then the blood of martyrs crowns the edifice.

> St. Jerome, Homily 66 (AACS 1 p. 71)

As His earthly course began with water, so it ended with it. His side is pierced by the spear, and blood and water flow forth, twin emblems of baptism and martyrdom.

> St. Jerome, *Letter 69 to Oceanus*, 6 (NPNF 2:6, p. 146)

The Lord was wounded in His Passion, and from that wound there went forth blood and water...water for washing, blood for drink, the spirit for His rising again. For Christ alone is to us hope, faith and love—hope is His resurrection, faith in the laver, and love in the Sacrament.

St. Ambrose of Milan, *Concerning Virgins*, 3.5.22 (NPNF 2:10, p. 385)

"Blood and water came out" –not simply without a purpose, or by chance, did those fonts come forth, but because by means of these two together the Church consists. And the indicated in the Mysteries know it, being by water indeed regenerated [in Baptism], and nourished by the blood and the flesh [in the Eucharist]. Hence the Mysteries take their beginning; that when you approach to that fearful Cup, you may approach as drinking from His very side.

St. John Chrysostom, *Homily 85* (PG 59:507; ONT, p. 547)

Twelfth Hour: "Burial"

Lam. 3:1-66; Jonah 1:10-2:7; Psa. 87:4, 22:3. 44:9, 11

Matt. 27:57-61, Mk. 15:42-16:1; Lk. 23:50-56; Jn. 19:38-42

Overview

"God descended, He was humbled for us so that we may ascend in safety and in confidence."

St. Jerome[32]

After the death of one crucified, it was customary for the Romans to leave their bodies on the crosses until the birds or beasts of the desert could eat them. The Jews, on the other hand, used to throw those bodies killed in a pit called the *Hannoum* valley, which means "Hell." The body of Jesus would have been thrown with the two thieves, but Joseph of Arimathea requested the Body from Pilate and took It with the help of Nicodemus, who was a member of the Sanhedrin.[33] We commemorate the burial of our Lord one hour after taking His Body from the Cross—for it took some time to acquire the approval of the Sanhedrin, prepare the tomb, gather the spices, and cleanse the Body for burial.

Although the Israelites had never practiced embalming, the more affluent made greater preparations for burial. They wrapped the body in long strips of linen and treated it with a mixture of spices. When they finished, the body looked somewhat like a mummy. This is how Nicodemus and Joseph of Arimathea prepared the body of Jesus (Jn. 19:39–40).[34] He came bringing a mixture of about 100 pounds of myrrh and aloes, fulfilling the prophesy in Isaiah that they would make "His grave...with the rich at His death" (Isa. 53:9).[35]

Burial normally took place the same day, since the hot climate brought quick decomposition and offensive odors. Wealthier families buried their beloved ones in either natural or man-made caves in the hillsides of Palestine, often times on their own estates. Joseph of Arimathea had cut the

---

[32] St. Jerome, *Commentary on the Psalms*, Homily 41 (FC 57).
[33] Fr. Pishoy Kamel, *JTG*, 73.
[34] Howard F. Vos, *Nelson's New Illustrated Bible Manners and Customs* (Nelson, 1999).
[35] *Ibid.*

tomb in which Jesus was put (Matt. 27:60), no doubt planning it for himself or his family.[36]

The First Old Testament Reading is from **Lamentation,** where the prophet speaks of the pains and sufferings of our Lord inside the tomb. We all await His resurrection.

The second reading is from the first book of **Jonah,** a well-known symbol of the Lord's burial and resurrection.

Two **Psalms** are then chanted, both relating to the pit of Hades and His death on the Cross. This is chanted in the most beautiful hymn of *Pekethronos* (mentioned several times above).

The **Gospels** then explain the burial of our Lord.

Church Tradition and Rites

The priest covers the icon with a white linen cloth and places the cross over it. He then covers them with rose petals and spices, as remembrance of the Hebrew burial tradition. He places two candles on each side of it—representing the two angels at the tomb of Christ. The priests, according to their ranks, start reading the Psalms 1, 2, and 3 until they reach "I lay down and slept" (Psa. 3:5). Then the curtain of the altar is closed and the 150 psalms are read in their entirety.

Readings and Patristic Meditations

LAMENTATIONS 3:1-66

Now I am the man who has seen affliction by the rod of His wrath. He has led me and made me walk in darkness and not in light. Surely He has turned His hand against me time and time again throughout the day.

He has aged my flesh and my skin, and broken my bones. He has besieged me and surrounded me with bitterness and woe. He has set me in dark places like the dead of long ago.

He has hedged me in so that I cannot get out; He has made my chain heavy Even when I cry and shout, He shuts out my prayer. He has blocked my ways with hewn stone; He has made my paths crooked.

---

[36] *Ibid.*

He has been to me a bear lying in wait, like a lion in ambush. He has turned aside my ways and torn me in pieces; He has made me desolate. He has bent His bow and set me up as a target for the arrow.

He has caused the arrows of His quiver to pierce my loins. *I have become the ridicule of all my people— their taunting song all the day. He has filled me with bitterness, He has made me drink wormwood.*

He has also broken my teeth with gravel, and covered me with ashes. You have moved my soul far from peace; I have forgotten prosperity. And I said, "My strength and my hope have perished from the Lord."

Remember my affliction and roaming, The wormwood and the gall. My soul still remembers and sinks within me. This I recall to my mind, therefore I have hope.

Through the Lord's mercies we are not consumed, because His compassions fail not. They are new every morning; Great is Your faithfulness. "The Lord is my portion," says my soul, "Therefore I hope in Him!"

The Lord is good to those who wait for Him, to the soul who seeks Him. It is good that one should hope and wait quietly for the salvation of the Lord. *It is good for a man to bear the yoke in his youth.*

Let him sit alone and keep silent, because God has laid it on him; Let him put his mouth in the dust— There may yet be hope. **Let him give his cheek to the one who strikes him, and be full of reproach.**

For the Lord will not cast off forever. Though He causes grief, yet He will show compassion according to the multitude of His mercies. For He does not afflict willingly, nor grieve the children of men.

To crush under one's feet all the prisoners of the earth, to turn aside the justice due a man before the face of the Most High, Or subvert a man in his cause— The Lord does not approve. Who is he who speaks and it comes to pass, when the Lord has not commanded it? Is it not from the mouth of the Most High that woe and well-being proceed? Why should a living man complain, a man for the punishment of his sins?

Let us search out and examine our ways, and turn back to the Lord; Let us lift our hearts and hands to God in heaven. We have transgressed and rebelled; You have not pardoned.

You have covered Yourself with anger and pursued us; You have slain and not pitied. You have covered Yourself with a cloud, that prayer should not pass through. You have made us an offscouring and refuse in the midst of the peoples.

All our enemies have opened their mouths against us Fear and a snare have come upon us, desolation and destruction. My eyes overflow with rivers of water for the destruction of the daughter of my people.

My eyes flow and do not cease, without interruption, till the Lord from heaven looks down and sees. My eyes bring suffering to my soul because of all the daughters of my city.

My enemies without cause hunted me down like a bird. They ended my life in the pit and they have laid a stone over me.[37] The waters flowed over my head; I said, "I am cut off!"

I called on Your name, O Lord, from the lowest pit. You have heard my voice: "Do not hide Your ear from my sighing, from my cry for help." You drew near on the day I called on You, and said, "Do not fear!"

O Lord, You have pleaded the case for my soul; You have redeemed my life. O Lord, You have seen how I am wronged; Judge my case. You have seen all their vengeance, all their schemes against me.

You have heard their reproach, O Lord, all their schemes against me, The lips of my enemies and their whispering against me all the day. Look at their sitting down and their rising up; I am their taunting song.

Repay them, O Lord, according to the work of their hands. Give them a veiled heart; Your curse be upon them! In Your anger, Pursue and destroy them from under the heavens of the Lord.

In its beautiful and touching tune, the Church cries out its lamentation for Her beloved. In this hour, we see the Holy Virgin Mary carrying The Lamb of God, we see Joseph of Arimathea and the women anointing the Holy and Pure Body with spices, dressing It for burial. "My eyes overflow with rivers of water...my eyes flow and do not cease, without interruption...my eyes bring suffering to my soul because of all the daughters of my city." Truly this is the cry of the Church, who is weeping with the holy women, the daughters of the city.

The Church sings from the Book of Lamentations, full of the prophesies of this burial, and foreshadows the Decent of our Lord into Hades to free Adam and Eve from the bondage of sin. Yes, there is much grief, but there is also much hope. Death and sin attack me saying, "But call out, if there is anyone who will answer you?" (Job 5:1). Is there anyone to answer me? "But surely as for me, I will beseech the Lord, and call upon the

---

[37] Septuagint translation, which is quoted by the Fathers, like St. Cyril of Jerusalem below.

Lord and Master of all, Who does great, incomprehensible, and marvelous things without number. He causes rain on the earth and sends waters on all the places. He sets the lowly on high and raises up the lost" (Job 5:8-11).

For we shall call for You, and You shall answer. You answer me as You answered the Psalmist, who testifies, "In the day of my trouble I will call upon You, for You will answer me" (Psa. 86:7). Lord, You assure me always saying, "He shall call upon Me, and I will answer him, I will be with him in trouble I will deliver him and honor him. With long life I will satisfy him and show him My salvation" (Psa. 91:15-16). And again, saying "The LORD is near to all who call upon Him, to all who call upon Him in truth" (Psa. 145:18). Thus, Jeremiah tells us Him, "I called on Your name, O Lord, from the lowest pit. You have heard my voice." Lord, you heard my voice when I was in the pit of sin, not only because You hear my voice in every place, but especially now, for You have descended into the lowest pit to lift me up from my sin and to give me the power of Your Resurrection.

You lift me as You lifted St. Peter from the waters, from the anguish of his doubt and straying from Your holy precepts. You lifted the man beside the pool of Bethesda from his suffering, anguish and pain. You lifted the sinful woman from her weeping, and told her, "Go, and sin no more." You lifted Lazarus and many others from the dead on earth, now You shall do the same for those who are in the tombs.

JONAH 1:10-2:7

Then the men were exceedingly afraid, and said to him, "Why have you done this?" For the men knew that he fled from the presence of the Lord, because he had told them. Then they said to him, "What shall we do to you that the sea may be calm for us?"—for the sea was growing more tempestuous. And he said to them, "Pick me up and throw me into the sea; then the sea will become calm for you. For I know that this great tempest is because of me." Nevertheless the men rowed hard to return to land, but they could not, for the sea continued to grow more tempestuous against them. Therefore they cried out to the Lord and said, "We pray, O Lord, please do not let us perish for this man's life, and do not charge us with innocent blood; for You, O Lord, have done as it pleased You." So they picked up Jonah and threw him into the sea, and the sea ceased from its raging. Then the men feared the Lord exceedingly, and offered a sacrifice to the Lord and took vows.

Now the Lord had prepared a great fish to swallow Jonah. And Jonah was in the belly of the fish three days and three nights.

Then Jonah prayed to the Lord his God from the fish's belly. And he said: "I cried out to the Lord because of my affliction, and He answered me.

"Out of the belly of Sheol I cried, and You heard my voice. For You cast me into the deep, into the heart of the seas, and the floods surrounded me; all Your billows and Your waves passed over me.

Then I said, 'I have been cast out of Your sight; yet I will look again toward Your holy temple.' the waters surrounded me, even to my soul; the deep closed around me; weeds were wrapped around my head. I went down to the moorings of the mountains; the earth with its bars closed behind me forever; yet You have brought up my life from the pit, O Lord, my God.

"When my soul fainted within me, I remembered the Lord; and my prayer went up to You, into Your holy temple."

Events did not just happen without Divine Providence; for God sent strong winds which caused great gales announcing God's anger against disobedience. He sent a big fish to the ship to swallow Jonah and thus supply him with a safe sleeping place rather than death, and to show him God's care for him.

St. Jerome says: "The Lord showed His anger when Jonah was in the ship, and showed His joy when he entered unto death," explaining that there he represented Christ the Lord Who trampled death by His death. Truly Jonah appeared as a victim of death who was swallowed by Hades, that could not stomach him for more than three days and three nights, but spat him out from its depth so that the prophet would say, "O death, I will be your plagues! O grave, I will be your destruction" (Hosea 13:14).

Inside the fish, Jonah entered into death to discover the mystery of Christ's resurrection which is victory over death. In the great fish, Jonah gave us the most beautiful song of praise which expressed Christ's redeeming work during the moments of His death on the Cross and His burial. Thus, the Church sings that hymn at the beginning of the 12th hour on Great Friday following the chanting of Jeremiah's Lamentations. So if the Lamentations express what bitterness our sins have done to the Lord, then Jonah's hymn lifts up the partition to reveal God's victory over hades and His redeeming work which lifts the believers to the Holies in an unspeakable glorious joy.

Fr. Tadros Malaty, *Patristic Commentary on Jonah*, 10-11, 31.

How are the three days and three nights calculated? (Jn. 1:17)

Christ emphasized that what happened to Jonah inside the whale was a symbol of what would happen to Him: "For as Jonah was three days and three nights in the belly of the great fish, so will the Son of Man be three days and three nights in the heart of the earth" (Matt. 12:40)...

There are three possible ways to calculate or interpret the three days and three nights.

First, St. Jerome says that the Jews consider a part of the day as a whole day and thus the repose of Christ is calculated from Friday to Sunday despite the fact that He died on the Cross on Friday at the end of the day and arose at dawn on Sunday. St John Chrysostom says that if the Lord had waited till the end of the day on Sunday to rise from the dead, the soldiers would have been off duty by then and the Jews would have believed that the soldiers left their posts; but He arose while they were guarding the tomb.

St. Jerome also presents another argument, which was supported by some, that the darkness, which came over the land when Christ was on the Cross, was a different, unique kind of night.

A third interpretation is that others consider the time of burial started when the Lord gave His Body to His disciples at the Last Supper, as though He was buried inside human bodies in order to raise it up with Him...

Regardless, the Lord was buried for three days and rose again. This is the reality which the disciples witnessed and which God validated with many evidences, so that we may live it as the mystery of our daily resurrection and our victory over death and Hades. Jonah was used as a living proof of the resurrection of the body at the end of time by his encountering death and emerging from it.

Fr. Tadros Malaty, *Patristic Commentary on Jonah*, 10-11

Scripture again witnesses that the space of those three days did not imply whole days in their entirety. Rather the first day is counted as whole from its last part, and the third day is itself also counted as a whole from its first part. But the intervening day, i.e., the second day, was absolutely whole with its twenty-four hours, twelve of the day and twelve of the night. For He was crucified first by the voices of the Jews in the third hour, when it was the sixth day of the week. Then He hung on the Cross itself at the sixth hour, and yielded up His Spirit at the ninth hour.

St. Augustine, *On the Holy Trinity*, 4.6.10 (NPNF 2:3, p. 74)

Next let us remark in what way, when asked in regard to one sign, that He might show it from heaven, to the Pharisees and Sadducees who put the question, He answers and says, "A wicked and adulterous generation seeks after a sign, and no sign shall be given to it except the sign of the prophet Jonah. And He left them and departed" (Matt. 16:4). But the sign of Jonah, in truth, according to their question, was not merely a sign but also a sign from heaven; so that even to those who tempted Him and sought a sign from heaven He, nevertheless, out of His own great goodness gave the sign. For if, as Jonah passed three days and three nights in the fish's belly, so the Son of man did in the heart of the earth, and after this rose up from it—from where but from heaven shall we say that the sign of the resurrection of Christ came? And especially when, at the time of the passion, He became a sign to the robber who obtained favor from Him to enter into the paradise of God; after this, I think, descending into Hades to the dead, "as free among the dead" (Psa. 88:6).

The Savior seems to me to conjoin the sign which was to come from Himself with the reason of the sign in regard to Jonah when He says, not merely that a sign likened to that is granted by Him but that very sign; for attend to the words, "And there shall no sign be given but the sign of Jonah the prophet." Accordingly, that sign was this sign, because that became indicative of this, so that the elucidation of that sign, which was obscure on the face of it, might be found in the fact that the Savior suffered, and passed three days and three nights in the heart of the earth.

At the same time also we learn the general principle that, if the sign signifies something, each of the signs which are recorded, whether as in actual history, or by way of precept, is indicative of something afterwards fulfilled; as for example, the sign of Jonah going out after three days from the fish's belly was indicative of the resurrection of our Savior, rising after three days and three nights from the dead; and that which is called circumcision is the sign of that which is indicated by Paul in the words: "We are the circumcision..." (Philip. 3:3). Seek you also every sign in the Old Testament as indicative of some passage in the New Testament, and that which is named a sign in the New Covenant as indicative of something either in the age about to be, or even in the subsequent generations after that the sign has taken place.

The Scholar Origen, *Commentary on Matthew*, 2.12.2 (ANF 10)

PSALM 87:6, 22:4; 44:9, 11

They laid Me in the lowest pit, in dark places, and in the shadow of death. Yes, even if I should walk through the valley off the shadow of death, I will fear no evils; for You are with me."

*Your throne O God, is forever and ever, the scepter of Your kingdom is a scepter
of righteousness. Myrrh, and allows and cassia are exhaled from Your garments.*

This hymn is chanted several times throughout Pascha, but at times to
the words of Psalm 54, "His words were softened above oil..."

As mentioned in the passage above, the Scholar Origen connects this
psalm with the other readings in this hour. For as the Psalmist speaks about
the "lowest pit" it represents Hades and the grave, which are represented
symbolically with Jonah in the belly of the fish and fulfilled actually when the
Lord was placed in the tomb.

See how God became man after the giving of the law by Moses? Hear
also a second testimony to Christ's Deity, that which has just now been read,
"Your throne, O God, is forever and ever." For lest, because of His presence
here in the flesh, He should be thought to have been advanced after this to
the Godhead, the Scripture says plainly, "Therefore God, even Your God,
has anointed You with the oil of gladness above Your fellows." See Christ as
God anointed by God the Father?

St. Cyril of Jerusalem, *Catechetical Homilies*, 11.15 (NPNF 2:7, p. 220)

His "Throne is forever and ever." Why? For that first throne of the
Kingdom was but a temporal one. From where then have we a "throne
forever and ever"? Because it is God's throne. O divine Attribute of Eternity!
for God could not have a temporal throne. "Your throne, O God, is forever
and ever — a scepter of direction is the scepter of Your Kingdom."

"The scepter of direction" is that which directs mankind: they were
before crooked, distorted. They sought to reign for themselves: they loved
themselves, loved their own evil deeds. They submitted not their own will to
God, but would gladly have bent God's will to conformity with their own
lusts. For the sinner and the unrighteous man is generally angry with God,
because it does not rain! And yet would not want God to be angry with him
because he is reckless. And it is pretty much for this very reason that men
daily sit, to dispute against God: "This is what He should have done; this He
has not well done."

Do you know what you are doing? He knows what He is doing. You
are the one who is crooked! His ways are right. When will you make the
crooked coincide with the straight? It cannot be made to coincide with it.
Just as if you were to place a crooked stick on a level pavement; it does not
join on to it; it does not cohere; it does not fit into the pavement. The
pavement is even in every part, but it is the stick that is crooked; it does not

fit into that which is level. The will of God then is "equal," your own is "crooked." It is because you cannot be conformed to it, that it seems "crooked" to you. Rule yourself by it; seek not to bend it to your own will for you cannot accomplish it since it is at all times "straight"! Would you abide in Him? "Correct yourself;" so will the scepter of Him who rules you, be unto you "a rule of direction." From this reason is He also called a "ruling" King. For that is no "ruler" that does not correct. Up until now He is our King, a King of "right ones." Just as He is a Priest (Secedes) by sanctifying us, so is He our King, our Ruler, by "ruling" us...

St. Augustine, *Commentary on Psalm* 45,15 (NPNF 2:8, pp. 340-341)

MATTHEW 27:57-61

Now when evening had come, there came a rich man from Arimathea, named Joseph, who himself had also become a disciple of Jesus. This man went to Pilate and asked for the body of Jesus. Then Pilate commanded the body to be given to him. When Joseph had taken the body, he wrapped it in a clean linen cloth, and laid it in his new tomb which he had hewn out of the rock; and he rolled a large stone against the door of the tomb, and departed. And Mary Magdalene was there, and the other Mary, sitting opposite the tomb.

MARK 15:42-16:1

Now when evening had come, because it was the Preparation Day, that is, the day before the Sabbath, Joseph of Arimathea, a prominent council member, who was himself waiting for the kingdom of God, coming and taking courage, went in to Pilate and asked for the body of Jesus. Pilate marveled that He was already dead; and summoning the centurion, he asked him if He had been dead for some time. So when he found out from the centurion, he granted the body to Joseph. Then he bought fine linen, took Him down, and wrapped Him in the linen. And he laid Him in a tomb which had been hewn out of the rock, and rolled a stone against the door of the tomb. And Mary Magdalene and Mary the mother of Joses observed where He was laid.

Now when the Sabbath was past, Mary Magdalene, Mary the mother of James, and Salome bought spices, that they might come and anoint Him.

LUKE 23:50-56

Now behold, there was a man named Joseph, a council member, a good and just man. He had not consented to their decision and deed. He was from Arimathea, a city of the Jews, who himself was also waiting for the kingdom of God. This man went to Pilate and asked for the body of Jesus. Then he took it down, wrapped it in linen, and laid it in a tomb that was hewn out of the rock, where no one had ever lain before. That day was the Preparation, and the Sabbath drew near. And the women who had come with Him from Galilee followed after, and they observed the tomb and how His body was laid. Then they returned and prepared spices and fragrant oils. And they rested on the Sabbath according to the commandment.

JOHN 19:38-42

After this, Joseph of Arimathea, being a disciple of Jesus, but secretly, for fear of the Jews, asked Pilate that he might take away the body of Jesus; and Pilate gave him permission. So he came and took the body of Jesus. And Nicodemus, who at first came to Jesus by night, also came, bringing a mixture of myrrh and aloes, about a hundred pounds. Then they took the body of Jesus, and bound it in strips of linen with the spices, as the custom of the Jews is to bury. Now in the place where He was crucified there was a garden, and in the garden a new tomb in which no one had yet been laid. So there they laid Jesus, because of the Jews' Preparation Day, for the tomb was nearby.

Joseph of Arimathea

This was Joseph of Arimathea, who had been hiding his discipleship up to this time. Now, however, he had become very bold after the death of Christ. Joseph was not an obscure person. He was highly visible, a member of the council and highly distinguished. From this it becomes clear that he was a man of special courage. For he exposed himself to death, taking upon him the enmity of all by his affection for Jesus. He not only dared to ask for the body but he did not desist until he obtained it. He did more than receive it and bury it in a splendid manner. He even laid it in his own new tomb. Joseph thereby showed both his love and his courage. This did not occur randomly or without purpose. It occurred so that there should not be any unsupported suspicion that He had risen instead of another.

St. John Chrysostom, *Commentary on Matthew*, Homily 88.2 (NPNF 2:10, p. 522)

Joseph of Arimathea is referred to as a rich man not because the writer of the Gospel wanted to boast that very wealthy and noble men were disciples of Jesus but rather in order to show why he was able to obtain Jesus' body from Pilate. For the poor and obscure did not have the right to approach Pilate, the representative of Roman power, and obtain the body of the Crucified. In another Gospel, the same Joseph is called βουλευτής, which means "councilor" or "senator" (Mk. 15:43, Lk. 23:50) Some think that the first psalm was composed with him in view: "Blessed is the one who does not walk in the counsel of the impious." (Psa. 1:1)

St. Jerome, *Commentary of Matthew*, 4.27, 57 (AACS 1b, pp. 299-300)

The Shroud and the Tomb

He was wrapped in a clean linen shroud and put it in a new tomb where no one was buried, thus preserving the body of Jesus for its glorious resurrection. But I think that this shroud was much cleaner from the time it was used to cover Christ's body than it ever had been before. For the body of Jesus retained its own integrity, even in death, so that it cleansed everything it touched and renewed even the new tomb which had been cut from the rock... Joseph did not roll many stones over the entrance to the tomb but only one great stone. [This stone] was greater than the power of those who lay in wait, but not greater than the power of the angels who descend from heaven and removed the stone and sat on it (Matt. 28:2). For all things which surround the body of Jesus are thereby clean and new and not simply "great" but surpassingly great.

The Scholar Origen, *Commentary on Matthew*, 143 (AACS 1b, pp. 300-301)

Notice the clean linen in which the pure Body of Jesus was wrapped and the new tomb that Joseph had hewn out of the rock, where "no one was yet lying,"... It suited Him who was unlike other dead people but who even in death revealed signs of life in the water and the blood. He was, so to speak, a new dead man, laid in a new and clean tomb. His birth was purer than all the others, since He was not born in the ordinary way, but of a virgin. At His burial, the new tomb where they deposited His body also symbolically indicated His purity. It was not built from stones gathered from various quarters not having natural unity. It was quarried and hewed out of one rock, united together in all its parts.

The Scholar Origen, *Against Celsus*, 2.69 (AACS 3, p. 372)

This above all shows the foolishness of those who say that the Word was changed into bones and flesh. For if this had been so, there would have been no need of a tomb. For the body would have gone by itself to preach to the spirits in Hades. But as it was, He Himself went to preach while the body that Joseph wrapped in a linen cloth laid away at Golgotha. And so it is demonstrated to all that the body was not the Word, but body of the Word.

St. Athanasius the Apostolic, *Letter 59 to Epictetus*, 6 (NPNF 2:4 p. 572)

We are able to discern from the spiritual sense of Scripture that the Body of the Lord must not be covered in gold nor jewels and silk, but pure linen. This may also mean, however, that the one who wrapped Jesus in clean linen is he who received Him with a pure mind...His body was placed in a new tomb lest it be imagined after the resurrection that one of the other interred bodies had arisen. The new tomb, however, may also signify Mary's virginal womb. The great stone was placed at the entrance to the tomb in order to show that it could not be opened without the help of several persons.

St. Jerome, *Commentary of Matthew*, 4.27.59-60 (AACS 1b, p. 300)

Joseph of Arimathea, having asked Pilate to return Jesus' body, wrapped it in a shroud, placed it in a new tomb carved out from a rock and rolled a stone in front of the entrance to the tomb. Although this may indeed be the order of events and although it was necessary to bury Him who would rise from the dead, these deeds are nevertheless recounted individually because each of them is not without some importance. Joseph is called a disciple of the Lord because he was an image of the apostles, even though he was not numbered among the twelve apostles. It was he who wrapped the Lord's body in a clean linen shroud; in this same linen we find all kinds of animals descending to Peter from heaven.[38] It is perhaps not to extravagant to understand from this parallel that the Church is buried with Christ under the name of the linen shroud (Rom. 6:4, Col. 2:12). Just as in the linen, so also in the confession of the Church are gathered in the full diversity of living beings, both pure and impure. The Body of the Lord, therefore, through the teaching of the apostles, is laid to rest in the empty tomb newly cut from a rock. In other words, their teaching introduced Christ into the hardness of the Gentile heart, which was uncut, empty and previously impervious to the fear of God. And because He is the only one who should penetrate our hearts, a stone was rolled over the entrance of the tomb, so that just as no one previous to Him had been introduced as the Author of divine knowledge, neither anyone be brought in after Him.

St. Hilary of Poitiers, *On Matthew*, 33.8 (AACS 1b, p. 300)

The Savior is placed in the sepulcher of another because He died for the salvation of others. For what could He have to do with a sepulcher, to

---

[38] This sheet is mentioned in Acts 10:11-12 symbolized the Church, according to Hilary, for it wraps and holds the Body of the Lord.

Whom death did not belong? What has He to do with a tomb upon the earth, Whose set is in heaven? What had He to do with a sepulcher, Who was only in the grave three days, not so much like one lying in death, as like one resting in a bed? (Isa. 53:9)

St. Augustine, *Harmony of the Gospels*, 3.22 (NPNF 2:6, p. 208)

We seek to know exactly where He was buried. Was His tomb made with hands? Did it rise above the ground, like the tombs of kings? Was the sepulcher made of stones joined together? What was laid upon it? O prophets, tell us exactly about His tomb. Where is it? Where should we look for it? The answer, "Look at the solid rock that you have hewn" (Isa. 51:1). Look and see. You have in the gospels, "in a rock-hewn tomb." What is next? What kind of door does the sepulcher have? Again, the prophet says, "**They have ended my life in the pit, and they have laid a stone over me**" (**Lam. 3:53**). I am "the chief cornerstone, chosen, precious" (1 Pet. 2:6; Isa.28:16); He Who is "a stone of stumbling" (1 Pet. 2:8) to the Jews but of salvation to those who believe was for a while within a stone. **The Tree of Life was planted in the earth to bring blessings for the earth which was cursed and to bring release for the dead.**

St. Cyril of Jerusalem, *Catechetical Lectures*, 13.35 (FC 6, pp. 27-28; AACS 3, p. 371)

Anointing His Body

Why do the two Mary's wait beside the sepulcher? Because they did not fully know His greatness. They had brought ointments. They were waiting at the tomb so that if the madness of the civil authorities should relax, they might go and care for the Body. Do you see these women's courage? Do you see their depth of affection? Do you see their noble spirit in providing? Do you see their noble spirit even to death? Let us imitate these women! Let us not forsake Jesus in time of trial! These women exposed their lives so much for Him when He was alive. But we men, I repeat, neither feed Him when hungry nor clothe Him when naked. See Him begging, we pass Him by. And yet if we might really behold Him in the neighbor, we would divest ourselves of all our goods.

St. John Chrysostom, *Gospel of Matthew*, Homily 88.2-3 (NPNF 2:10, p. 522)

Wise women followed our common Savior Christ, gathering whatever was both useful and necessary for faith in Him. When He gave His flesh as a ransom for the life of us all, they wisely committed themselves to care for His Body. They supposed that the corpse would continue to remain in the grave.

St. Cyril of Alexandria, *Commentary on Luke*, Homily 153 (AACS 3, p. 373)

Yesterday the lamb was slain and the door posts sprinkled with its blood, while Egypt mourned for her firstborn. But the destroying angel and his sacrificial knife, fearful and terrifying, passed over us (Exod. 12), for we were protected by the Precious Blood. This day we have wholly departed from Egypt and from Pharaoh its cruel tyrant and from Pharaoh's oppressive overseers. We are freed from laboring with bricks and straw (Exod. 5), and no one forbids us to celebrate the festival of our passing over, our Pasch, and not to celebrate with the leaven of malice and wickedness, but with the unleavened bread of sincerity and truth (1 Cor. 5:8).

Yesterday I was crucified with Christ; today I am glorified with Him. Yesterday I died with Him; today I am given life with Him. Yesterday I was buried with Him; today I rise again with Him.

St. Gregory Nazianzen, *On the Holy Pasch and His Own Reluctance* (AACS 1b, pp. 237-238)

III

BRIGHT SATURDAY

"He lifts us up…"

Overview

"If He descends into Hades, descend with Him. Learn to know the mysteries of Christ there also, what is the providential purpose of the twofold descent, to save all people absolutely by His manifestation, or there too only them who believe."

St. Gregory Nazianzen, Second Oration (NPNF 2:8)

Passover is a joyful celebration, from which we pass over from death to life, from sin to holiness, from Hades to Paradise. The glorious Church provides us with the same path from Great Friday to Easter through Apocalypse Saturday or "Bright Saturday." On this day, the Church is dressed in white, and filled with joyful hymns.

Although we are hoping to celebrate the Resurrection, we still remember the death of our Savior and His resting in the tomb. Thus, the mood is still one of restraint and reflection.[39]

History[40]

The Apostolic Canons promoted the assembly of the Church on Bright Saturday, wherein the Law, the Prophets, and the Psalms were read until dawn.[41] Thus far, the Church has read through the entire book of Isaiah, the Psalms, and most of the other prophesies and gospels. During this festival of joy, the Church continues in its prayerful meditations by reading the praises from the Old Testament—spanning the entire breadth of the Bible, from the Historical Books (Exodus), the Prophetic Books (Isaiah, Samuel, Daniel, Habakkuk, Baruch) the poetical books (Lamentations, Job) and the Deuterocanonical books (Bell and the Dragon, Susanna).

Chromatius of Aquileia[42] also speaks of the importance of this vigil, as compared with other vigils:

---

[39] Kevin W. Irwin, *Easter: A Guide to the Eucharist and Hours* (Collegeville, MN: Liturgical Press, 1991), 87.

[40] Also see the Introduction to Midnight Psalmody in the introduction to Volume 4 of this series, *The Holy Fifty Days*.

[41] *Apostolic Constitutions*, 5:19.

[42] Chromatius, *Sermon 16: on the Great Night*, 1. Chromatius was bishop of Aquileia, near modern Trieste in northwest Italy from 387-407. More than fifty of his sermons are extant, and were rediscovered only in the twentieth Century. The English translation of this sermon is taken from A. Hamman, T*he Paschal Mystery: Ancient Liturgies and Patristic Texts*, ed.

Every vigil celebrated in honor of the Lord is welcome and pleasing to God, but this vigil is so more than all other vigils. In fact, this night has a distinctive name, "the Vigil of the Lord." For we have read in the Scriptures, "This is that night of vigil to the Lord for all the children of Israel throughout their generations" (Exod. 12:42). This night is properly called "the vigil of the Lord" because He was awakened to life lest we should sleep in death. For our sake He took upon Himself the sleep of death, through the mystery of His Passion. But that sleep of the Lord has become the vigil of the whole world because Christ's death staved off from us the sleep of eternal death. He Himself says this when He speaks through the prophet, "Therefore I slept and I kept watch, and My sleep was made sweet to Me" (Psa. 3:5; Jer. 31:26 38:26). That sleep of Christ was obviously made sweet, because from the bitterness of death He called us to the sweetness of life.

Hence this night is called "the Vigil of the Lord" because even in the very sleep of His passion He kept watch. He shows this when He says through Solomon, "I sleep and my heart keeps watch" (Song 5:2). This clearly shows the mystery of divinity and flesh in His own person. For He slept in His flesh and kept watch in His divinity, since divinity could not sleep. For we read this, said of the divinity of Christ, "Behold, he who guards Israel shall neither slumber nor sleep" (Psa. 121:4). He says, "I sleep and my heart keeps watch" (Song 5:2) because in the sleep of His Passion, He slept in His flesh, but His divinity was scouring the underworld, so that He could carry off humanity, which was imprisoned in hell.

For our Lord and Savior willed to scour every place, to have mercy on all. Form heaven He came down to earth, to visit the world. From earth, again, He went down to the underworld to bring light to those who were bound in Hades, according to the word of the prophet, who said, "A light has dawned for you who sit in darkness and the shadow of death" (Isa. 9:2). So this night is rightly called, "the Vigil of the Lord." In it, He brought light not only to this world, but also to those who were in the underworld.

Thomas Halton (Montreal: Palm, 1969) 135-138; Cantalemessa, *Easter in the Early Church*, 106-107.

Church Tradition and Rites

After completing the Psalms of David the prophet, the clergy dress in their vestments and light candles. The highest ranking priest faces towards the east and chants Psalm 151 in Coptic. While the Psalm is read in Arabic or English, the book of Psalms is then wrapped in a white linen cloth, carried by the elder priest at the altar door with candles lit. After its completion, the priest, along with the priests and the deacons chant the hymn of the Second Canticle (Marenouwnh `ebol, "Let us give thanks") while circuiting the church. After circling the church, they start chanting the Midnight Praises from the First Canticle.

After the First Canticle is chanted, the priests and deacons sit in two rows, with the candles lit in their midst, and begin the Old Testament readings. The readings here focus on the gateway of the Cross from death to life—the bridge from the suffering of our Lord on the Cross, to His glorious Resurrection. We enter into this celebration of the Cross and Resurrection through two main means: *baptism* and *repentance.*

Those catechumens planning to be baptized on the Feast of Resurrection were thoroughly prepared through the readings of Bright Saturday, which focused on baptism. The Crossing of the Red Sea and the story of the Three Holy Youth are symbolic of baptism—in which God saves His people both through the crossing of water and through the fires of temptation and sin. For those who were already baptized, this was a reminder of their baptism. Being reminded of this first state, they were called to repentance.[43]

Readings and Patristic Meditations

The first seven Old Testament readings are as follows:

1. The Praise of Moses after crossing the Red Sea (Exod. 15)— the Lord will rise up and "pass over" the waters of baptism[44] into life. By this

---

[43] The Eastern Orthodox, Roman Catholic, and Anglican Churches also celebrate Holy Saturday, but according to different rites and traditions. It is common for most, however, to also baptize the catechumens on this day. In the Catholic tradition, a special candle, *"the paschal candle"* is lighted and placed on the altar. It stays on the altar until Ascension Day (the Thursday 40 days after Easter) when Christ left His followers after 40 days of living among them in His resurrected body.

44 Passing over death and corruption for all humanity through His life-giving death and resurrection as we experience in the baptism.

song of praise, the Church declares it has been given the essence of this immortal praise mentioned in the book of Revelation: "They sing the song of Moses, the servant of God, and the song of the Lamb" (Rev. 15:3). The Church chants this praise with a feeling of transfiguration, as someone standing before the Throne of God on the sea of glass. He carries God's harp and praises God with those ones who overcame the dragon, its image, its qualities, and its many names.[45] Thus, this praise represents the victory of the Cross over any tribulation, controversy or turmoil. The Church reminds us of the beginning of our journey to salvation through Baptism, in which our Lord has led us from Hades to Paradise, from Egypt to Israel, from this world to heavenly Jerusalem.

2. The Praise of Hannah, the mother of Samuel, who thanked the Lord for giving her a son in her barren state (1 Sam. 2:1-10).

3. The Prayer of Hezekiah: (Is. 38:10-20) In this prayer, we declare with Hezekiah, to the Lord, "I will praise you all the days of my life."

4. The First Praise of Isaiah the Prophet: (Is. 25:6-8) This praise speaks of the Sacrifice of the Cross and the Blood. This "feast" of wines symbolizes the feast of the Cross, the ultimate fulfillment of the Passover meal.

5. The Second Praise of Isaiah the Prophet: (Is. 26:1-9) Here we declare that He will swallow up death. This is our God for whom we waited, and in Him we will rest. This praise speaks of the Resurrection when "He shall spread forth His hands."

6. The Third Praises of Isaiah the Prophet (Is. 10-20) is another joyous praise surrounding the sacrifice of the Cross and the end of death.

7. The Praise of Manasseh, the son of King Hezekiah, explains the mystery of repentance as well as the passing over from death to life.

After these seven readings, the three Hymns for the Three Holy Youth are chanted: the Third Canticle, `Ari'alin, and Tenen. Just as these youth were saved from the blazing fire by the Angel of God in their midst, so too are we saved from the fires of hell by the Messiah who lives and dwells within us and among us. In the prayer of Azariah, we remember the prayer that presents God's supporting hand in the midst of His suffering and even His burial (Dan. 3:20-28).

---

[45] His Grace Bishop Mettaos, *Meditations on the Midnight Praise*, trans. by Margaret Rafla.

As indicated earlier, the reference of the Three Holy Youth has a long-standing tradition dating back to the Early Church. This tradition survives today in the Eastern Orthodox Churches. There, the excerpt from the Septuagint chapter of Daniel is one of three passages from the Old Testament which are read after the "Little Entrance."[46] As Fr. Lev Gillet writes: "Miraculously protected from death, [the three holy youth] symbolize the victory of the risen Christ. Their song of thanksgiving enjoins all nature to praise God...Thus, we will include the entire universe in the joy of the Resurrection.[47]

Saint Irenaeus also explains that the three youth, like Jonah and Elijah, are symbolic of our resurrection from the dead: Jonah emerged from the sea, Elijah ascended into the highest, and the three youth emerge from the fiery flames.

St. John Chrysostom says, "For the three youth were cast into the furnace, and did not even for this forget their piety. The flames did not frighten them—while that fire encircled them, instead of frightening them, they sent up those sacred prayers to heaven. Therefore, the fire became a wall to them, and the flame a robe; and the furnace was a fountain. Although it received them bound, it restored them free. It received bodies that were mortal, but abstained from them as if they had been immortal! It knew their nature, yet it reverenced their piety! The tyrant bound their feet, and their feet bound the operation of the fire!..."[48]

After these hymns, the reading from Daniel is continued from where it was left off. The following readings are read as well:

1) *The Praise of Daniel* (Dan. 6:1-23). Just as God rescued Daniel from the lions, so too has He saved us from destruction, agony, and pain. Daniel also repents for the sins of all of his people; as the Lord took for Himself the sins of the world. This prayer also mentions that the Lord's deliverance of His people out of Egypt, again a symbol of our deliverance from sin.

2) *The Prayer of St. Mary.* The Theotokias are not chanted on this day since they speak in detail of the Incarnation, as related through the Holy Virgin Mary. Since we are focused instead this evening upon the Crucifixion,

---

[46] The other two are the account of creation (Gen. 1:1-13), and the Passover from Exodus 12. These readings are read on Holy Thursday and Great Friday in the Coptic Orthodox Church.
[47] Gillet, *The Year of Grace*, 176.
[48] St. John Chrysostom, *Homilies on the Statues to the People of Antioch*, Homily 4 (NPNF 1:9, pp. 610-617).

Burial and Resurrection, we read here the prayer St. Mary which relates to the Crucifixion.

3) *Simeon's Prayer.* Simeon lived only to see the glory of God. Once He beheld the Messiah, he departed in peace. The Church has us read this prayer at the end of each day (in the 12th hour of the Agpeya, the Midnight Prayer and the Midnight Psalmody) to remind us of our death in Christ.

4) *The Story of Susanna* (Dan. 13:1-64). Then we read how Daniel saved Susanna from the sentence of death, a symbol of Christ who saved us from our death sentence. The prayer of Susanna reminds us of our own prayer to our Savior for this deliverance. Susanna is freed of her false accusation when Daniel asks about the tree that she rested on. The tree is none other than the Cross which saves us from the enemy.

5) *The Story of Bell and the Dragon* (Dan. 14:1-42). Here, Daniel reveals to the king the secret of "eating" of the idol, prompting the king to cancel Daniel's death sentence. St. Cyril of Jerusalem relates the fifth chapter to the ascension of the Lord: "Remember the Prophet who said, "Who builds His ascension unto heaven" [5:33: cf. Ezek. 8:3] and all the other particulars mentioned yesterday because of the denying of the Jews."

6) *The Praise of Habakkuk* (Hab. 3:2-19) speaks of the Lord returning in glory: "His glory covered the heavens, and the earth was full of His praise. His brightness was like the light He had rays flashing from His hand."

7) *The Praise of Jeremiah* (Lam. 5:16-22) shows His immortality against His enemies, "You, O Lord, remain forever; Your throne from generation to generation."

8) *The Praise of Baruch* (Baruch 2:7-16).

9) *The Praise of Elijah* (1 Kings 18).

10) *The Praise of Job* (Job 19:1-13).

11) *The Praise of Solomon* (1 Kings 8:32).

Matins and the Book of Revelation

After these praises are read, candles and lit and the hymn *Ten-owi enthok* ("We Follow You") in its annual tune is chanted. Matins is then prayed, as preparation for the Divine Liturgy. Afterwards, the Book of Revelation is read in its entirety.

By reading the Book of Revelation, we are reminded of the Lord's Second Coming. We remember His amazing Resurrection from the Dead and His Second Coming. This mysterious book also encapsulates the entire

Bible into one. As the entire week of Pascha was full of prophesies from the Old Testament, this last day is full of prophesies from the New Testament.

This is perhaps one of the most powerful books in the Holy Bible, for it was given from God the Father, to Christ, to an angel, to John. It is a book of symbols and mystery, a book in which the past, present and future unite. There is victory, death, and pain.

As Fr. Pishoy Kamel says: "The Church moves us to the delight of the resurrection and beyond, when it finishes the service by reading the Book of Revelation. The priests, the deacons, and the congregation stay amid the seven oil candles before the throne of God (Rev.1: 4). These seven candles are symbols of the seven lamps of fire burning before the throne, which are the seven Spirits of God (Rev 4:5). The seven candles are also the seven golden lamp stands (Rev. 1:12) and the seven stars in His right hand, which are the angels (bishops) of the seven Churches. The seven golden lamp stands also represent the seven Churches (Rev. 1:16,20). The readings of this book reveal the mysteries of what is beyond the resurrection. Much can be said regarding this night, but it is the night of personal experience. No one can give a full account about the concepts of this night unless you live it personally and live the readings as well as the tunes of this wonderful rite. "To him who overcomes I will grant to sit with Me on My throne, as I also overcame and sat down with My Father on His throne. He who has an ear, let him hear what the Spirit says to the Churches."[49]

Thus we see that by remembering the Descent into Hades, we gather to witness the Resurrection unto eternal life. The Divine Liturgy is then celebrated. The psalm and gospel of the day is sung in a mixed tune, half in the mournful tune of Holy Pascha, and half in the annual tune. This shows the mixture of joy and sadness that we began the week with.

Those who would be baptized on this day remember that they are baptized into His death, declaring with St. Paul: "Or do you not know that as many of us as were baptized into Christ Jesus were baptized into His death? Therefore we were buried with Him through baptism into death, that just as Christ was raised from the dead by the glory of the Father, even so we also should walk in newness of life (Rom. 6:3-4). And again, "you were also ...buried with Him in baptism, in which you also were raised with Him through faith in the working of God, who raised Him from the dead" (Col.

---

[49] Fr. Pishoy Kamel, *JTG*, 76.

2:11-12). The fathers also spoke about this relationship between our baptism and His burial:

Baptism is the Cross. What the Cross and Burial is to Christ, Baptism has been to us, even if not in the same respects. For He died Himself and was buried in the flesh, but we have done both to sin…Here [St. Paul] hints, along with the duty of a careful walk, at the subject of the Resurrection…For if you have shared in His Death and Burial, much more will you share in the Resurrection and Life…After the Resurrection to come had been set before us, he demands of us another, a new conversation, which is brought about in the present life by a change in habits.

St. John Chrysostom, *Commentary on Romans* (5), Homily 10 (NPNF 1:14)

The soul when it was deified descended into Hades, in order that, just as the Sun of Righteousness rose for those upon the earth, so likewise He might bring light to those who sit under the earth in darkness and shadow of death. In order that just as He brought the message of peace to those upon the earth, and of release to the prisoners, and of sight to the blind, and became to those who believed the Author of everlasting salvation and to those who did not believe a reproach of their unbelief, so He might become the same to those in Hades: that every knee should bow to Him, of things in heaven, and things in earth and things under the earth. And thus after He had freed those who had been bound for ages, straightway He rose again from the dead, showing us the way of resurrection.

John of Damascus, *An Exact Exposition of the Orthodox Faith*, 3.29 (NPNF 2:9)

IV

CONCLUSION
"Come, Lord Jesus!"

Concluding thoughts are best expressed by St. Gregory Nazianzen. We were created that we might rejoice. We rejoiced when we were created. We were entrusted with Paradise that we might enjoy life. We received a Commandment that we might obtain a good repute by keeping it; not that God did not know what would take place, but because He had laid down the law of Free Will. We were deceived because we were the objects of envy. We were cast out because we transgressed. We fasted because we refused to fast, being overpowered by the Tree of Knowledge...We needed an Incarnate God, a God put to death, that we might live. We were put to death together with Him, that we might be cleansed; we rose again with Him because we were put to death with Him; we were glorified with Him, because we rose again with Him.

St. Gregory Nazianzen, *On the Holy Pascha*, Oration 45.1 (NPNF 2:80)

Through this praise and prayer, we may declare with the Psalmist, "We went through fire and through water; but You brought us out to rich fulfillment" (Psa. 66:12). Through this Holy Week, O Lord, we went through the fire of the Cross, as the Three Holy Youth. We experienced the pain, suffering, and heartache. We went through the baptismal waters, the place of rejoicing and victory. Now, we ask You, O Lord, take us into this rich fulfillment. We long to go into the land where grief, sorrow, and groaning have fled away. We saw You work miracles on earth, and we were crucified with You. But You lifted us in Your Resurrection and Ascension. Lift us up forever with You, O Lord as You lifted Adam and Eve from their graves. We lived in darkness, You gave us light. We lived in sin, You gave us holiness. We dwelt in sadness and gloom; You have given us eternal joy.

Δοξαϲι ὸΘεοϲ ἡμων

Made in United States
North Haven, CT
07 April 2023